BRITISH CINEMA OF THE 90s

Edited by

Robert Murphy

 Publishing

For Sophie and Allie

First published in 2000 by the
British Film Institute
21 Stephen St, London W1P 2LN

Reprinted 2001, 2002

The British Film Institute is the UK national agency with
responsibility for encouraging the arts of film and television
and conserving them in the national interest.

Cover design: Paul Wright/Cube
Cover images: (Front) *Trainspotting*; (back) *The Long Day Closes*; *Nil by Mouth*; *My Name is Joe*;
Elizabeth; *Sense and Sensibility*; *Shooting Fish*

Set in 10/12pt Minion by Wyvern 21
Printed in Great Britain by St Edmundsbury Press, Bury St Edmunds

British Library Cataloguing-in-Publication Data
A catalogue record for this book is available from the British Library
ISBN 0–85170–763–7 (hbk)
ISBN 0–85170–762–9 (pbk)

Contents

Acknowledgements

I would like to thank Steve Chibnall, Tim O'Sullivan, Chris Goldie, Jo Mills, Richard Dacre, Paul Marris, Sam Rennie, Sophie and Edward Noel, Pius Hume, Eileen Murphy, Julia Chamberlain and Anne Eardley, for tempering and shaping my views on 90s British films; Steve Gamble, John Mackintosh and the man in the the audio-visual department of Cole Brothers, Sheffield, for solving my computer problems; Carol Barron and Stephen Creigh-Tyte for providing me with elusive government reports; Cathy Poole at the Watershed, Bristol and Erik Hedling at the University of Lund for allowing me opportunities to try out ideas about 90s British cinema; Chantal Latchford for her diligent copy-editing; my editor Andrew Lockett for his unfailing help and support; and, of course, all the contributors to this book who responded with good humour to my chiding and criticism. In venturing beyond the territory served so valiantly by Dennis Gifford's *British Film Catalogue 1895-1985*, I have relied extensively on the BFI's *Film and Television Handbooks* and the *Time Out Film Guide*. Thanks are also due to De Montfort University, Leicester and the Arts and Humanities Research Board, London whose Research Leave Scheme allowed me time to complete the editing of this book.

Notes on Contributors

Karen Alexander is currently working in the Collections Department of the BFI. She has worked extensively in independent film and video as a producer, writer and teacher.

Geoff Brown writes film and music criticism for *The Times*. His studies of British cinema include *Walter Forde* (BFI, 1997) and *Launder and Gilliat* (BFI, 1977). He is a contributor to *Michael Balcon: The Pursuit of British Cinema* (Museum of Modern Art, 1984) and *The British Cinema Book* (BFI, 1997) and author with Tony Aldgate of *The Common Touch: The Films of John Baxter* (NFT, 1989).

Charlotte Brunsdon teaches in the Department of Film and Television Studies at Warwick University. Her publications include *Screen Tastes* (Routledge, 1997), *Feminist Television Criticism* (Clarendon Press, 1997) and *The Feminist, the Housewife and the Soap Opera* (Clarendon Press, 1999).

Stella Bruzzi teaches film at Royal Holloway College, University of London. She is a regular contributor to *Sight and Sound* and the author of *Undressing Cinema: Clothing and Identity in the Movies* (Routledge, 1997) and *New Documentary: A Critical Introduction* (Routledge, 2000).

Ian Christie is Professor of Film Studies at Birkbeck College, London. He is the author and editor of a number of books on Michael Powell and Emeric Pressburger, including *Arrows of Desire* (Faber, 1994); and he wrote and co-produced the television series *The Last Machine*. His latest book is *A Matter of Life and Death* (BFI, 2000).

Pamela Church Gibson is a Senior Lecturer in Contextual Studies at the London College of Fashion. She has co-edited *Dirty Looks: Women, Power, Pornography* (BFI, 1993) and *The Oxford Guide to Film Studies* (OUP, 1998). She is currently working on a book for Routledge, together with Stella Bruzzi, entitled *Fashion Cultures: Theories, Explorations and Analysis*.

Stuart Hanson was a Youth and Community Worker before becoming a Lecturer in the Department of Cultural Studies and Sociology at Birmingham University. His research interests are in cinema as a social and cultural practice, the development of multiplexes and post-war British cinema.

John Hill is Professor of Media Studies at the University of Ulster. His publications include *Sex, Class and Realism: British Cinema 1956–63* (BFI, 1986), *Cinema and Ireland* (Croom Helm, 1987), *Border Crossing: Film in Ireland, Britain and Europe* (IIS/BFI, 1994), *Big Picture, Small Screen: The Relations Between Film and Television* (John Libbey, 1996), *The Oxford Guide to Film Studies* (OUP, 1998) and *British Cinema in the 1980s: Issues and Themes* (Clarendon Press, 1999).

Moya Luckett is Assistant Professor of Film Studies in the English Department at the University of Pittsburgh. With Hilary Radner, she is the co-editor of *Swinging Single: Representing Sexuality in the 1960s* (University of Minnesota Press, 1999). She is currently completing a book on spectatorship, the city and modernity entitled *Cities and Spectators: An Historical Analysis of Movie Going in Chicago, 1907–1917* and a volume on national identity and femininity in 1960s British and American film and television.

Karen Lury teaches in the Department of Theatre, Film and Television Studies at the University of Glasgow. She is an editor of *Screen* and author of *British Youth Television: Cynicism and Enchantment* (OUP, forthcoming).

Geoffrey Macnab is a freelance writer based in London. He contributes regularly to *Sight and Sound, Moving Pictures International* and *Time Out* and is the author of *J. Arthur Rank and the British Film Industry* (Routledge, 1993) and *Searching for Stars* (Cassell, 1999).

Toby Miller is Associate Professor of Cinema Studies at New York University. He is the author of *The Well-Tempered Self: Citizenship, Culture, and the Postmodern Subject* (Johns Hopkins University Press, 1993), *The Avengers* (BFI, 1997), *Technologies of Truth: Cultural Citizenship and the Popular Media* (University of Minnesota Press, 1998) and *Popular Culture and Everyday Life*, with A. McHoul (University of Minnesota Press, 1998). He is co-editor of *Social Text*.

Claire Monk is a Lecturer in Film and Media Studies at De Montfort University, Leicester. She is completing a doctorate on British heritage films and their reception, at Middlesex University. She has contributed to *Sight and Sound*, the *Journal of Popular British Cinema*, and to *British Crime Cinema* (eds Steve Chibnall and Robert Murphy, Routledge, 1999). She is currently co-editing a collection on representations of the past in British cinema.

Robert Murphy is the author of *Realism and Tinsel* (Routledge, 1989), *Sixties British Cinema* (BFI, 1992) and *British Cinema and the Second World War* (Continuum, 2000), editor of *The British Cinema Book* (BFI, 1997) and co-editor of *British Crime Cinema* (Routledge, 1999). He is Senior Research Fellow at De Montfort University, Leicester.

Kate Ogborn has been the Executive Producer of the BFI and Channel Four's New Directors scheme since 1989. In 1996 she set up a production company, Strange Dog, with Carine Adler and produced Carine Adler's debut feature film *Under the Skin*, which was released in the UK in 1997. Strange Dog currently has three features in development.

Claire Smith graduated with an MA in Cinema Studies from Nottingham Trent University. She currently lives and works in London.

Peter Todd is Information Service Manager of the BFI National Library. His short film, *Diary* (1998), was shown at the Rotterdam International Film Festival. He curated the touring programme of short films, *Film Poems* in 1999.

Neil Watson is a writer and researcher specialising in the film industry. He collaborated on David Puttnam's book, *The Undeclared War*, published by HarperCollins in 1997.

Introduction

Robert Murphy

The revival of British cinema in the past five years has aroused both hopes and fears which are expressed in about equal parts in the essays in this book. Economic revival is welcomed but its durability questioned; box-office success acknowledged but doubts voiced over whether it is going to the right films.

Peter Todd accepts internationalisation as a *fait accompli* which is not necessarily bad for British cinema but he stresses the dangers of neglecting the well-springs of talent among film-makers whose first priority is not to please the market if our film culture is not going to be an entirely *ersatz* one. Geoff Brown, mapping out the changes of the past ten years, questions whether we still have a film culture – and citing the influence of Tarantino and *Empire* magazine – surmises that, if we do, it is already American. Toby Miller places less emphasis on Americanisation and blames government – both the irresponsible *laissez-faire* attitude of the Tories and the commerce-as-culture attitude of New Labour for fostering a cinema of false values.

Stuart Hanson looks at the multiplexes, the most obvious sign of change. He condemns their homogenisation of the cinema-going experience – part of a world-wide process of 'McDonaldization' – but he also welcomes the revival they have brought about and the opportunities they offer for greater flexibility.

Kate Ogborn uses her experience running the BFI New Directors scheme to write about the sort of low-budget films which rarely reach the multiplexes. She worries that the current stress of marketability might squeeze out originality and experimentation, but she concedes that this might be balanced by increases in funding and technological developments which will allow films to be made more cheaply and easily.

Ian Christie charts a course through the murky world of European funding initiatives and reveals that despite the hazards of Europuddings and bureaucracy, there is much to be gained from co-operating with our European partners. Neil Watson, examining the relationship between Britain and Hollywood, also believes that the benefits outweigh the dangers and argues that greater internationalisation of the film industry puts Britain in a strong position to mediate between Hollywood and Europe. But he also expresses concern about the makeshift nature of the British film industry and the talent drain that results from its instability.

The remaining ten essays shift their emphasis from the industry to the films. Moya Luckett measures the balance between heritage and modernity, realism and stylisation and looks at the troubled and complicated ways in which a British national identity is expressed in films such as *The Full Monty* (Peter Cattaneo, 1997) and *Twin Town* (Kevin Allen, 1997), *Elizabeth* (Shekhar Kapur, 1998) and *Sliding Doors* (Peter Howitt, 1998).

Karen Lury examines the extent to which films like *Trainspotting* (Danny Boyle, 1996) and *Shopping* (Paul Anderson, 1994) can be viewed as part of a global youth culture and explores *Trainspotting*'s success in turning itself into a 'brand' capable of attracting a wide following into its intensely parochial world.

Karen Alexander looks – with some dismay – at the limited opportunities open to black film-makers and how moves towards a more multicultural society have been paid scant regard by the new British cinema. She argues that such narrowing perspectives not only foster nostalgia and illusion but miss out on the dynamism black culture has brought to other art forms, particularly music.

Pamela Church Gibson studies the heritage film and finds it surprisingly healthy. Late-90s manifestations such as *Jude* (Michael Winterbottom, 1997), *The Wings of the Dove* (Iain Softley, 1997), *Elizabeth* and *Shakespeare in Love* (John Madden, 1999), break free of the restrained Merchant–Ivory idiom that characterised the previous decade to become more adventurous and more playful.

Stella Bruzzi, looking at the ways in which non-heterosexual relationships have been depicted in 90s cinema, finds a shift away from the radical queer cinema of the 80s to a more subdued exploration of sexual plurality. She examines three films – *Priest* (Antonia Bird, 1994), *Sister My Sister* (Nancy Meckler, 1995) and *Love and Death on Long Island* (Richard Kwietniowski, 1998) – which explore the division between repression and openness and show the process of coming out as a troubled and difficult one.

Geoffrey Macnab tackles the problem of why so many British films never reach the cinema screen. By following the fate of four films – *Bullet to Beijing* (George Mihalka, 1995), *Bob's Weekend* (Jevon O'Neill, 1996), *Donald Cammell: the Ultimate Performance* (Kevin Macdonald and Chris Rodley, 1998) and *The Serpent's Kiss* (Philippe Rousselot, 1997) – he uncovers a knot of issues, from underfunding and heavy American competition, to inflexibility in distribution and exhibition and the proliferation of other markets, which illustrate the problem and show there is no easy solution.

Claire Smith looks at the changing face of art cinema and the avant-garde in the 90s and celebrates the work of a new generation of film-makers typified by Patrick Kieller and Andrew Kotting whose work defies categories of documentary and fiction. She also finds that the climate for innovation and experimentation is far from ideal and, like Karen Alexander, warns that the silencing of a voice from the margins will impoverish British cinema.

Claire Monk looks at the way in which images of men have changed in 90s British films, charting the stunted career of the 'new man' and the rather more lively one of the 'new lad'. She also examines the disturbing portrayals of male violence in Mike Leigh's *Naked* (1995) and Gary Oldman's *Nil by Mouth* (1997) which indicate that the crisis of masculinity in society has prompted an unprecedented self-examination by men in the cinema.

Charlotte Brunsdon's complementary piece on women compares the way in which lone female protagonists in three low-budget productions – *The Girl with Brains in her Feet* (Roberto Bangura, 1998), *Stella Does Tricks* (Coky Giedroyc, 1998) and *Under the Skin* (Carine Adler, 1998) – fare in comparison with the group protagonists of popular television drama series such as *Real Women* (wr. Susan Oudot, 1998) and *Playing the Field* (wr. Kay Mellor, 1998). She concludes that while the television series remain optimistic by splitting aspects of female identity – mother, working woman, single girl etc. – amongst its cast, the desperate heroines of the films have a hard time playing the multiple roles expected of them.

John Hill looks at the return of the spectre of class conflict, which never really went away in the films of Ken Loach, but which also underlies more populist films such as *Brassed Off* (Mark Herman, 1996) and *The Full Monty*. He compares both the Loach films and the social comedies to the 'kitchen sink' realist films of the 1960s and sees a seismic shift in the way in which the working class has been represented.

Contributors disagree on the significance and the way ahead for British cinema and I have not attempted to impose an orthodox view nor suppressed contradictions. Occasionally the same films or the same factual information reappear in more than one essay and there are lacunae which I have only been able to partially cover over in my own chapter. Britain's animation film industry, spearheaded by Wallace and Gromit has flourished so abundantly in the 90s that its achievements would have been worth chronicling. Similarly, there has been a creative revival in documentary film-making, though in Britain documentary is seen as a televisual rather than a cinematic form and the relationship of television to the film industry is too big a topic to deal with here.

The decision not to commission essays on individual directors and particular genres, while necessary in terms of keeping the book down to a manageable size, has meant that some key films and some important directors have been regrettably neglected. The most important casualty is Mike Leigh, whose contribution to British cinema has been immense, though Derek Jarman, Terence Davies and Peter Greenaway have also received less attention than they deserve.

In retrospect, comedy which has been Britain's most important contribution to world cinema in the 90s, ought to have had its own chapter. The reader might fill this gap by reading Andy Medhurst's articles in *Sight and Sound*, particularly those on *Funny Bones* (1997) and *Little Voice* (Mark Herman, 1999) and wading through the plethora of writing on *Shakespeare in Love* and *Notting Hill* (Roger Michell, 1999).[1]

I have not attempted the traditional task of defining what is and what is not a British film. There is certainly a problem in how to categorise films like Anthony Minghella's *The English Patient* (1996) and Ang Lee's *Sense and Sensibility* (1996) but in an industry which is becoming increasingly international, the economic wrangles over which national cinema can claim which film become less interesting than those over why some representations of Britain – in *Four Weddings and a Funeral* (Mike Newell, 1994) or more surprisingly in *The Full Monty* – appeal to an international audience while others don't. What these essays show is that whatever the disappointments, the dangers, the mistakes made, British cinema in the 90s is an unexpectedly exciting and complex field of study.

Notes

1 Andy Medhurst 'Unhinged invention', *Sight and Sound*, October 1995, pp. 6–10; and 'Spend a little time with me', *Sight and Sound*, January 1999, pp. 38–9.

Chapter 1
A Path through the Moral Maze

Robert Murphy

> ... it may be no bad thing that the British film industry is suffering a near terminal
> decline. The weaker it gets, the more likely it is that the philistines will be driven out
> and the old methods of work – so inimical to creativity – will be defeated. In their place
> will come, with luck, new creative and entrepreneurial talents.
>
> (Terry Ilott, 1992)[1]

The British film industry in 1990 seemed a sickly plant unlikely to survive the millennium.
The number of films produced – sixty – was double that of the previous year and, despite
a blip in 1991, numbers continued to rise. But the euphoria brought about by the Oscar
success of *Chariots of Fire* (Hugh Hudson, 1982) and *Gandhi* (Richard Attenborough, 1983)
and the first wave of Channel Four films had long evaporated. Goldcrest had been brought
down by the failure of *Revolution* (Hugh Hudson, 1985) and Palace Pictures, which had
seemed to represent a daring, thrusting new generation of cine-literate film-makers expired
amidst a cloud of acrimony in 1992.[2] David Puttnam, despite being knighted by the government, complained that 'In Nicholas Ridley, we've got a Secretary of State who gives the
impression that he would regard his greatest success at the Department of Trade and Industry if he could close the British film industry down.'[3]

Cinemagoing had continued to expand with the proliferation of the multiplexes, but
what most people were going to see were Hollywood movies. Between 1990 and 1993 the
only British films to figure in the top twenty box-office films in Britain were Alan Parker's
The Commitments – an American-backed film shot in Ireland and Kenneth Branagh's *Much
Ado About Nothing* (1993), shot in Tuscany with American money. Whereas *The Commitments* grossed nearly £7 million (and an American box-office hit like *Robin Hood: Prince of
Thieves* grossed over £20 million) a typically British film, such as Ken Loach's *Riff-Raff*
(1991) took £61,069.[4] Hardly surprising then that budgets were kept low and most films
were aimed at the television audience.

In this depressing environment the emergence of a 'Brit-pack' of young British directors
determined to launch themselves into the industry without serving a laborious and frus-
trating apprenticeship was seen as a promising sign.[5] There were two rather different
impulses – to make films on shoestring budgets which might – like those of contemporary
American independents Sam Raimi, Steven Soderbergh and the Coen brothers – achieve a
cult success; and rather more hard-headed attempts to emulate American action movies
which it was hoped would attract a measure of financial backing and a mainstream
audience.

Of the micro-budget films, Vadim Jean and Gary Sinyor's *Leon the Pig Farmer* (1992) attracted the most attention, though it was the unpretentious *Staggered* (1993), directed by and starring the television comedy actor Martin Clunes, that was commercially most successful. *Leon the Pig Farmer*, an ethnic comedy which reverses the message of Hanif Kureishi's *My Beautiful Laundrette* (Stephen Frears, 1985) to advocate sexual conformity and the importance of family values, now seems primarily of interest for the way in which it embodies a 'Majorite' ethos of mild, middlebrow conservatism.[6] It lacks the subtlety and originality of the Frears/Kureishi film, but it is uncannily prescient of future trends, beginning among smart but rather wacky young people in London and then moving up to Yorkshire for broad comedy. Made on a budget of £160,000, it earned enough to make a profit, as did Stefan Schwartz's road movie, *Soft Top, Hard Shoulder* (1994) but most of these films were disappointingly amateurish and fared badly. *Blonde Fist* (Frank Clarke, 1992), *Beyond Bedlam* (Vadim Jean, 1993), *Mad Dogs and Englishmen* (Henry Cole, 1994), *White Angel* (Chris Jones, 1994), *The Mystery of Edwin Drood* (Timothy Forder, 1993) and *Clockwork Mice* (Vadim Jean, 1994) took little over £200,000 between them and others like *Savage Hearts* and *Seaview Knights* failed to reach the cinema screen. They also attracted industry criticism about their abuse of the system of deferred payments which encouraged technicians and actors to work for nothing in the hope of future rewards.[7]

Of the bigger budget genre films aimed at the multiplex market – *Young Americans* (Danny Cannon, 1993), *Dust Devil* (Richard Stanley, 1994), *Crime Time* (George Sluizer, 1994) and *Shopping* (Paul Anderson, 1994) – only *Young Americans* made much impact on the box-office, and it was an Anglo-American adaptation of a Stephen King story, *The Lawnmower Man* (Brett Leonard, 1993), which really cleaned up, taking £3.6 million in Britain (compared to *Shopping*'s £101,286 and *Dust Devil*'s £2,836) and $32 million in America. However, Cannon and Anderson sufficiently impressed Hollywood to win themselves major blockbuster assignments, Cannon directing *Judge Dredd* (1995), Anderson directing *Mortal Kombat* (1995) and *Event Horizon* (1997).

The early 90s renaissance seemed even weaker and shorter-lived than the one a decade earlier. Thus the unprecedented box-office success of *Four Weddings and a Funeral* (Mike Newell) in 1994 (it earned £28 million in the UK, somewhere around US $250 million world-wide) was treated with a degree of scepticism.[8] The fact that it had proved a success in America before it reached Britain, that it had an American female lead, that it was nominated for Oscars, marked it out as a fluke, a single swallow which was not going to make a summer. The impression was confirmed when Newell's next film, *An Awfully Big Adventure* (1995) made the modest sum of £600,000 and he went off to Hollywood to direct Johnny Depp and Al Pacino in *Donnie Brasco*.

Fortunately there were other signs of change. *Shallow Grave* (Danny Boyle, 1995), a slick, cynical black comedy was rapturously received by the critics and became an unexpected hit. Danny Boyle had a respectable record as a television director but the project was initiated by producer Andrew Macdonald (the grandson of scriptwriter Emeric Pressburger) and writer John Hodge. From the start it was conceived as a clever commercial package rather than a deeply personal film. But as Ian Conrich points out, whereas the 'Brit-pack' films had failed by modelling themselves too closely on American films, *Four Weddings* and *Shallow Grave* succeeded 'by drawing on their environment or the attributes of British culture'.[9] *Shallow Grave* could be seen as a reworking for the 90s of the darker elements of Hamer and Mackendrick's Ealing comedies and, although *Four Weddings* has been criticised as a 'heritage' view of Britain, packaged for the American market, Richard Curtis's

An unexpected hit, *Shallow Grave* (1995)

script is a direct descendant of the well-made comedies of upper-middle class life epito-mised by Dodie Smith's *Dear Octopus* and Esther McKracken's *Quiet Wedding*, and Hugh Grant's bumbling hero is a worthy successor to the sort of silly asses played by Ralph Lynn, David Tomlinson and Ian Carmichael.[10]

Hodge, Boyle and Macdonald followed up their success with *Trainspotting* (1996), which made £12.3 million at the British box office (*Shallow Grave* had taken just over £5 million) In retrospect it seems an obvious choice – a cult novelist with particular appeal to the youth market, an opportunity to do visually interesting things around the activities of its drug-taking protagonists, an appeal to trendy rebelliousness in the dog days of a discredited Tory government. But success was by no means guaranteed. Of the cast, only Ewan McGregor and Robert Carlyle were known, and Carlyle's character was an irredeemably vicious hard man. Though the action was again based in Edinburgh, the switch from yuppies to junkies risked alienating the affluent thirtysomethings who had applauded *Shallow Grave* – and there were precedents to warn that Irvine Welsh's Scottish vernacular might not reach beyond the relatively small circle of his admirers. David Leland's adaptation of William McIlvanney's *The Big Man* (1990) had flopped and James Kelman's Booker Prize-winning *How Late It Was, How Late* (1995) had not sold well. A brilliant marketing campaign over-came these obstacles and though *Trainspotting*'s box-office earnings were less than half those of *Four Weddings*, it could be seen as innovative and different, a harbinger of a real renaissance in British film production. As Tom Charity told his *Time Out* readers: '*Trainspotting* is the movie we have all been waiting for, the first British film of the '90s gen-eration to speak to the way we live here and now.'[11]

Even so, there were worrying signs. Of the forty-five feature films made in 1979, all but one were released theatrically, in 1996 eighty-five films were made but only forty per cent of them received theatrical distribution.[12] As production grew, the distribution logjam worsened. Thirty-three of the films made in 1996 had failed to secure a distribution deal by June 1998, seven had bypassed the cinema and been shown on television, three had been glimpsed only briefly, at the National Film Theatre in London and six had been abandoned uncompleted.[13]

The way in which films are distributed and exhibited cinematically has been fundamentally changed by the multiplex revolution. In the heyday of cinemagoing from the 1920s to the early 1960s, most films were slotted into a place on the circuits and guaranteed an audience. Some films did much better than others but a circuit release guaranteed a return of sorts and it was rare for a film to be excluded entirely.[14] Theoretically the multiplexes offered greater flexibility and greater choice, but according to one estimate, 'of the 30–40 films on release in Britain at any one time, 90 per cent of revenues are taken by the top three, the next four take 9 per cent, and the remaining 25 scramble for the last 1 per cent'.[15] Despite the proliferation of markets, film-making seems to be more of a gamble than ever. Neil Jordan's *The Crying Game* (1992), for example, which took over £2 million at the UK box-office (and a huge amount world-wide) may be a better film than his previous one, *The Miracle* (1991), which took only £15,000. But it is not a hundred times better. Because of Jordan's redeemed reputation and its modest budget (£2.7 million, compared to *The Crying Game*'s £2.1 million) subsequent video and television sales might eventually bring *The Miracle* a small profit. But most films made by fading or not yet established directors find it as difficult to get into the video stores and onto the television channels as they do to reach the cinema screen.

In 1969 Alan Lovell claimed that critical neglect had led to British cinema being an 'unknown cinema'.[16] British cinema of the 90s deserves the epithet simply because a substantial portion of the films made have never been released and many of those that have, reached only a tiny audience. Box-office returns indicate that I am not the only one who missed seeing interesting-sounding films like Mike Sarne's *The Punk* (1994), Udayan Prasad's *My Son the Fanatic* (1997), Beeban Kidron's *Amy Foster* (1997), Roger Michell's *Titanic Town* (1997) or Mike Radford's *B Monkey* (1998) in the cinema.

In 1997 *The Full Monty* (Peter Cattaneo) took a staggering £46.2 million at the box-office and it was followed by a phalanx of films which enjoyed considerable commercial success and established securely a number of directors, producers and actors in the industry. *Mrs Brown* (John Madden, 1997), *Shooting Fish* (Stefan Schwartz, 1997), *Sliding Doors* (Peter Howitt, 1998), *Lock Stock and Two Smoking Barrels* (Guy Ritchie, 1998), *Elizabeth* (Shekhar Kapur, 1998), *Hideous Kinky* (Gillies MacKinnon, 1999), *Little Voice* (Mark Herman, 1999), *This Year's Love* (David Kane, 1999), *Shakespeare in Love* (John Madden, 1999) and *Notting Hill* (Roger Michell, 1999) give the impression of a genuine new wave of British films with the potential to change the nature of British film culture and break the Hollywood stranglehold.

Stewart Till of PolyGram Filmed Entertainment, the most successful company operating in the British market in the 90s, complained that, 'It's tough to make films for $2 million to $4 million and compete head-on with $80 million American productions.'[17] Through its subsidiary production company, Working Title, PFE had been primarily responsible for *Four Weddings and a Funeral,* but the company sought to shorten the odds against success by making bigger-budgeted films aimed squarely at the American market. Initially, results were disappointing; of its 1995 productions, *Moonlight and Valentino* (David Anspaugh), *Death and the Maiden* (Roman Polanski), and *Carrington* (Christopher Hampton) did reasonably well in America but not well enough to cover losses from the £25 million flop *French Kiss* (Laurence Kasdam). In 1997 the company was much more successful with no less mainstream but more recognisably British productions. The £4 million spent on *Spice World* (Bob Spiers), £16 million on *Bean* (Mel Smith) and £29 million on *The Borrowers* (Peter Hewitt) paid off when the three films were only topped at the UK box-office by *The Full Monty*. These are not the sort of films critics get excited about but they are important in assuring the economic viability of the British film industry. Rowan Atkinson's comic television character – like those of Norman Wisdom and George Formby before him – was able to appeal to an international market (in Europe and Japan as well as the United States) and *Bean* earned US $198 million world-wide, even more than *The Full Monty*.

Though the British market is once again – as it wasn't from the mid 70s to the late 80s – big enough to support well thought-out projects made on budgets of under £3 million. This depends on them being shown in the multiplexes, which in turn depends on British films having a high enough profile to attract the attention of audiences away from an exclusive concern with Hollywood blockbusters. Some films with a very limited appeal – *Twin Town* (Kevin Allen, 1997), *Up'n'Under* (John Godber, 1998) – have made enough to turn a profit from the British market alone, but they have only been able to do so by following in the footsteps of their predecessors, *Trainspotting* and *The Full Monty*. The trend towards greater internationalism would make it impossible to reintroduce the quota system which between 1928 and 1985 forced cinema owners to show a percentage of British films, and without it there is no real alternative to closer ties with Europe and America.

American money was responsible for funding such successful British films as *Much Ado About Nothing, Sense and Sensibility* (Ang Lee, 1996), *The Full Monty, Sliding Doors* and *Shakespeare in Love* as well as what might be considered entirely American productions such as *Judge Dredd* and *Evita* (Alan Parker, 1995) despite their British directors. Such an inflow of funds is useful in maintaining an infrastructure of craftsmen, technicians, facilities, and allowing actors and film-makers the opportunity of linking up with Hollywood while remaining based in Britain. Alan Parker, for example, has combined making big-budget American backed films with the chairmanship of the BFI; and Ridley and Tony Scott, though essentially Hollywood directors, have invested in British film production through their ownership of Shepperton Studios. Actors like Kenneth Branagh, Emma Thompson, Minnie Driver and Kate Winslett have alternated between big-budget Hollywood films and much smaller British films. And with Gwyneth Paltrow there is the extraordinary phenomenon of an American actress becoming an international star by playing English characters in British (albeit American-financed) films. Nevertheless, too close a dependence on Hollywood can be dangerous. The withdrawal of American finance at the end of the 60s contributed to the rapid decline of the British film industry in the following decade; and the location of big-budget American movies in Britain is susceptible to the vagaries of international finance. It is important not to underestimate the monopolising tendencies of American capitalism. PFE, since its take-over by the Canadian drinks conglomerate, Seagram, could easily be bullied or snuffed out by what is now a sister company, the Hollywood major, Universal.

European finance has been crucial in fostering the careers of Ken Loach, Mike Leigh, Sally Potter, Peter Greenaway and Gillies MacKinnon, all of whom have made economical, enterprising and innovative European co-productions. But their films have to be set against an array of expensive and unwanted Europuddings – *The War of the Buttons* (John Roberts,

1993), *Mesmer* (Roger Spottiswoode, 1995), *Dancing at Lughnasa* (Pat O' Connor, 1998) – which indicate that films aimed explicitly at a European market still have difficulty attracting audiences.

The 1998 government report, *A Bigger Picture*, complains that production appears to be stuck at a 'cottage industry' stage of development and calls for the building up of integrated corporations handling production, distribution and exhibition.[18] But this understandable desire to tidy up and rationalise the industry has its dangers. Anyone with a memory of the 70s, when independent producers like David Puttnam, Jeremy Thomas, Don Boyd, Jake Eberts and Sandy Lieberson struggled in tiny Soho offices to raise enough money for their next low-budget production, while the conglomerate giants poured their millions into a string of disastrous extravaganzas, culminating in *Raise the Titanic* (Jerry Jameson, 1980) and *Can't Stop the Music* (Nancy Walker, 1980), might have qualms about the idea of concentrating power and resources in corporate hands. Ministerial desire for a happy and efficient ship ignores the fact that creative waves of film-making – the German Expressionist cinema after 1918, French cinema in the mid-30s, Italian Neo-Realism after the war, the French Nouvelle Vague, even the early days of New Hollywood – come from the sort of chaotic, small-scale set-up which at the moment characterises British film production.

One only has to consider the fate of Orion and the Ladd Company, well-financed American corporations which for a time functioned as big players in the international film industry, or of the attempt by Bernard Delfont's Thorn-EMI and Lew Grade's ITC to storm the American market, to see what happens to those who try to muscle in on the Hollywood majors. Attacks on Lottery-funded films such as the *Daily Mail*'s 'Fool Britannia', which lists 'two dozen turkeys' and acerbically condemns them all (*Shooting Fish* is 'little more than a lazily assembled series of sketches', *Love is the Devil* the 'sadomasochistic adventures of painter Francis Bacon') and the *Sunday Times's* (inaccurate) report that 'Lottery's 200 funded films all lose cash', might be embarrassing to government ministers but the uncomfortable truth is that making films is a gamble and there are always far more losers than winners.[19]

While those on the outside of the industry bemoan the loss of public money on films with few commercial prospects, insiders see the solution in terms of fewer, bigger-budgeted films. Nick James, editor of *Sight and Sound*, endorses the views expressed in *A Bigger Picture*, arguing that 'in order to compete at the box-office both here and abroad, British films need to increase their budgets to ensure the kind of production values that cinemagoers expect'.[20] But increasing budgets sometimes seems like a panacea rather than a real solution. It is difficult to see how bigger budgets would have improved *Four Weddings, Shallow Grave, Trainspotting* and *The Full Monty*, which cost less than £10 million between them. And one of the most attractive qualities about Mike Leigh and Ken Loach – a key to their survival when many of their contemporaries have drifted into oblivion – is their readiness to work with modest, unpadded budgets.[21] Films backed by American companies in the £5–15 million budget bracket such as *Much Ado About Nothing* and *Sense and Sensibility*, have done well and there is an obvious need in internationally marketed projects such as *Bean* and *The Borrowers, Notting Hill* and *Shakespeare in Love* to ensure they have high production values. But with other films it sometimes looks as if money has been used as a substitute for imagination and ingenuity. One can see why *Mrs Brown* only cost £1 million while *Wilde* (Brian Gilbert, 1998) cost £6.4 million, but audiences obviously preferred the committed acting and the quirky originality of the former to the sumptuous decor of the latter. And if imaginative, visually stimulating films like *Orlando* (Sally Potter, 1992), *Land*

and Freedom (Ken Loach, 1995) and *Hideous Kinky* can be made for £3 million or less, is there any real justification for *Jefferson in Paris* (James Ivory, 1995) or *Victory* (Mark Peploe, 1998) costing over £8 million? Even at the low-budget level it is difficult to see why, if *Sliding Doors* cost £1.8 million, its inferior clone, *Martha: Meet Frank, Daniel and Laurence* (Nick Hamm, 1998) had to cost £3 million; and it is instructive to recall that *Leon the Pig Farmer*, which was originally budgeted at £3 million, was made for £160,000 (with deferrals of costs and salaries) while a later offering from one of its directors, *Stiff Upper Lips* (Gary Sinyor, 1997), squandered nearly £4 million on a ponderously unfunny parody of a 'heritage' film.

It is not simply a matter of extravagance. A film like *The Wings of the Dove* (Iain Softley, 1997) – a true 'heritage' movie in the sense that its literary origins and its sumptuous setting is its *raison d'être* – can justify an £8.7 million budget, especially as its American backing ensured it an expensive marketing campaign. Michael Winterbottom's *Jude* (1996) – even though it is one of the finest films of the decade – is too grim and parochial a tale to stand much chance of recouping the £5.7 million spent on it. The *Daily Mail* might be unfair in contrasting commercially successful films like *The Full Monty* and *Lock Stock and Two Smoking Barrels* with Lottery-funded films that fail – it took faith and perception to recognise that a tale of unemployed Sheffield steel workers could appeal to a mass market and that this particular larky caper movie was different from the hundreds of other Tarantino-copies – but too often the commercial viability of many of the films supported is either ignored or misperceived. There is some justification in providing small amounts of finance for controversial low-budget films like *Stella Does Tricks* (Coky Giedroye, 1997) and *Love is the Devil* (John Maybury, 1998) which seem to have artistic significance even if they have little commercial appeal (ironically, *Love is the Devil* has won sufficient international acclaim to ensure its profitability) but there seems to be a confusion of cultural and commercial considerations in the backing granted to projects like *Keep the Aspidistra Flying* (Robert Bierman, 1998).

Though the huge waste of talent and resources which occurs when a film is made and hardly seen is regrettable, it is not the generally modest Lottery-funded films which will bring down the industry. Much more dangerous are the grandiose projects which compete openly with Hollywood and which can very quickly bring the industry to its knees when they go wrong. The Hollywood majors are by no means immune to such mistakes themselves – Warner Bros.' $45 million *The Avengers* (Jeremiah Chechik, 1998), for example, probably looked like a good idea at the time – but they have financial reserves which can absorb such losses. British producers need to be more cost-conscious and cautious.

For Nick Roddick the important question is 'Not "what future for British cinema?" but "What future, at the dawn of the digital age, for a genuinely innovative cinema whose motive is aesthetic, political, experimental – anything but commercial?"'[22] Many of the contributors to this book share his concern that film culture is becoming narrower, more commercial and less adventurous and experimental. The death of Derek Jarman in 1994 and the silence of Terence Davies after *The Neon Bible* (1995) has dented the reputation established in the 80s for British art cinema, although the hostility accorded Peter Greenaway's uncompromisingly modernist *The Baby of Maçon* (1993) was more than balanced by the welcome given *Prospero's Books* (1991) and *The Pillow Book* (1997). One could cite the flourishing careers of Mike Leigh and Ken Loach as an encouraging sign, but there has been little in the way of new talent capable of emulating or challenging the old masters. Whether one views the work of Patrick Kieller, Andrew Kotting and Chris Petit as postmodern whimsy or cutting edge avant-garde art, it seems unlikely that enthusiasm for their

work will spread beyond a relatively narrow circle.[23] The promise Sally Potter showed with
Orlando was not fulfilled by her next film, *The Tango Lesson* (1997), and talented black
directors such as John Akomfrah, Maureen Blackwood, Isaac Julien and Menelik Shabazz
have found it difficult to get projects off the ground.

From a more populist point of view, however, the situation is far from bleak. In his
review of *Shakespeare in Love*, Gilbert Adair comments on how the film's publicity concentrated on the actors and writers, virtually ignoring the director, John Madden. The same
was true of Mike Newell with *Four Weddings* and Roger Michell with *Notting Hill*, Peter
Cattaneo with *The Full Monty*, and even Danny Boyle with *Trainspotting, Shallow Grave*
and *A Life Less Ordinary* (1997). Nineties directors seem to have taken as their model unass-
uming professionals like Mike Newell and Stephen Frears rather than flamboyant,
idiosyncratic directors like Ken Russell and Nicolas Roeg. Adair complains that 'John Madden is a perfectly competent organiser of visual material and an effective director of actors.
But there's not a spark of specifically cinematic invention in his work.'[24] But Adair's art cinema concept of the director as artist obscures Madden's achievement in holding together
a complex narrative and a cast of cameo performers; and ensuring a degree of wit and ele-
gance in a film burdened by the need to show off its expensive sets and pleasing a
mainstream audience without alienating Shakespeare aficionados.[25]

Direction at this level of competence enables a film to carry meaning and significance.
The steadfastness, for example with which Viola accepts, in the midst of her *amour fou* with
Shakespeare that she must obey the dictates of her family, her Queen and the audience (for
whom she must fulfil a destiny which is complicit with rather than contradictory to his-
torical authenticity) and leave him for the obnoxious Wessex, gives a core of integrity to
Shakespeare in Love which makes it more than a fluffy piece of historical nonsense.

Similarly, the sleek, smug surface of Peter Howitt's *Sliding Doors* and the slickness with
which David Kane switches between his characters in *This Year's Love* is easily underesti-
mated.[26] In *Sliding Doors*, Howitt, helped by Irish John Lynch, Scottish John Hannah and

The sleek surface of a cinematic parable – *Sliding Doors* (1998)

American Gwyneth Paltrow, seems to suspend the English class system. A film which displayed greater fidelity to reality might be less winsome, but it would also be less effective as a parable. Within this magic world, the moral message is clear. The Helen who turns her back on her old life and (helped by the Business Expansion Scheme) lurches into a New Labour fantasy of the good life, dies. The Helen who is degraded into low-paid casual employment and suffers exploitation, betrayal and humiliation, survives and earns the right to happiness.

This Year's Love's achievement in balancing sympathies between six disparate interacting characters is a regular enough occurrence in television drama series and soap operas. But one has only to sit through the clunkingly obvious plot moves of *Martha: Meet Frank, Daniel and Laurence* or *A Life Less Ordinary* to recognise how infrequently it is transferred from television to cinema. The surefootedness with which Kane handles his characters, allowing them time and space to reveal the flaws which make their relationships so combustible, helps *This Year's Love* throw out a shower of sparks illuminating contemporary society. Unobtrusive directorial effectiveness of this sort might seem closer to the competence Mel Smith displays in directing *Bean* or Danny Cannon demonstrates in *Judge Dredd* than to the deeply personal work of Peter Greenaway or Derek Jarman but it is not to be sniffed at.

Of course the writer can be as much a creative force as the director and no doubt Tom Stoppard contributed as much to *Shakespeare in Love* as, say, Colin Welland did to *Chariots of Fire* or Joe Eszterhas to *Basic Instinct* (1992). Richard Curtis, as the writer of *Bean* and *The Tall Guy* (Mel Smith, 1990), *Four Weddings and a Funeral* and *Notting Hill* (as well as the television series *Blackadder* and *The Vicar of Dibley*), is something of a special case and deserves more serious consideration. If, in his collaborations with Rowan Atkinson, it is Atkinson's persona which dominates, *Four Weddings* and *Notting Hill* explore Curtis's own world, with Hugh Grant standing in for him in the way Jean-Pierre Leaud did for Truffaut in his Antoine Doinel films. Nick Roddick's report on the aftermath of *Four Weddings* predicted that 'for 12 months or so, literally hundreds of half-completed films and even half-written scripts will be pitched as "this year's *Four Weddings and a Funeral*..." '.[27] Few of these projects materialised (though Tim Sullivan's 1995 film, *Jack & Sarah*, used elements of the same formula) and it was left to Curtis to write his own sequel.

Surprisingly in view of its much bigger budget, *Notting Hill* seems a more personal film than *Four Weddings*. Its plot premise – what would happen if a beautiful Hollywood movie star began a romance with a very ordinary Englishman? – might look like a cynical attempt to produce a sugary romance designed to flatter American sensibilities, but in practice the film makes cheekily few concessions to Hollywood. It is not just the way in which the film industry is represented as crass, cynical and superficial – this counts as affectionate mockery in comparison with the venomous exposé of Robert Altman's *The Player* – it is the assurance with which a messy, unambitious, British lifestyle is shown as preferable to the gloss and glamour of Hollywood.

Nick Roddick, countering accusations that *Four Weddings* represents a tourist's eye view of Britain, points to Curtis's acute observation of social details. 'You have to know the British upper-middle class pretty well before you send them off to a smart wedding in a battered Land Rover.'[28] Nonetheless, part of the film's appeal came from its exploitation of an international conception of Britain as a country of odd rituals and dotty aristocrats. Despite the trendy location, *Notting Hill* offers a less obvious milieu to buy into for a non-British audience.[29] The Britain of *Four Weddings* is inhabited by aristocratic bohemians and eccentrics, but *Notting Hill*'s gallery of determinedly non-achieving characters are not far removed from the struggling stoics of Mike Leigh's *Life is Sweet* (1991). William's friends emerge as characters with lives of their own rather than as lovably cute caricatures. Max's proud insistence in carrying Bella around, with its unspoken hint that her disability has perhaps made them more equal. Bella's puncturing of William's nostalgic romanticism with her admission that she never really fancied him. Honey and Spike's unpredictability. This cosy little world is very much Curtis's creation, but Roger Michell and Julia Roberts deserve credit for bringing alive the disruptive presence who overturns it. In *Four Weddings*, Andie MacDowell is characterised by vitality, spontaneity and classless unstuffiness, the sort of qualities American actresses like Constance Cummings and Evelyn Dall brought to British films in the 30s and 40s. Julia Roberts is entirely different. Nick James speaks of her 'discreet portrait of the modern movie star as enigmatic alien being', of her 'other-worldliness' and 'her spooky glamour'.[30] Like William we are intrigued by what might lie beneath the sphinx-like smile, the chameleon-like switches (from tough cookie to friendly girl-next-door to sophisticated and tempestuous star). She is potent and dangerous enough to be a femme fatale and she makes life hell for William. His rejection of her offer of love because she causes such disruption to his quiet existence that his heart can't cope, scrapes a degree of plausibility and sympathy because we share the blast of emotional intensity Michell's directing and Roberts' acting generate around her appearances – at his door, in his shop, glimpsed through her minders and publicists – and understand his awe and distrust. But in contrast to Andie MacDowell, who serves as a deus ex machina, allowing Hugh Grant's Charles a chance to escape from a drearily conventional marriage, Roberts' Anna Scott emerges as a complex character and it is her needs and her vulnerability which determine the course of the film.

If William has difficulty coming to terms with being in love with a woman who is a sort of goddess, Anna's problem is how to know whether William is strong and steadfast in his love for her or a fool dazzled and flattered by her image. Thus the key issue is one of trust. Anna's first kiss is a thank-you for the warmth William exudes in spite of his nervousness. Her aloofness at the interview at the Ritz is a punishment for him not calling her back soon enough. She comes to his bed because he offers her a refuge, and the virulence of her rejection of him when the photographers arrive reflects the magnitude of the betrayal she feels. Ironically, what William sees as her betrayal of him – her dismissal of him to a fellow actor as an insignificant figure from her past – she sees as an automatic protection of her real feelings.

Notting Hill repeats many of the elements of *Four Weddings* – the on/off Anglo-American romance, the group of wacky friends – and follows the same emotional trajectory. There is also a similar time span, but whereas in *Four Weddings* the gap between one night stand and long-term consummation is busily filled with weddings and funerals, in *Notting Hill* it is an empty space. Michell's long, season-changing track down Portobello Road neatly covers it over, but this time gap is crucial, allowing them both a proper period of regret and loss.[31] William's speech to Bella and Max – after dinner with a 'perfect' woman in whom he isn't even slightly interested – about the improbability of love being reciprocated, displays his constancy, but the real change happens off screen with Anna. Her return to Britain to make the Henry James film and her gift of the Chagall painting show that the breach of trust has healed and she is ready to commit herself to him. If the overheard conversation on the film set seems to reveal that all William has been fostering is a sad fantasy, Anna's reappearance in the shop, stripped of all the accoutrements of stardom, is a confirmation of the reality of their love, albeit one which William initially refuses to accept.

Nick James, querying the view of Britain purveyed by *Notting Hill*, cites the scene at the end of the film where William sits reading, on a bench in the private communal garden they had trespassed into earlier, with a pregnant Anna resting her head in his lap:

> Anyone versed in the iconography of the English immediately thinks of *The Secret Garden* with its 'little bit of earth', of *The House at Pooh Corner*, of *Peter Pan*, of Kipling and all the other literary touchstones of Empire contentedness – things we all enjoy, but keep the inhabitants of these islands half in love with their now distant past.[32]

But with Pooh Corner and Never Never Land colonised by Disney it is arguable how potent their iconography now is, and the Notting Hill secret garden seems more redolent of a privileged London existence – which presumably Anna's wealth now gives them access to – than to Frances Hodgson Burnett's novel (or Agnieszha Holland's film). There are few other indications that the film is nostalgic; rather it belongs to the growing band of films which celebrate the pleasures of middle-class life in London which began with Anthony Minghella's *Truly, Madly, Deeply* (1990) and Les Blair's *Bad Behaviour* (1992) and continues with films like *Sliding Doors* and *This Year's Love*. Thus there is a sly extra-textual message. Anna isn't being asked to give up her career to become a supportive wife, she is being offered the opportunity to share the lifestyle enjoyed by Curtis and his fellow luminaries at the top end of the British film industry: a lucrative and internationally prestigious career combined with a comfortable, happy life in one of London's smartest urban villages.[33]

I actually like *Four Weddings* and *Notting Hill* and *Sliding Doors* and though I don't feel quite so warm about *Jack & Sarah*, *Martha: Meet Frank, Daniel and Laurence* or *Leon the Pig Farmer* they still appear to offer fascinating insights into British society. There is an element of appalled fascination here, but I suspect that film works in the opposite way to that proposed in the old 'opium for the people' argument, that even when they seem to celebrate an ideological hegemony, they open up gaps and allow fantasies of opposition to flourish. In *Who Dares Wins* (Ian Sharp, 1982), a rare example of a Thatcherite film in an 80s dominated by anti-Thatcherite films, this works simply on the level of caricatured characters and ludicrous plotting. But in a film like *Jack & Sarah* the process is more complex. Jack can be a yuppie working in a glass tower in Docklands and living in a big house in Islington and still retain our sympathies because his wife has died in childbirth and he's left with a sweet little baby; because the down-and-out who sleeps in his skip and the incompetent but sexy American waitress can both see good in him; because his mum is Judi Dench, and (for some people at least) because he is played by Richard E. Grant, still trailing aspects of Withnail's disreputability. We don't have to approve to be interested in the attitude the film expresses – that the workmen who do up your house are loveable scoundrels, that female bosses are manipulative, sex hungry and don't like babies, that it's all right to have servants, especially if they are wayward and funny, that the classless society means upper middle-class men can look beyond their usual circle to cheeky, free-spirited American girls – to find them revealing.

A Life Less Ordinary (which borrows its rich girl/poor boy romance from Frank Capra's *It Happened One Night*) and *Martha: Meet Frank, Daniel and Laurence* (which, like Terence Rattigan and Anthony Asquith's *French Without Tears* has its lovesick schoolchums all chasing the same woman) have slacker narratives and one-dimensional characters. But the way in which they update their 1930s models and promote an ineffectual and indecisive man as their hero raises interesting questions about continuity and change in the way in which masculinity is depicted in the cinema.

In 1999 it is too early to know if John Madden, Peter Cattaneo, David Kane and Peter Howitt will produce a significant body of films or whether they will drift into anonymity, but a handful of directors have emerged in the 90s who one can single out as potential auteurs. It is difficult to find much common ground between Anthony Minghella's low-budget, BBC-funded *Truly, Madly, Deeply* (1991) and his lavish, American-financed *The English Patient* (1996) and the link doesn't appear to lie in his little-seen second film, *Mr Wonderful* (1992). His talent is unquestioned but it is by no means certain that he can be claimed for British cinema. Like Mike Figgis and John Boorman before him, he might become an international film-maker wandering the world searching out backers for films which cross the line between art and commerce.[34]

Peter Chelsom's two full-length British films – *Hear My Song* (1991) and *Funny Bones* (1994) – are exactly the sort of ambitious, adventurous, visually stylish films Gilbert Adair claims we lack. But his is a distinctly Lancastrian vision and it holds little attraction for London critics. *Hear My Song* was generally dismissed as mawkish, and *Funny Bones* – which complicates its narrative line with incomprehensible sub-plots and presents an array of bizarre characters (from Lee Evans, Leslie Caron and the two sad brothers at the heart of the film, to the Bastard Son of Louis XIV and the Bagpipe Playing Dwarf at its peripheries) – as a jumbled mess.[35]

Gilles MacKinnon is more acceptable and was honoured with a National Film Theatre retrospective in June 1999. His adaptation of *Hideous Kinky* (1999), Esther Freud's sketches of life in Morocco with a hippy mother, brought him into the limelight, but he had been quietly building a reputation with a well-received television film *The Grass Arena* (1992) and a sensitive adaptation of Pat Barker's *Regeneration* (1997). However, it is his evocation of the recent past – the 50s in *The Playboys* (1992), the 60s in *Small Faces* (1995) and the

Gillies MacKinnon's acute adaptation – *Hideous Kinky* (1999)

70s in *Hideous Kinky* – that marks him out as an original and interesting director. Deliberately avoiding the sort of surface detail dwelt upon by heritage films, he recreates the period through the dilemmas and decisions faced by his characters.[36] In *Hideous Kinky*, for example, he eschews the usual clichés about hippies, Englishwomen abroad, cute children, exotic drug cultures, to make a marvellously acute study of the tensions between the responsibilities of parenthood and the search for personal fulfilment outside a conventional family structure.

Along with *The Grass Arena*, the BBC's 1992 'Screen Two' series boasted another outstanding film, Michael Winterbottom's *Love Lies Bleeding*. Winterbottom stayed on in television to direct a four-part drama series written by Roddy Doyle, *The Family* (1995). Doyle's fiction had been popularised by Alan Parker's adaptation of *The Commitments*, a key film, not only for its box-office success when the fortunes of British cinema were at a low ebb, but for its genuinely populist appeal and the example it set (particularly in its audition sequence) to films as different as *Shallow Grave* and *The Full Monty*. The two other novels in Doyle's Barrytown trilogy – *The Snapper* and *The Van* – were filmed by Stephen Frears. Although they allow more of Doyle's attention to the corrosive effects of poverty to seep through, they remain essentially optimistic. *The Family* is different, more uncompromisingly realistic in showing how the poor live than anything since Ken Loach's *Up the Junction* (1965) and *Cathy Come Home* (1965).[37] Along with Loach's *Riff-Raff, Raining Stones* (1993), *Ladybird Ladybird* (1994) and *My Name is Joe* (1998), it helped provoke cinematic interest in portraying life on the council estates where those who hadn't benefited from Thatcherite prosperity were confined. Films range from the relatively sunny *Beautiful Thing* (Hettie MacDonald, 1995), to the stylishly brutal *Bumping the Odds* (Rob Rohrer, 1997) and the astonishingly bleak *Nil by Mouth* (Gary Oldman, 1997).

It was hardly surprising that Winterbottom's first feature film should be the spiky, uncomfortable *Butterfly Kiss* (1994) set in the wasteland of Britain's motorways. He followed this with *Jude* (1996) a bold, moving, literary adaptation unexpectedly full of cinematic allusions; *Welcome to Sarajevo* (1997), a brave attempt to look at the Balkan war in a way which doesn't shy away from the implications of Western bungling; and *I Want You* (1998), an odd melodrama set in the South coast seaside resort of Hastings.[38] Winterbottom's intensity and integrity of vision marks him out as an important and talented director. But his lack of sentimentality makes his films seem difficult and harsh and he has yet to have a commercial success.

By contrast, the three very different films directed by Mark Herman in the 90s have all done well at the box-office. The first two, *Blame it on the Bellboy* (1992) and *Brassed Off* (1996), he wrote himself, though it is difficult to imagine more of a contrast between a black farce set in Venice and a poignant tale of a Yorkshire mining community and its brass band. There is little continuity between either of them and Herman's third film *Little Voice* (1999) which was adapted from a play by Jim Cartwright. The play had depended heavily on Jane Horrocks's uncannily accurate impersonations of Judy Garland, Shirley Bassey and Marilyn Monroe. In the cinema, with its potential for tricks and illusions, such virtuosity might be regarded more sceptically. Although Jane Horrrocks does all her own singing, and the film was shot on location in Scarborough, Herman sacrifices verisimilitude in favour of an artificial world of larger (or, in the case of Horrocks and Ewan McGregor, smaller) than life caricatures. Herman makes his film dark and dangerous enough to work as a fairy story, with Little Voice undergoing a baptism by fire which enables her to break free of the thraldom she is held in by her mother. He aroused accusations of misogyny, particularly for the coarsened mother character played by Brenda Blethyn, but his evocation of a world beyond the air-brushed political correctness of New Labour where people are honest enough to admit they are gross, desperate, manipulative and human is refreshing.[39]

Nick Roddick gloomily complained at the end of 1998 :

> I have spent a lot of my working life arguing that film is not an art form created by an individual in a garret but is manufactured by a capital-intensive industrial system. But I never thought it was *only* that. And I never expected to see that definition adopted as a prescription by a Labour government.[40]

One can share his impatience with DCMS rhetoric on 'market shares' and 'export performances' and his worries about commerce overwhelming culture. But interspersed among the mobile phone-wielding wannabes, hard-nosed cynics, Hollywood rejects and Oxbridge luvvies who have always sought a home in the British film industry, there are a number of very interesting film-makers. Fondly looking back isn't really an option. There has been a substantial and encouraging growth in the study of British cinema over the past fifteen years, but it has yet to uncover a Golden Age. As Terry Ilott reminds us, there was much that was reprehensible about the industry in the 'good old days', that: 'Grown fat from the years of plenty and dominated by old men, it had, by the mid seventies, lost the will to respond to changes in audience tastes.'[41] Nineties British cinema might not be the repository of a cornucopia of masterpieces we would desire, but it is growing out of a disastrous period of decay and decline. An industry which has found commercial success with films as different as *Four Weddings, Trainspotting* and *The Full Monty*, which has allowed the production of a range of films stretching from *Blue* (Derek Jarman, 1993) to *Judge Dredd* and which has attracted back audiences once feared lost forever, deserves at least two cheers. To come to an optimistic conclusion one has to overlook worrying trends – a cinema where only half the films made reach an audience can hardly be too proud of itself – but not since the late 1950s have we reached the end of a decade when it was possible to look forward to things getting better rather than worse.

Notes

1 Terry Ilott, 'Essentials that money can't buy', *Guardian*, 25 April 1992.
2 For the Palace story see Angus Finney, *The Egos Have Landed* (London: Heinemann, 1996).
3 Quoted in Simon Garfield, 'British film on the cutting room floor', *Independent on Sunday*, 10 June 1990, p. 20.
4 Box-office and budget figures are taken from the relevant *BFI Film and Television Handbooks*. A number of early 90s films such as Mike Newell's *Enchanted April* (1991), which was allowed only a token release in the UK by the BBC and Neil Jordan's *The Crying Game*, were considerably more successful in the United States than they were in Britain.
5 See Nick Roddick, 'Welcome to the multiplex', *Sight and Sound*, June 1994, pp. 26–8.
6 John Major was Prime Minister of Britain between November 1990 and May 1997.
7 Janice Turner, 'Exposed: The great British film industry rip-off', *Stage, Screen & Radio*, July/August 1994, pp. 10–12.
8 Terry Ilott mentions *Four Weddings and a Funeral*'s '$350 million world-wide gross' in Eddie Dyja (ed.), *BFI Film and Television Handbook 1996* (London: BFI, 1995), p. 22; but

Nick Roddick adds everything up to give a figure of $234,389,467, 'Four Weddings and a final reckoning', *Sight and Sound*, January 1995, p. 15.

9 Ian Conrich, 'Art or entertainment: British cinema in the nineties', unpublished research paper.

10 *Dear Octopus* was filmed by Anthony Asquith in 1943, *Quiet Wedding* by Harold French in 1945 and by Roy Boulting in 1957. Kenworthy reports that the script for *Four Weddings* was dismissed in Hollywood as 'Noel Coward-like', *Independent on Sunday*, 26 March 1995, p. 24.

11 Tom Charity, 'The other side of the tracks', *Time Out*, 31 January–7 February 1996, pp. 16–19.

12 See Alan Parker, 'Don't get me wrong. . .', *Guardian Media Section*, 27 October 1997, p. 8.

13 Eddie Dyja (ed.), *BFI Film and Television Handbook 1999* (London: BFI, 1998), p. 27.

14 *Chance of a Lifetime* (Bernard Miles and Alan Osbiston, 1950), a mildly pro-worker film, had to enlist government support to get a circuit release; and in the early 60s Sydney J. Furie's *The Leather Boys* (1963) and a number of other films handled by the independent distributor British Lion, found they were waiting an inordinately long time for a release date but these are memorable examples because they are exceptional.

15 Melanie Clulow, 'A tear-jerker at the movies', *Independent on Sunday Business Section*, 5 April 1998, p. 3.

16 Alan Lovell, *British Cinema: the Unknown Cinema*, BFI Education Seminar Paper, 1969.

17 Dawn Hayes, 'Credits set to roll for a local hero', *Independent on Sunday Business Section*, 3 May 1998, p. 3.

18 *A Bigger Picture – The Report of the Film Policy Review Group* (London: DCMS, 1998).

19 *Daily Mail*, 28 April 1998, p. 37; *Sunday Times*, 25 April 1999, p. 7. As an alternative form of financial support, the unfairly maligned National Film Finance Corporation, privatised and downgraded into British Screen in 1985, might provide a useful model. Between 1949 and 1959 it lost an average of £127,000 a year on the £40 million it invested in 438 feature films, *NFFC Annual Report for the year ended 31 March 1959*, p. 4.

20 *BFI Film and Television Handbook 1999*, p. 17.

21 Neither Loach nor Leigh has been tempted to make a film budgeted at over £3 million. *Secrets and Lies* (Mike Leigh) was one of the most profitable films of 1996, costing $4.5 million and bringing in $39.6 million, Eddie Dyja (ed.), *BFI Film and Television Handbook 1998* (London: BFI, 1997), p. 41.

22 Nick Roddick, 'Show me the culture!', *Sight and Sound*, December, 1998, p. 23.

23 Nick Roddick reports that Patrick Kieller sees his future in the art gallery rather than the cinema: 'There are only so many people in the world who are going to pay £8 to watch a geography lesson'. Ibid., p. 23.

24 Gilbert Adair, 'Shakey? It's pretty thin', *Independent on Sunday*, 31 January 1999, p. 5.

25 *Shakespeare in Love*, backed by the American Miramax company, cost $25 million. John Madden's previous film, *Mrs Brown*, cost £1 million.

26 Peter Howitt worked as an actor in Carla Lane's television comedy series, *Bread*. David Kane wrote the script for Frank Clarke's television film, *Shadow on the Earth* (1992), and for *Finney* (David Hayman, 1994), an impressive drama series inspired by Mike Figgis's *Stormy Monday* (1987).

27 Nick Roddick, 'Four Weddings and a final reckoning', p. 15.

28 Ibid.

29 There are several Notting Hill films. The most sociologically significant is *The L-Shaped*

Room (Bryan Forbes, 1962); the most enjoyable is Dick Clement's *Otley* (1969); the oddest is *Moon over the Alley* (Joseph Despins, 1975); the most disappointing, *Absolute Beginners* (Julian Temple, 1985); the most interesting for a double bill, Hanif Kureishi's *London Kills Me* (1994), a good example of a writer not being able to bring his own script to life on the screen.

30 Nick James, 'Farewell to Napoli', *Sight and Sound*, May 1999, p. 20.

31 *Otley* begins with a similarly long tracking shot down Portobello Road, though the number of people staring at the camera and the occasional difficulties Tom Courtenay has pushing his way through the crowds explains why *Notting Hill*'s producers relied on a studio set.

32 Nick James, 'Farewell to Napoli', p. 22.

33 The idea that London might be a better place to live than Hollywood is not a new one. In 1930 Alexander Korda, wrote disgustedly from Los Angeles, 'Boredom, terrible boredom. It's hot, I have insomnia.... At night there is nothing to do, nowhere to go, it's like being in the Foreign Legion at Sidi-bel-Abbes, waiting for one's enlistment to run out'. Michael Korda, *Charmed Lives* (London: Allen Lane, 1980), p. 83.

34 John Boorman's three 90s films - *Where the Heart is* (1990), *Beyond Rangoon* (1995) and *The General* (1999) – were all made outside the UK. Mike Figgis made *The Browning Version* (1994) and *The Loss of Sexual Innocence* (1999) in Britain; *Internal Affairs* (1990), *Liebestraum* (1991), *Mr Jones* (1994) and *Leaving Las Vegas* in the US.

35 The exception is Andy Medhurst's sensitive and knowledgeable piece, 'Unhinged invention' in *Sight and Sound*, October 1995, pp. 6–10.

36 Apart from his low-budget debut feature, *Conquest of the South Pole* (1989) and his first television film, *Needle* (1990, with a script by Jimmy McGovern), MacKinnon also directed *A Simple Twist of Fate* (1994) an updated adaptation of George Eliot's *Silas Marner* starring Steve Martin, and *Trojan Eddie* (1995) a film about Irish racketeers which prefigures Paddy Breathnach's *I Went Down* (1997) and John Boorman's *The General*.

37 John Boorman pays tribute to the realism of *The Family* by incorporating Johno (Sean McGinley) and his daughter Nicola (Tina Kellegher) in virtually the same parts – and with the same abusive relationship – in his impressive film biography of Dublin gangster Joe Cahill, *The General*.

38 With *Bhaji on the Beach* (Gurinder Chadha, 1994), *Funny Bones, Bob's Weekend* (Jevon O'Neill, 1996), *I Want You*, and *Little Voice*, the English seaside resort seems to have come into its own as a film location, though nobody has yet discovered the potential of Cleethorpes.

39 Andy Medhurst's review article, 'Spend a little time with me' deals perceptively with *Little Voice, Sight and Sound*, January 1999, pp. 38–9.

40 Nick Roddick, 'Show me the culture!', p. 24.

41 Terry Ilott, 'Essentials that money can't buy'.

Chapter 2
The British Film Industry in the 1990s

Peter Todd

we have recognised a very simple fact about movie-making: that it is *both* a cultural and an economic activity.'

(Chris Smith)[1]

Current trends

The end of the 1990s sees uncertainty about what the millennium holds. In the UK the number of films produced doubled and the amount of money invested in UK feature film productions rose from £169 million in 1992 to £560 million in 1996.[2] In 1998 the number of films in production dropped but budgets for UK and UK-linked films increased.[3] Print runs dramatically increased with wider launches of films for shorter periods to capitalise on marketing and media interest.[4]

Marketing skills and campaigns have become increasingly important. The poster campaign for *Trainspotting* was crucial in fostering its box-office success and has been widely copied. For *Lock Stock and Two Smoking Barrels* (Guy Ritchie, 1998), PolyGram was reported to have used posters on 1,500 sites in fifteen key conurbations and television advertising to promote its wide release on 221 screens. By contrast, the same company's *Elizabeth* (Shekhar Kapur, 1998) was given a much slower build up opening on fourteen screens in London and gradually increasing to a peak of 197 in its fourth week.[5] Other films handled by PolyGram in 1998, such as *Dad Savage* (Betsan Morris-Evans, 1998) and *I Want You* (Michael Winterbottom, 1998), did much less well, indicating that even for an experienced company there is no guarantee of box-office success.

Films produced in 1996, the year of peak production in the 1990s include not only artistic and economic successes like *Mrs Brown* (John Madden, 1997) and *The Full Monty* (Peter Cattaneo, 1997), but large numbers of films that failed to get any significant release like *The Slab Boys* (John Byrne, 1997) – possibly the only film to be funded by both the English and Scottish Arts Councils – and *The Scarlet Tunic* (Stuart St Paul, 1998), or went straight to television like Amber Associates' *The Scar*.

The Oscar success of *Shakespeare in Love* in 1999 was the culmination of a decade spent acknowledging the contributions of UK talent to the international film industry, echoing the awards won by Anthony Minghella's *The English Patient* in 1997, by Nick Park for his animated shorts *Creature Comforts* and *A Close Shave* in 1991 and 1996 and the numerous awards won by British composers and art directors.[6] According to the Minister of Culture,

The Oscar-winning *Shakespeare in Love* (1999)

Chris Smith, 'British talent has carried off 30 per cent of all the Oscars awarded in the last twenty years.'[7]

Rank Film Distributors, one of the long-standing stalwarts of British cinema, was sold to Carlton Television, and after initial optimism, closed down. With Rank gone, the names of the major distributors are essentially those of the American majors, Twentieth Century-Fox, Warner Bros., Universal, Columbia Tri-Star, and Buena Vista (Disney). In 1999, PolyGram Filmed Entertainment, the most important independent distributor operating in Britain, was sold by its parent company, Philips, to the drinks conglomerate Seagram, which plans to merge it with another of its subsidiaries – Universal.

The Americans have also moved into the exhibition side of the industry, so long the pre-

Table 2.1 Cinema admissions (millions) and number of films produced in 1990–8 in the UK with financial involvement

Year	Admissions	Films produced
1990	97.37	60
1991	100.29	59
1992	103.64	47
1993	114.36	67
1994	123.53	84
1995	114.56	78
1996	123.80	128
1997	139.30	116
1998	135.50	89

Source: Screen Digest/BFI

Table 2.2 Budget breakdown of UK films (including international co-productions) Jan 1994–Dec 1998

Budget £ million	1994	1995	1996	1997	1998
Under 0.99	14 (2)	6 (1)	26 (5)	18 (-)	13 (1)
1–1.99	14 (6)	18 (6)	30 (8)	23 (6)	11 (-)
2–2.99	12 (8)	21 (14)	16 (8)	15 (7)	17 (2)
3–3.99	10 (6)	7 (4)	8 (4)	27 (10)	8 (-)
4–4.99	1 (1)	6 (2)	5 (3)	9 (4)	12 (4)
5–5.99	2 (1)	4 (3)	7 (3)	5 (2)	4 (1)
6–6.99	4 (1)	2 (-)	5 (1)	1 (-)	2 (1)
7–7.99	1 (-)	3 (3)	3 (1)	2 (-)	4 (3)
8–8.99	7 (2)	2 (1)	4 (1)	- (-)	3 (2)
9–9.99	2 (2)	2 (-)	2 (-)	- (-)	- (-)
10–14.99	1 (1)	2 (1)	3 (1)	4 (-)	2 (1)
15 and over	2 (2)	4 (1)	5 (2)	2 (-)	4 (1)
Total	70 (32)	77 (36)	114 (37)	106 (29)	80 (16)

Figure in brackets is number of international co-productions between one or more UK companies and foreign partner(s). The UK element can be the majority or the minority. *Source: Screen Finance/X25 Partnership*

serve of the Rank and ABC cinema chains. The multiplex revolution has been essentially an American one, with National Amusements' Showcase Cinemas joining Warner Bros. and UCI in dominating the cinema market. Richard Branson's Virgin Corporation has been able to launch something of a fightback and there have been encouraging signs that the specialised art/avant-garde market is picking up. London Electronic Arts and the London Film Makers Co-Op combined to found The Lux in Hoxton, East London, and the Europa Cinemas network, dedicated to the screening of non-mainstream films, has expanded. Film clubs such as Kino in Manchester, Peeping Tom's, and Uncut at the ICA in London have been established and film festivals are increasing in number, such as those in Birmingham, Bradford, Chichester and Leeds. In April 1999, the British Film Institute launched a festivals' fund specifically aimed at supporting and developing these initiatives; and Chris Smith has expressed his concern at 'the narrowing of the cinema audience in Britain', pledging to support initiatives which will 'reach out to those former cinema devotees who have stopped going to the pictures for one reason or another and encourage them to come back'.[8] Film society membership has been maintained and distribution on 16mm continues, despite the competition from video. For the majority of cinemagoers, though, the multiplex has become the main venue for viewing films and multiple screens don't necessarily mean greater choice. Big-budget films such as *Titanic* tend to fill a number of screens, though where there is a specialised demand it can be catered for by less obvious films. *Dil Se..* (Mani Ratnam, 1998), the first Hindi film to appear in the top ten box-office charts in Britain, played for its first two months five times a day at staggered intervals at the fourteen-screen Cineworld cinema in Feltham and was followed by another Hindi film, *Kuch Kuch Hota Hai* (Karan Johar, 1998) starring Shah Rukh and Kajol, which opened on six screens six times a day.[9]

There has been increasing intervention by television companies into film production and Channel Four and the BBC have, throughout the 90s, been major financiers of British films. However, their demands are primarily for films which can be showcased in cinemas, used for repeated television screenings, become part of a library of films and, ideally, have the potential for a spin-off television series. Channel Four has launched its own film distribution company, an echo of the integrated industry of the past but also a response to the growing threat from satellite and cable companies with their own specialised film channels.

Beyond what could be called the mainstream industry, workshops such as Amber Associates in Newcastle (making features like *Dream On, Eden Valley* and *The Scar*) and Leeds Animation Workshop (making films on social issues such as *Through The Glass Ceiling* and *A World of Difference*) continue to produce work, though now with much-diminished support from Channel Four. It is difficult to gauge changes in levels of low-budget and independent film activity but looking at New British Expo featured alongside the Edinburgh International Film Festival in 1998, over two hundred shorts were featured on both film and video from across the country.[10] The end of the 1990s has seen the arrival of the digital era with DVD and digital broadcasting which could transform the process and the economics of film-making.

There has been a huge expansion in the number of students recruited to university courses in film and media studies and with the creation of professorships at the Universities of Westminster, Stirling, Southampton, Sheffield, Ulster, East Anglia, Warwick and Kent and Birkbeck College, London these disciplines are beginning to acquire academic respectability.[11] This, with the increase in film screenings on television via the development of specialised films channels offered by the cable and satellite companies means that viewing, studying and making films has become increasingly accessible to a growing number of people.

The development of 'time based' work in British art has led to the regular screening of film and video in galleries. Gillian Wearing, who won the Turner Prize in 1997, works in this way as do three of the four candidates for the 1998 prize. This sort of work is widely seen abroad and perhaps attendance figures for shows given by such artists should be added to box-office figures? How these works are viewed officially as separate from the film industry can be seen in terms of censorship. A film or video needs to be certified by the British Board of Film Classification; a work of art in a gallery does not. These artists, like a range of those working in film, from the animator Nick Park and art cinema auteurs like Peter Greenaway, John Maybury, Sally Potter and the late Derek Jarman, to mainstream directors such as Ridley and Tony Scott, illustrate the importance of art schools as a training ground for creative film-makers.

The statistical revolution

Both globally, and locally, the utilisation and development of cheap and easy to use spreadsheets and graphics, has released more statistics than ever before, but do the statistics most commonly quoted really represent the state of the British film industry? Statistics are used to back decisions by government, investors, industrial and cultural agencies but they do not give the whole picture of a varied industry and culture, and areas where there are few statistics tend to be unrepresented and ignored.

Governments in the 1990s have sometimes found it difficult to gather the statistical information they need to make and defend policy. Figures for employment in the film industry are vague. They have to cover not only those workers actually employed in film-making but those involved in cinemas and cinema-building, as well as those providing advertising, marketing, PR, insurance, legal and professional services (often not exclusively to the film industry). Many people involved in film work as directors, writers and actors also work in advertising, theatre and television. The Census of Employment is the main source of information but trade associations and annual industry publications also present statistics to ensure that government recognises their sectors' work.[12] The Census of Population to be carried out in 2001 will perhaps retrospectively record changes in employment in the 1990s. Details of employment are needed by government in order to develop training strategies and investment.[13]

Government agencies monitor and report on the industry through a range of publications. In 1987 the Office for National Statistics (ONS) started a quarterly survey, *GB Cinema Exhibitors Inquiry*, and in 1990 it took on the responsibility for surveying all UK film and television broadcasting companies who have overseas transactions.[14] The Office for National Statistics is now supported and advised by the Analytical Services Unit of the Department for Culture, Media and Sport (DCMS).

The BFI Film and Television Handbook has sought to provide an overview of the situation in the UK, drawing upon a range of information from journals like *Screen Finance, Screen Digest, Variety, Screen International, AC Nielsen EDI* and from organisations like the British Video Association and the Cinema Advertising Association. If box-office is seen as the most important statistic, the information has never been so abundant.

It is now possible to find details in these kind of publications on the budgets of UK films and the amount they took at the UK box-office. Figures for advertising costs are more difficult to obtain.[15] The amount cinemas make on top of box-office income through the sale of food, drink and confectionery is also elusive. Mintel has suggested that for the years 1993 and 1995 almost a quarter of UK cinema consumer revenue (excluding income from on-screen advertising) came from merchandising and catering.[16]

There is also interest in the impact of film-making in terms of spending by film crews. The various film commissions and media development agencies have started to produce figures such as those in *Scottish Screen Data* which show the beneficial impact of *Braveheart* and *Rob Roy* in terms of tourism.[17]

Britain and the international film industry

In 1990 the weekly UK trade paper *Screen International* carried a London Top Ten on its front page and a few more statistics on the back page. By 1998 the North American top ten and an international top ten were on its front page and an array of statistics covering the rest of the world on the back – though ironically the London breakdown is now only available by additional subscription from AC Nielsen EDI. From a parochial concern with what was happening in the UK, there has been a shift to an international perspective.

Statistical information covering film, television, video and new media in Europe will be used to develop initiatives and choices. The *Statistical Yearbook* produced by the European Audiovisual Observatory set up in 1992 with 'a view to promote the transparency of information in the audio-visual industry in Europe' can draw its information from particular schemes, such as the Europa Cinemas network and the European Media Development Agency (previously the European Script Fund) which have developed from initiatives to encourage development, production, marketing, distribution and exhibition of European films. The figures from the *Yearbook* for admissions for European films in Europe show

Table 2.3 Top 10 of admissions of European films distributed in Europe 1997.
Based on analysis of 70% of admissions in European Union in 1997

Original Title	Country	Admissions
1 Bean	UK	21,500,270
2 The Fifth Element	FR	18,519,222
3 The Full Monty	UK	18,100,481
4 The English Patient	US/UK	14,673,687
5 Tomorrow Never Dies	UK/US	8,368,416
6 Evita	UK/US	5,700,294
7 Fuochi D'Artifichio	IT	5,444,136
8 La Vérité si je Mens	FR	4,955,037
9 Le Pari	FR	4,017,576
10 Knockin' on Heaven's Door	DE	3,544,820

Source: European Audiovisual Observatory

that films from the UK or with UK involvement fill five of the top ten films and that no other European country has a film with US involvement among the top twenty films recorded in 1997.[18] The UK has a unique involvement with Hollywood but this could well change as European film-makers develop English language product aimed at the English-speaking market (as Luc Besson did with *The Fifth Element*), and studios elsewhere in the world begin to compete with UK facilities in handling US films as Rupert Murdoch is doing in Australia where new studios are being built to accommodate the next *Star Wars* film.

Europe is physically much closer to Britain than the USA but language is a major barrier. Europa Cinemas has managed to create a network of cinemas showing a proportion of European films throughout Europe, and in 1997 six cinemas in Bradford, Croydon, Ipswich, Leicester, Norwich and York were added to the circuit, making a total of twenty-five in Britain.[19] The European Audiovisual Observatory reports that the number of European films being shown on British screens is increasing, but despite the expansion of the Europa network, they remain rare outside London, which generates seventy-one per cent of art house national box-office.[20]

The preface to a 1995 UK government report suggests that 'The British film industry has become uncertain about its future', contrasts the integrated industry of the past with the one-off films of today and quotes Sir Stephen Tallents in 1932 complaining that the Americans, 'enjoying special advantages, have turned every cinema in the world into the equivalent of an American consulate'.[21] Three years later, the next government report, *A Bigger Picture*, was more upbeat but warned that 'at the moment our success is precarious. We do very well in some years and less well in others. We need to ratchet up our performance – our films still have only 23% of our own audience, while US films have 73%.'[22]

One problem of this way of viewing things is that it implies a view of Hollywood production as American production. This in a decade which has seen Hollywood studios owned by French, Japanese and Canadian companies. That Hollywood is becoming a global rather than an American concern is shown by the success of Australian-born magnate Rupert Murdoch whose media empire includes major television interests around the world and the Hollywood major, Twentieth Century-Fox.

Hollywood is becoming less American but the big studios remain 'theatre-driven': the showing of films in cinemas is seen as the gateway to potentially huge revenues from videos, merchandising, games, theme parks and multiple television screenings. As it is impossible to compete as an equal to Hollywood, the implication might be to invest in Hollywood companies thereby gaining a proportion of their profits. As the figures for European co-productions with the USA show, for the moment the UK has a unique share in contributing to Hollywood production.

Much future decision-making by the government in the UK depends on the success of the three Lottery-funded franchises awarded to Pathé Pictures, The Film Consortium and DNA Films. These corporations are guaranteed production finance over a six year period and it is hoped that they will provide continuity and stability to the industry. The inclusion of the French-based Pathé was controversial but could be seen to reflect the concerns of Chris Smith for Britain to use its unique position 'as a bridge, geographically, culturally and economically, between Europe and the United States'.[23]

The way in which people see films is changing. In the future, audiences will have greater choice than ever in how they view films: in cinemas, on television, on video, on the web and via the new formats and delivery systems being developed. Income from video retail and rental is already higher than that of cinema box-office and though the independent video shop has been replaced by the local branch of a national or multinational chain, the market remains buoyant.[24]

Different ways of working, like those of regional workshops such as Amber Associates, or the Orkney-based film-maker Margaret Tait who devoted a lifetime to creating a body of largely self-financed work remain marginal in terms of the statistics available but could be important for the future.[25] The success of a film such as *Following* (Christopher Nolan, 1998), with exteriors shot on a 16mm clockwork-driven Bolex camera, indicates that

Different ways of working. Amber production team's regionally generated feature – *The Scar* (1997)

Working Title's success *Elizabeth* (1999). Australian actress Cate Blanchett under the direction of Indian director, Shekhar Kapur

imagination is even more important than money, technology and marketing in the production of worthwhile films. As Nick Roddick argues: 'every memorable achievement to come out of UK cinema since the war has come out of someone's desire to say something, not to sell it'.[26] How these non-industry areas of work can interact with the mainstream industry can be seen in the way a television advertising campaign such as that for BSkyB draws – much to her annoyance – on the experimental work of Gillian Wearing.

The non-Hollywood independent sector in the USA has drawn upon a long established culture of regional and state funding. In the USA funding has gone to support festivals, to regional film funds, to distributors, to community production facilities and to public television. At key festivals abroad there has been a co-ordinated marketing of American independent films.[27] Oscar winner Barbara Kopple, David Lynch and Spike Lee all received funding early on in their careers from organisations such as the American Film Institute and New York State Council for the Arts. Hollywood looks on the American independents festival, Sundance, as a source of new talent and product. In the UK the value of this sector has hardly been recognised and the lack of a government strategy for independent and experimental work limits the possibilities for the future. UK independents will still be here if the entertainment production dollars go abroad and might prove useful in reinvigorating the industry.

Mainstream players in the UK industry fully realise the need for flexibility. As Eric Fellner, co-chairman of Working Title, puts it:

> The business here is a cyclical cottage industry done in dollars. If the exchange rate is good, business is good; if not, business is bad. Perceptions are also cyclical: if a *Four Weddings* or a *Full Monty* come out, everyone wants small British films; if not, they don't. If Merchant

Ivory scores a hit, everyone wants frock-flicks or tea-and-cucumber flicks; if there's a *Trainspotting*, everyone screams for hip, cutting-edge contemporary movies. It's shifting sands. There is no clear-cut British Film Industry.[28]

Working Title's most recent success, *Elizabeth*, was financed by PolyGram (at that time a Dutch company), with an Indian director, and an Australian lead actress.

Expenditure on cinemagoing has increased but it is still below other leisure activities and the amount of time people have to spend on leisure has increased little.[29] The British Video Association lists cinema at the bottom of a leisure expenditure chart after (in descending order) television licence, music, video, satellite, cable and computer software. The European Leisure Software Publishers' Association suggests that the games market is greater than the cinema market and, according to Nick Wray, 'computer games sales now support an industry which, in the States, alone, generates $1 billion more in revenue than US cinema takings'.[30]

The first survey of the service sector by the Office of National Statistics revealed total revenue from film and television exports increased annually by an average rate of approximately seven per cent between 1993 and 1997. The largest consumer of British film and television is the USA accounting for £330 million. With music, software, fashion, design, publishing, arts and antiques these sectors employ approximately a million people in the UK and account for some sixteen per cent of the global market in creative goods and services.[31]

From the earliest days of cinema, British directors and actors and technicians have gone to where the opportunities are. At the end of the 90s, it remains a tantalising possibility that the UK can build a film culture and a film industry which is distinctively British but part of a world-wide entertainment industry and strong enough to retain the undoubted talent generated in this country.

Notes

1 Chris Smith, *Creative Britain* (London: Faber and Faber, 1998) p. 86.

2 Eddie Dyja (ed.), *BFI Film and Television Handbook 1999* (London: BFI, 1998), pp. 28 and 42.

3 *Screen Finance*, 21 January 1999, p. 1.

4 'British films come to rely on strong opening week', *Screen Finance*, 12 October 1998, pp. 8–9.

5 Nick Roddick, 'Shotguns and weddings', *Mediawatch 99*, with *Sight and Sound*, March 1999, p. 13.

6 See *BFI Film and Television Handbook 1999*, pp. 80–5 for a listing of British Oscar achievements.

7 Chris Smith, *Creative Britain*, p. 88.

8 Ibid., pp. 214–25 and 209–12.

9 Vivek Chaudhary, 'Film's greatest fans', *Guardian*, 4 December 1998.

10 *NBX (New British Expo) 1998* (Edinburgh: Edinburgh Film Festival, August 1998).

11 Lavinia Orton, *Media Courses UK 1999* (London: BFI, 1999).

12 Office for National Statistics, *Annual Employment Survey* (London: Office for National Statistics, 1997). *The Pact Directory of Independent Producers*, PACT (London: PACT, 1998). *The Production Guide*, EMAP Media. (London: EMAP Media, 1998).

13 London Economics, *Employment in the Film Industry in the UK* (London: London Economics, 1993). Myra Woolf and Sara Holly, *Employment Patterns and Training Needs 1993/4* (London: Skillset, 1994).

14 *GB Cinema Exhibitors* (London: Office for National Statistics, 1987). *Overseas Transactions of the Film and Television Industry* (London: Office for National Statistics, 1990).

15 Nick Roddick makes good use of information on advertising expenditure in 'Shotguns and weddings'.

16 Mintel, *Cinemas* (London: Mintel International Group Ltd, 1996), pp. 14-15.

17 Jamie Hall, *Scottish Screen Data* (Glasgow: Scottish Screen, 1997).

18 André Lange, *Statistical Yearbook 1998* (Strasbourg: European Audiovisual Observatory, 1998). The European Audiovisual Observatory is an initiative of the Council of Europe. The European Union has its own Eurostat publications and also the *European Cinema Yearbook* produced by Media Salles (Milan: Media Salles, 1997).

19 *The Network*, Europa Cinemas 1997 (Paris: Europa Cinemas, 1997).

20 Chris Chandler, 'Beyond a London thing', *Vertigo*, Autumn 1997, Issue 7, pp. 58–9.

21 National Heritage Committee, *The British Film Industry, Vol. 1: Report and Minutes of Proceedings* (London: HMSO, 1995), p. vii.

22 *A Bigger Picture – the Report of the Film Policy Review Group* (London: DCMS, 1998), p. 10.

23 Chris Smith, *Creative Britain*, p. 87.

24 *British Video Association Yearbook 1998* (London: British Video Association, 1998), p. 67.

25 Margaret Tait died in April 1999, aged eighty.

26 Nick Roddick, 'Show me the culture!', *Sight and Sound*, December 1998, p. 26.

27 Peter Todd, 'Funded in the USA', *Moving Pictures*, May 1995, Issue 9, pp. 34–5.

28 Rory Ross, 'Buying in to the Technicolor dream', *Financial Times*, 6/7 February 1999, p. 6.

29 The Henley Centre, *Media Futures 99* (London: The Henley Centre, 1998).

30 *British Video Association Yearbook 1998* (British Video Association, London 1998). European Leisure Software Publishers' Association (UK) Ltd, *Playing for success. A white paper on the UK leisure software industry* (Offenham: ELSPA, 1998); Nick Wray, quoting from *Variety*, 'When dinosaurs ruled the earth', *Audiovisual Librarian*, February 1995, vol. 21, no. 2.

31 Department for Culture, Media and Sport, *Creative Industries Mapping Document* (London: DCMS, 1998).

Chapter 3

Something for Everyone: British Film Culture in the 1990s

Geoff Brown

Early in September 1998, several broadsheet newspapers carried obituaries of the veteran film journalist F. Maurice Speed, founding father of the listings magazine *What's On in London* and the *Film Review* annuals, published since 1945, which survey all films released in Britain. For any film enthusiast of a certain age, the news of Speed's death at the age of eighty-six evoked memories of a vanished world: a world where you talked of 'going to the pictures', where there were no film buffs but only film fans, people who flocked to their Odeon and ABC cinemas and had as their idols handsome chaps like Ronald Colman or Stewart Granger, or Technicolored ladies like Betty Grable or Ava Gardner, whose bright red lips regularly scorched *Film Review*'s pages of coloured plates.

Speed's first *Film Review* was implicitly addressed, in his words, 'to those who are interested in the cinema as entertainment, as art, or merely as a cheap and pleasing manner of passing the time'.[1] The categories of entertainment and art are still with us, if hugely altered, but the last concept reads very strangely. Few except senior citizens with grey afternoons to spare would own up to going to a cinema in Britain simply to pass the time: for the young bulk of the population, bombarded by media advertising and product from the earliest age, keeping up with the movies, particularly the American ones, is a sheer necessity, like breathing.

So what about 'cheap and pleasing'? On average, going to the cinema remains cheaper than visiting the theatre or opera, though the sum involved (£8 or so in the West End) can hardly be called negligible. For those some way beyond the 15–25 age range that is Hollywood's chief constituency, a cinema visit may not always be pleasing either. Consider briefly the experience from an old-timer's viewpoint. You reach your seat after running an olfactory obstacle course past the lobby's popcorn dispensers: the old orange drink Kia-Ora, metallic in taste, but at least odourless, has long disappeared. A disinterested employee tears your ticket and leaves you to tumble into a viewing space that might have the dimensions of a shoebox. And then what do you see? It could, with luck, be *Saving Private Ryan*, or *Love is the Devil*. It could also be *Species II*, *Lethal Weapon 4* or *The Real Howard Spitz*. These were some of the films being released when Speed died.

Fifty years of social shifts and upheavals have obviously transformed Britain's film culture, like the country at large, almost beyond recognition. Yet the interesting point is that you do not even have to be F. Maurice Speed, with a mindset formed in the 1930s, to feel the changes. The landscape today looks far different even if your only reference point is the 1980s.

Let us turn back the clock just ten years, to the beginning of the 1990s. This, too, seems far distant, almost as remote as the age of Ava Gardner and Kia-Ora. In 1990 no-one has heard of Quentin Tarantino. The latest British film renaissance has not yet materialised; and the Conservative government seems deaf to industry pleas for a constructive approach to tax concessions and other means of encouraging growth. In 1989, just thirty British films managed to get made, one less than the figure achieved at the start of the 80s.[2] Scriptwriter Frank Cottrell Boyce, later teamed with Michael Winterbottom in *Butterfly Kiss* and *Welcome to Sarajevo*, considers opportunities for production so restricted that he jestingly considers moving to Burkina Faso, in West Africa, where film-making seems in better health.[3] In 1990 itself, the number of British films jumps to sixty, the biggest total since 1979, though there is more diversity than quality in a list that includes *Nuns on the Run*, *The Big Man*, *Bullseye!*, *The Fool* and *Memphis Belle*.

At the start of 1990 Penelope Houston is still scrupulously editing the British Film Institute's *Sight and Sound*, then the country's most widely read organ for serious film writing, and a magazine more alive to the totality of cinema than popular myth suggests. But an old-world bias is clear. Look at the cover for Autumn 1990: 'Nicholas Ray on directing. Lindsay Anderson on Mary Astor. James Ivory on spiders' (a review of *Arachnophobia*): all this superimposed over an image of John Gielgud, resplendent in costume for Greenaway's *Prospero's Books*. This is Houston's last issue as editor, after thirty-four years; next spring a new team will sweep in, with a radically different approach.

As the decade advances, the changes will multiply. In time there is more of everything: more British films (over a hundred per year from 1996), more money to make them, more screens (1,685 in 1990, 2,383 in 1997), more cinemagoers (97.37 million in 1990, 139.3 million in 1997), more educational courses, more media outlets for film promotion and reviewing. In 1990, Barry Norman, an old Fleet Street hand, reigns supreme as the television's favourite movie pundit, handing out bland judgements on the week's releases. Ten years later he is still in business, on a different channel (the satellite channel BSkyB, not the terrestrial BBC). All around, though, are youngsters on sofas, sounding off to the camera. They lack wide experience, but they have the benefit of being the same age as the target audience for most of the films released. They penetrate broadsheet newspapers too. From February 1996, *The Times* begins supplementing its film critic's views with 'Snap Verdicts' from cinemagoers aged around 20, gushing over some mainstream product ('cool soundtrack, sexy Jonny Lee Miller...') while fearlessly trashing art-house product like Theo Angelopoulos's *Ulysses' Gaze*. The film-maker they worship more than anyone – and they are not alone – is Quentin Tarantino.

Unknown in 1990, he soon becomes the flavour of the decade. In the first week of January 1993, *Reservoir Dogs* is released in Britain after twelve months at large in the States. One year later, *Pulp Fiction* debuts at the Cannes Film Festival, and gets a British release by November. Two months later, in January 1995, Tarantino arrives in Britain to be treated like a God, drawing the kind of ecstatic crowds usually reserved for evangelists or rock stars. He is interviewed at the National Film Theatre, prompting such a pressure for tickets that another auditorium is used to relay God's words through a video-feed. Then the Tarantino imitators move in, eager to copy his laid-back brand of violence, post-modern spirit and obsession with low-life criminality. Every other young British film-maker wants to make a Tarantino movie, and for some their wish comes true, most successfully with *Lock Stock and Two Smoking Barrels*, made in 1997.

Aside from Tarantino, the decade also brings a serious decline in repertory programming and opportunities for importing foreign films. The independent distributor and exhibitor becomes increasingly squeezed by the major companies with the muscle and

The British film-maker's wish come true – *Lock Stock and Two Smoking Barrels* (1998)

money. The changing priorities of the BBC and Channel 4 play a part too. In the 70s and 80s their acquisition of television rights had been a key component in financing the theatrical distribution of foreign films, and when TV companies start to lose heart over subtitled films the cost of distribution can become prohibitive. An audience increasingly unwilling to risk its money on new and unknown foreign film-makers also takes its toll. By the end of the decade the Camden Plaza and the Lumière in St Martin's Lane, two London cinemas owned by Artificial Eye, will have closed, joining a melancholy list of venues topped in popular memory by the Academy cinemas in Oxford Street (a casualty in 1986).

The BFI's National Film Theatre goes through its own changes, as it variously responds to perceived shifts in its audience and the financial requirements of a parent body that, even though bolstered by government funds, insists its cinemathèque runs at a profit. In 1990, it is still possible to find an NFT season devoted to esoteric world cinema figures like the Russian director Jacob Protazanov. As the decade advances, the monthly schedules are more likely to feature seasons like 'Sean Connery: The Later Years', or, most famously, 'Fabulous Pfeiffer', a season of twelve Michelle Pfeiffer films shown in December 1992 which immediately becomes a useful stick for journalists to use if they want to beat the BFI.

'Buffs accuse film theatre of mediocrity and vulgarity', runs a startling headline in *The Times* on April 18, 1995. The British Film Institute has long attracted criticism for some of its activities, merited or not; but it is a new and significant phenomenon of the 1990s for the complaint to be about undue pursuit of popular appeal and bums on seats. In the 1970s, the most vocal complaint was about the theorists roosting in the Institute's education department, who filled the pages of *Screen* magazine with tortuous articles written with jargon and methodologies absorbed from French linguistic theory (with a little Marxism thrown in). Complaints about élitist intellectuals were still abroad in 1986 when Alan Parker took the occasion of his TV contribution to British Film Year, *A Turnip-head's Guide to British Cinema*, to deliver sometimes wild swipes at the BFI's publications and production policies.[4] But now the structuralists, like the communists after 1989, have run to ground, or recanted their sins. The field is clear for more prosaic complaints about money and resources: about 'dumbing down' at the NFT or the revamped *Sight and Sound*; or the use of funds, including Lottery money, for the construction of an IMAX cinema, one of several past BFI endeavours seen as needlessly duplicating activities best left to the commercial sector. And Alan Parker, old gripes forgotten, served as the BFI's chairman from 1998 to late 1999, eager to promote the two new buzzwords: education and access.

Such are some of the surface signs of the changes in British film culture in the 1990s. But to understand their full significance we need to acknowledge some underlying changes to people's very awareness of cinema during the decade. From one standpoint, the 90s have been marked by an explosion of general interest and knowledge in contemporary films, in step with the increased hold the media exert over our lives. The more TV channels there are, terrestrial or satellite, the more they use films to fill out the schedules and pull in viewers. The glossy magazine *Empire*, first published in Britain in 1989, develops during the decade into the country's best-selling film publication, with star profiles and Hollywood releases prominently featured. Pages of broadsheet newspapers are spattered with 'soft' news stories about Kate Winslet, Ewan McGregor, or the trivial doings of some Hollywood stars, previously thought the tabloids' preserve ('Kate Winslet on sex, drugs, and losing weight': *The Times*, January 23, 1999). Film, especially Hollywood film, is the world's universal language.

Things seem equally booming away from the bright lights. Courses in media studies at Britain's universities and art colleges have increased. The 1990 edition of the *BFI Film and TV Handbook* lists some 166 courses. By the 1998 edition, there are 270 to take into account, some offering elements of practical training, many more wrestling with selected areas of film history and theory, including matters of race, gender and social stereotyping, national identity, postcolonial cinema, and British cinema. More people are walking the streets with degrees in film and media studies than ever before. More people buy film books too: aside from other publishers' celebrity biographies, Faber and Faber keep the shop shelves stocked with their film scripts, anthologies of directors' thoughts (*Scorsese on Scorsese*, etc.), and their own quirky film annuals, *Projections*, begun in 1992 as a way for film-makers to speak their mind about the turmoil of world cinema.

From another standpoint, however, people's awareness of cinema has contracted, not expanded. As each year's releases pile up, cinema accumulates more past, and more gets forgotten, never known about, even in academic spheres. The smart put-down used to be that for many film enthusiasts cinema begins in 1977 with *Star Wars*. But that gibe is now out-of-date. Richard Holmes, producer of *Shooting Fish* (1997), in which some critics identified a freewheeling 1960s feel, proudly declares that both he and his director, Stefan Schwartz, had 'almost no knowledge of films before 1980'.[5] Cinema's history can still be glimpsed at the NFT, on video, on television, but there is a shrinking incentive to explore areas of cinema off the beaten track, unsanctified by fashion. Students across the country pile up papers on the films of Peter Greenaway; but no-one, teacher or student, finds an opportunity to dig up an earlier intellectual at large like Adrian Brunel, a bright spark of the 1920s who never found a proper footing in the commercial film industry.

Indeed, there is some argument for questioning whether in the 1990s it is correct to refer to a film culture at all, especially if we remember Matthew Arnold's Victorian hymns of praise to a culture offering 'the best knowledge and thought of the time, and a true source, therefore of sweetness and light'.[6] Perhaps what swirls around us in the air as we watch or read about our films is merely the hot gas produced by an explosion of marketing and hype.

When British films enjoyed a creative surge in the early 60s, with new directors from stage or television, and fresh actors with northern accents, it was possible to see connecting threads in the body of work. Film-makers like Tony Richardson and John Schlesinger were determinedly shaking off old habits and donning new ones, some imported from the French New Wave. They had a purpose. But however striking each individual film, the latest British boom has no similar thrust: the pile of miscellaneous product is simply larger, bolder, and occasionally more profitable, than the small heaps produced in the 70s and 80s.

Outside the cinemas, the spirit of the age discourages debates about ideas and values, traditional components in any culture worth the name. Anything that smacks of élitism is out. Market forces, or pragmatism if you will, are in. The past is out, too; or at least so it seemed in the first editorial for the revamped *Sight and Sound*, published in May 1991. Philip Dodd, currently director of the Institute of Contemporary Arts, declared that the new magazine 'has no interest in nostalgia for the good old things; it wants to start from the bad new things'.[7] Bad new things like serial killer movies: pride of place in the first issue goes to an article by Amy Taubin of New York's *Village Voice* picking over the genre in the light of *The Silence of the Lambs*.

To readers who grew to cine-literacy with Penelope Houston's magazine, Philip Dodd's brash new creation seemed a distasteful upstart from the streets, little better than *Empire* with a sprinkling of pretensions. Yet all the new *Sight and Sound* was doing, for better or worse, was responding to the world outside its offices, reflecting a post-modern age that officially saw no distinction between high and low culture (and unofficially thought that low culture, being more popular, was better). In the same year, 1991, Julie Burchill and friends founded *The Modern Review*, filling its pages with sneering comments about 'sandal-wearing academics' and excited articles about the TV soap *Knots Landing*, or Keanu Reeves's 'bodacious sex appeal'.[8]

After May 1997, the new egalitarianism won the official endorsement of Tony Blair's Labour government. In a collection of his speeches, *Creative Britain*, Chris Smith, Secretary of State for Culture, Media, and Sport, was happy to tell readers that Noel Gallagher, of Oasis, and the contemporary classical composer George Benjamin are 'both musicians of the first rank'; nor could he acknowledge any distinction in value between Bob Dylan and John Keats. In the world of Cool Britannia they were all equal citizens.[9] Smith explained the new egalitarianism as a matter of 'bringing democracy to culture': hence the change in his government department from National Heritage to Culture, Media, and Sport. There may also be some 'political correctness' at work: a reluctance to declare that one thing has more value than another, for fear of offending those without the experience, education or skills to appreciate it.

In the film world, however, a scale of values certainly exists, especially for audiences. For all-round entertainment, Hollywood tops the scale. Hollywood also comes second, third and fourth. Britain delivers a few big pleasures. The rest of the world scarcely features. So perhaps our film culture, if we have one, is basically American, not home-grown at all? The point is worth considering.

Certainly, the industry and media-driven hype about our film renaissance obscures the fact that American films and fashions remain what the bulk of the population want and get. At the start of the decade, eighty per cent of the nationwide box office gross goes into the pockets of American distributors. In 1997, British films account for less than ten per cent of the home market, no better than their share in Scandinavia or Spain: Labour's declared goal on taking office was to double the figure.[10]

Writing early in 1998, Chris Smith could crow in his introduction to *Creative Britain* that films like *The Full Monty* and *Mrs Brown* have already brought the figure to twenty-three per cent. But the success of a few films distorts the general picture. As other chapters in this book reveal, over half the British films made never find any theatrical distributor; those that do face an unequal battle with Hollywood product to achieve a public profile and secure enough screen time to exploit their potential. Hollywood stars alone ensure that most American product arrives pre-sold to the public. On its release in the autumn of 1998, posters for *Lethal Weapon 4* bore the slogan 'The faces you love. The action you expect'. No British film could be advertised like that: in British cinema we never know what to expect. The sheer diversity of our film product in the late 90s may be a sign of artistic strength, but it presents a big marketing difficulty. Most British films must build up public perception from ground zero, unless they carry one of the few marketable stars, or can be pitched as a sequel to *Trainspotting* or *Four Weddings and a Funeral*.

The Americanisation of our film culture is nothing new. Ever since the 1920s, Hollywood films have been what the British public wanted, and what they were given, apart from the special circumstances of World War Two: even then, you only need turn to Speed's first *Film Review* annuals to see the appeal of Technicolor glamour to a country weary of war and its privations. But in film as in society at large America's influence has now reached levels and depths previously unimaginable. Take a typical phenomenon of the 1990s, *Empire* magazine. The dominant coverage of Hollywood releases, stars and fashions is to be expected. What is more striking is the kind of language used by its writers and readers, both enraptured by American usage and pronunciation. A glance through the letters pages of 1994, when the magazine was edited by Philip Thomas, reveals words and spellings like 'yeah', 'geddit', 'go figure', and, my favourite, 'cur-r*eeeepy*!'. The London listings magazine *Time Out*, long a crucial source of news and views for metropolitan buffs, speaks a similar language at times.

The multiplex cinema is another sign of the decade. Stand with me in the foyer of one of these still burgeoning complexes, the Warner Village at the O2 shopping mall in Finchley Road, West Hampstead, opened in the autumn of 1998. Bugs Bunny and other Warner cartoon characters wait to greet you, alongside the ranks of popcorn dispensers. Coloured lights play on the ground, suggesting Las Vegas or a club's dance floor, though the ambience in general presumes that the customer's average age is about thirteen. We could be in any American cinema; or any multiplex in the western world built by Warners, UCI, National Amusements or one of the other great chains.

The multiplex is not, of course, solely a 90s phenomenon: the first newly-built British multiplex, the ten-screen Point at Milton Keynes, dates from 1985, and existing cinemas had been giving birth to smaller auditoria since the late 60s. In January 1991, *Variety* reports that the building of multiplexes is tapering off.[11] But this is premature; by the end of the decade, buoyed by rises in admissions figures, the circuit chiefs are scouring inner and outer city sites for suitable land, and the multiplex gives birth to the megaplex (a term trademarked within the UK by Virgin Cinemas), capable of offering over twenty screens per building. In none of them, however, is there much space for films beyond the mainstream, something brazenly acknowledged in February 1999 by the magazine *Total Film* when it headlines one of its review pages with the words 'Round up. Those others: the arty farty smarties not at your multiplex . . .'). America rules inside the cinema and out.

This is a snapshot, perhaps inevitably subjective, of the climate in which British films during the 1990s have been conceived, made, and seen. The snapshot can be enlarged and tested by examining a representative cross-section of films from the late 1990s, the very films thrust into the shoebox cinemas, beefed up in *Empire*, pooh-poohed by Barry Norman, rhapsodised or scorned by *Sight and Sound*.

Pride of place goes to *The Full Monty* (1997), one of the flagships of the British renaissance, though there are shadows to its success story. Unemployed Sheffield steelworkers and friends band together to earn much-needed money and pride by stripping on stage like the Chippendales: profitable plot material, this, though imagine the extra sharpness it might have acquired had Simon Beaufoy's script been made in the 1980s, when the industrial north was truly in the grip of the recession. In the late 90s, the film seemed almost a period piece, like Mark Herman's *Brassed Off* (1996), another comedy that wraps up human deprivation in feel-good sentiment. British cinema has usually been slow at catching the pulse and feel of the moment, and the trumpeted arrival of Cool Britannia did not bring much change, unless one counts *Spice World: The Movie* (1997). There was also something typically and sadly British about the way the country failed to benefit financially from its own handiwork. *The Full Monty* was entirely financed and distributed by one of the US majors, Twentieth Century-Fox, who pummeled the land with teasing advertising, crucial for pulling in the crowds. The praise went to Britain, but all the film's profits went to America.

The power of America and the pull of the past can also be seen in John Madden's *Mrs Brown* (1997), the story of Queen Victoria's relationship with her manservant, John Brown. This was planned and executed as a BBC television film, with some of the expected ingredients: historical subject matter; actors in mutton-chop whiskers and crinoline galore; a leading performance by a theatrical notable (Judi Dench); and an eye-catching serious turn by a comedian (Billy Connolly). The film's heritage slant caught the attention of Miramax Films, who bought it for theatrical release in the States. An unveiling at the Cannes Film Festival in May 1997 crowned its transformation from small-screen drama to a movie event. Coincidentally, *Mrs Brown* was released in Britain in the week following the death of Diana, Princess of Wales, a time for much public thought about royalty and personal happiness. The film went on to achieve a small success at the local box-office (over two million pounds in its initial British release), and its well-bred nature meant *Mrs Brown* was well-positioned for the Oscar race. Judi Dench was duly nominated for Best Actress in 1998, but lost to Helen Hunt in *As Good As It Gets*. It is a sobering, if not horrifying, thought, but for a British film today the intimate, amusing, genteel *Mrs Brown* actually might be as good as it gets.

The decade's retreat from the cutting edge is certainly in evidence. Derek Jarman is dead. Peter Greenaway gets a withering rebuke from critics and audiences for *The Baby of Maçon*, restores some prestige with *The Pillow Book*, but overall expends more creative energy on art exhibitions and museum installations than film-making. And the BFI's production division withdraws from funding features after a decade of mixed fortunes. Some titles, once made, sit on the shelf; others, released, deserve to sit alongside. Still others, like *Under the Skin* and *Gallivant*, find a warm reception, and it is ironic that the closure announcement came as *Love is the Devil*, John Maybury's film about the gay loves and bitchy milieu of the painter Francis Bacon, co-produced with BBC Films, scored a notable hit at Cannes in May 1998. On release in October 1998, good reviews, media interest in Bacon, and a simmering row with the painter's estate ensured the film a high profile. In style, *Love is the Devil* showed an experimental film-maker, formerly an assistant to Jarman, confidently handling conventional dialogue and actors, and reaching out towards the mainstream. The film was released by Artificial Eye, in origins a company committed to high European art (who else would handle the films of Jean-Marie Straub?), but latterly forced by the market-place to fill their schedules with less testing, English-language product.

Love is the Devil found a niche, but there was less room for the films of Ken Loach. Yet he is a survivor, sticking to his sobering material and plain aesthetic no matter who his paymaster is. Throughout the 1990s, Loach's films almost consistently won critical approval, along with prizes at the major film festivals, yet they made little dent at the box-office. UIP, a company much attacked in Europe (France especially) for swamping cinemas with American product, chose to distribute *Ladybird Ladybird* (1994), but still the film made little headway. The multiplex experience draws audiences that want to be taken away from their drab urban surroundings towards the Hollywood pizzazz echoed by the buildings' architecture and decor. Loach's films drag them back to run-down council housing, to the benefits office, or back to school for a history lesson about the Spanish Civil War or Nicaragua: places audiences do not want to go to. Britain's film culture in the 90s tolerates Loach's spartan humanism, but does not endorse it. In 1997, Loach's Nicaragua film, *Carla's Song*, earned a box-office total of £322, 661. In the same year, a comparatively minor Mike Leigh film, *Career Girl*, earned £492,772, while in 1996 his *Secrets and Lies* earned over three times as much.[12] Leigh's gift for wrenching deep feelings out of social caricature brings him closer to the public pulse.

Leigh's box-office take pales, however, alongside *Bean* (£17 million in 1997), or even *Shooting Fish* (£4 million). The latter is one of many films that arrive carrying the tag, 'Supported by the National Lottery through the Arts Council of England'. Its Lottery contribution is £1 million, and the film becomes the first so funded to be in a position to repay its loan from box-office receipts. Stefan Schwartz and Richard Holmes' film earns its place in these case histories, however, more from the nature of the material. Lottery funding encourages films to rush into production before the script is in proper shape, and this

Shooting Fish (1997) sponsored by the National Lottery through the Arts Council of Great Britain

breezy tale of young con-artists in London suffers particularly from messy, superfluous detail: a real problem of the age, despite all the books and seminars offering practical help on writing and selling film scripts. The attitudes behind the script are also interesting. The film is Janus-faced. Part of it wants to be up-to-date: Britpop sounds parade on the soundtrack; cock-snooking, street-smart characters parade on the screen. The film also looks back to the past, not just to the 60s, but to older attitudes towards class and property (Stuart Townsend and Dan Futterman's characters want to buy a stately home: not something most spectators would easily identify with). The unevenness of *Shooting Fish* proves no impediment at the box-office; though it does make you question whether Britain gives enough help nurturing the requisite talent and thoughtfulness to back up the money now available to film-makers.

And then there is the cinema according to Irvine Welsh. In 1999 the dishevelled nihilism of *The Acid House* was too much for the public to swallow, but three years earlier, *Trainspotting*, adapted from his novel, topped the list of British films at the box-office: earning over £13 million. It came ninth in the year's overall top twenty, sandwiched between *Jumanji* and *The Nutty Professor*. An emerging pin-up, Ewan McGregor, helped: he is Renton, the leading character in a jumble of junkies, layabouts and psychos. So did the film's abrasive stance. It gives the audience no hiding place from the drug use, the violence, the pounding music by Pulp, Blur or Sleeper. Nor was there any blanket of morality cast over the characters' actions: they just do what they do. The film, widely pre-sold sight unseen on the strengths of the makers' *Shallow Grave*, was aimed squarely at youngsters willing to go with the flow, wherever it leads ('16 to 24, the cinema audience,' said its producer, Andrew Macdonald) and showed absolutely no interest in courting anyone else.[13] That there are limits to young audiences' endorsement of Welsh's world, however, was proved by *The Acid House*. Compared to this, *Trainspotting* is a film you would take your mother to. Welsh himself adapted three of his stories for the screen, stories of wild lives, drug excess and violence on Edinburgh's bleakest housing estates. The director Paul McGuigan hurled Welsh's world unfiltered onto the screen, producing a movie so alienating to its intended audience that it scarcely made a mark at the box-office. There was only one place for *Total Film* to put its negative review: in the round-up, among the 'arty farty smarties'.

Trainspotting and its success certainly displays the resonance of youth culture in 90s Britain, and cinema's place, on occasion, on that culture's front line. But it also demonstrates how British films and the thinking around them have become rigidly compartmentalised. The widely based audience that sustained British films in the days of mass cinemagoing, the heyday of F. Maurice Speed, has gone. Films are now aimed at very specific targets, niche markets determined by age, gender, and smaller markers of social behaviour: whatever culture floats around them is of little help in developing a distinctive national cinema in the face of the Hollywood onslaught. By a charming coincidence *Trainspotting* was released on the same day in 1997 as *Sense and Sensibility* (British material, scenery and cast; American finance; a Taiwanese director). Audiences, therefore, could choose between hearts fluttering and irony creeping among bonnets, top hats and grazing sheep, and Edinburgh's finest drug users showing their mettle, injecting and puking. Something for everyone, in fact.

Notes

1 'The year in the cinema', in *Film Review* (London: Macdonald and Co., 1945), unpaginated.
2 These and other figures come from Eddie Dyja (ed.), *BFI Film and Television Handbook 1999* (London: BFI, 1998) pp. 28–9.
3 Adam Dawtrey, 'Scripting a pic renaissance', *Variety*, 15 December 1997, p.11.
4 For coverage of the programme, see David Robinson, 'Cinema at war within itself', *The Times*, 12 March 1986, p.19, and Penelope Houston, 'Parker, Attenborough, Anderson', *Sight and Sound*, Summer 1986, pp. 152–4.
5 Sheila Johnston, 'British pic biz bounces back', *Variety*, 15 December 1997, p. 4.
6 Matthew Arnold, *Culture and Anarchy*, ed. Stefan Collini (Cambridge: Cambridge University Press, 1993), p. 79.
7 'No turning back', *Sight and Sound*, May 1991, p. 3.
8 See Clive Davis, 'Who put the camp in campus?', *The Times*, July 12, 1993, p. 27.
9 Chris Smith, *Creative Britain* (London: Faber and Faber, 1998), p.3. The comparison between Dylan and Keats is drawn from an interview in *Spectator*, 28 March 1998, mentioned in *The Times*, 27 March 1998, p. 8.
10 Figures for 1990 from *Variety*, 21 January 1991, p. 58 ('U.S. majors take 80% of the pic pie'); 1997 statistic from *Variety*, 11 August 1997, p. 7 ('Hollywood muscle pushes Brit pix blitz').
11 Don Groves, 'Cinema's multiplex fever cooling down', *Variety*, 21 January 1991, p. 62.
12 These and subsequent figures are drawn from Eddie Dyja (ed.), *BFI Television Handbook 1998* (London: BFI, 1997), p. 35, and *BFI Film and Television Handbook 1999*, pp. 32–3.
13 Robert Crampton, 'The Hit Squad', *The Times Magazine*, 20 January 1996, p. 21.

Chapter 4

The Film Industry and the Government: 'Endless Mr Beans and Mr Bonds'?

Toby Miller

> A cinematograph film represents something more than a mere commodity to be
> bartered against others.
>
> (*Palache Report*, 1944)[1]

When we talk about government film policy, we are referring to a network of practices and institutions intended to sustain and regenerate production, distribution and exhibition. These include technical training, tax breaks, local government assistance, copyright legislation, co-production treaties, European Community programmes, media education, archiving, ambassadorial services and censorship. Such practices are planned and executed through networks of institutions and discourses. In the domain of film, public debate over policy is minimal in comparison with arguments over whether television rots your brain, or videos turn you into a mass murderer. For Colin MacCabe, 'almost all appeals to "policy", like its repellent semantic cousin "management", are appeals away from a reality which is too various and too demanding'.[2] But getting to know film policy and intervening in it is an important part of participating in film culture.[3] Resistance goes nowhere unless it takes hold institutionally. For example, the gains made in British film by women and people of colour have come about through harnessing the work of social movements to a critique of state policies and programmes in actionable ways.

During the 1980s, the Conservative government unravelled a gradually accreted system of subvention which had protected and stimulated the British film industry since the 1927 Cinematograph Films Act. The system had operated under twin imperatives – to deal with the cultural impact of *le défi américain* (in 1926, the *Daily Express* suggested Hollywood was turning British youth into 'temporary American citizens'); and to shore up the domestic industry.[4] The Tories under Margaret Thatcher, however, were not interested in the screen as a site either of cultural diversity, or industrial development through state participation.[5]

Seventy years on from that first legislation, identical imperatives apply. The 1990s opened with the British film industry in a period of extreme fragility and uncertainty and a Tory government indifferent to its fate. But the news was not all bad. As one critic put it, the 'lumpen-monetarist approach to this industry has swept away some of the humbug', though he warned that 'the effect will be purely negative if the elimination of an industrial policy for the cinema is not used as an opportunity to promote a cultural policy in its place'.[6]

Has this happened? Or are public subsidies being given to support unspecified claims about cultural maintenance, diversity, and development? Was the commerce-culture demon of film policy under any sort of control in 1990s Britain? Absolute answers depend on textual and audience studies, but there are suggestive signs in the debates signalled and thrown up by government action. This chapter goes looking for them under three broad headings: the New International Division of Cultural Labour; Institutions; and Facing the Millennium.

The New International Division of Cultural Labour

I want to... ensure that film making in the UK remains a pleasurable and profitable experience for overseas companies.

(Chris Smith, 1997)[7]

In reviewing foreign films made in the UK, the *Independent* newspaper refers to Britain as 'Our green and profitable land', while David Bruce notes of Scotland that it 'has tended to be regarded more as a film location and source of stories than as a film culture'.[8] The same might be said for much of Britain. For apart from some efforts in support of a local film culture, the period under review saw bald attempts at a purely industrial policy to exploit the New International Division of Cultural Labour (NICL).

The NICL derives from reworkings of economic dependency theory that followed the inflationary chaos of the 1970s. Developing markets for labour and sales and a shift from the spatial *sen*sitivities of electrics to the spatial *in*sensitivities of electronics, pushed businesses beyond treating Third World countries as suppliers of raw materials, to look on them as shadow-setters of the price of work, competing among themselves and with the First and Second Worlds for employment. Just as manufacturing fled the First World, cultural production has also relocated, though largely within the industrialised market economies. This is happening at the level of film production, marketing and information. Across the screen industries, labour market slackness and developments in global transportation and communications technology have diminished the need for film industries to be concentrated in one place. Fragmentation reduces labour costs and allows multinational companies to take advantage of tax incentives, exchange rates and other factors of production, moving on when they are offered more favourable terms elsewhere. Communications technology permits electronic off-line editing across the world, but also facilitates increasingly sophisticated digital effects, problematising the very need for location shooting. The trend is clearly towards horizontal connections to other media and a break-up of public-private distinctions in ownership, control, and programming philosophy.[9]

Britain has been a major player in the NICL, as both foreign investor and recipient of off-shore production funds. In one sense none of this is new, since Hollywood has long tapped the UK for people, locations, settings and stories. But from the 1980s, it became impossible to recoup the cost of most British feature films domestically, and the industry was forced to look outside. The necessity of finding employment for skilled workers and their employers turned the industry into a welcome mat for foreign, particularly US, film-makers. In 1991 a British Film Commission (BFC) was formed to market UK production expertise and locations by providing overseas producers with a free service articulating local talent, locations and subsidies, and generating a national network of urban and regional film commissions. In 1997, seven Hollywood movies accounted for fifty-four per cent of the £465 million spent on feature film production in the UK. But Britain faces increasing competition to capture Hollywood production finance. Between 1990 and 1998, thirty-one film commissions were set up across the globe and many of them, such as the British Virgin Islands Film Commission, are solely concerned with attracting foreign capital. In 1998, the Government opened a British Film Office in Los Angeles in an attempt to facilitate traffic between Hollywood and Britain by offering liaison services to the industry and promoting British locations and talent. The BFC announced the new government's outlook on cinema: 'set firmly at the top of the agenda is the desire to attract more overseas film-makers'.[10]

One key agency, the London Film Commission (LFC), was formed in 1995 with a £100,000 grant from the Department of National Heritage to attract off-shore film production. It subsequently obtained funding from United International Pictures and the Corporation of the City of London, but needed a bail-out from the government of £95,000 in 1998 when it failed to attract sufficient private-sector money to continue operations. The LFC promotes the capital to overseas film-makers, arranges police permits, and liaises with local residents and businesses. Its defining moment was *Mission: Impossible*. According to the Commissioner, the film's Hollywood producers: 'came up with all these demands and I just went on insisting that, as long as they gave us notice, we could schedule it'.[11]

The hold on foreign capital is always tenuous, however, and depends heavily on foreign exchange rates. Of course, this too relates to state activity – the government's decision to float the pound and free the Bank of England from democratic consultation contributed to a situation in 1998 where a strengthening currency raised costs for overseas investors and encouraged locals to spend elsewhere, with severe implications for off-shore film funds.

In order to keep British studios going, regulations were promulgated under John Major that meant films entirely made in Britain counted as British, regardless of theme, setting, or stars. So *Judge Dredd* with Sylvester Stallone is 'British', but *The English Patient*, which did too much of its post-production work abroad to qualify, is not. Until 1998, ninety-two and a half per cent of a film had to be created in the UK. At the end of that year, the government reduced this requirement to seventy-five per cent to encourage those American companies unwilling to relinquish the right to use sophisticated Hollywood special effects and post-production facilities to make their films in Britain.[12]

Britain was a late starter as a co-production partner, although an intergovernmental treaty of 1965 spawned some Anglo-French productions. This agreement specified films of high cultural quality, but assistance was routinely granted to money-spinners when the local industries were in trouble (financing was made available for the James Bond film, *Moonraker*, for example). Increasing European co-operation in the early 90s stimulated new projects, though few of them were commercially successful. Ken Loach, Mike Leigh and Peter Greenaway have all made use of European co-production partners, but more money has been lavished on expensive costume pictures such as *Nostradamus* (Roger Christian, 1993), *Victory* (Mark Peploe, 1998) and *The Serpent's Kiss* (Philippe Rousselot, 1997) which have conspicuously failed to find an audience capable of recuperating their £6–8 million budgets. In 1993 Britain joined Eurimages, the continental film fund of the Council of Europe, which supports documentary, exhibition, distribution and marketing through interest-free loans, but the Conservative government thought it poor value for money and quickly withdrew.[13] During this period, the European Commission's MEDIA programme was launched, with the aim of pushing European film production towards responsiveness to local cultures while keeping a close eye on profitability – an attempt to blend culture and commerce.

What do film industry mavens make of this situation? Michael Kuhn, managing director of PolyGram Filmed Entertainment (PFE), the company which dominated the British film industry in the 90s, considers that 'Europe (when you talk about mainstream movies) is almost a vassal state to that Hollywood business' and argues that only 'supra-national government institutions' can turn this around, because of the lack of a firm financial base to compete with Hollywood's mix of production and distribution and the United States' cartel-like discrimination against European producers.[14] Ironically, PFE has now been taken over by the North American drinks conglomerate, Seagram, and will merge in some form with another of Seagram's subsidiaries, the Hollywood major, Universal.

In contrast to Kuhn, Rupert Murdoch welcomes 'new joint ventures between the Hollywood majors and both public and private broadcasting' in Europe, citing the numbers of European workers invisibly employed in the making of *Titanic*: 'this cross-border cultural co-operation is not the result of regulation, but market forces. It's the freedom to move capital, technology and talent around the world that adds value, invigorates ailing markets, creates new ones'.[15] This view finds support in the upper echelons of the EC, which has offered US film marketers unhindered access to the European marketplace – a new turn for the Commission, driven by the same neoliberalism that has characterised Tony Blair's Labour government and its predecessor.

Films can also function as plenipotentiaries for the state. The preferred image of Britain is one of heritage and tranquillity. The Foreign Office declined to fund black British films at the 1992 Carthage film festival because they were deemed 'not likely to be representative of British cinema' and might 'give a bad image of Britain. . . . After all, they're not exactly *Howard's End*'.[16] And for the first British-Bangla Film Festival, held in Dhaka in 1998, the British Council selected films with colonial echoes such as *Mrs Brown, Chariots of Fire, The English Patient* and *A Night to Remember*, to show alongside Bangla movies.

Institutions

Television has more or less become the film industry.
(John Hill and Martin McLoone, 1997)[17]

The divide between television and cinema is barely sustainable other than in very limited exhibitionary terms. When it comes to personnel, ideas, genres, funds, companies and the state, the lines are very blurred indeed. The 1990s saw the BBC cling to a vision of itself as a groundbreaker, but some critics saw it as stuck in a mentality of white domination, a world of colonialism *manqué* that still views diversity as an add-on. Isaac Julien notes how many black directors have felt unwelcome there, and don't fit into the Corporation's usual narrative for its successful employees.[18] Channel Four's Multicultural Department, initially hailed as an important intervention into Britain's screen whiteness, did not succeed in stabilising independent black film production and served as a token that let the mainstream of the station carry on with business as ever.

The BBC has worked with an annual budget for film production of approximately £5 million through the 90s. This is a tiny sum in film industry terms, though the BBC also buys TV rights to independently produced pictures.[19] BSkyB has invested small amounts in British films and has participated in film pre-sales from 1994 in order to fulfil obligations for European content.[20]

Toward the end of the decade Channel Four transformed its programming strategy and started a film company, Film Four Ltd, with funds freed up by the belated opportunity to reinvest profits rather than remit them to ITV. The new firm was envisaged as a movie studio, but it had much work to do – in 1998, Channel Four films accounted for just one per cent of UK box-office revenues. In February 1999, Film Four announced a London-based partnership for production and global distribution with Arnon Milchan and TF1, primarily designed to make and sell UK films.[21] It would be odd to rhapsodise Film Four's success as a commercial bridgehead, but it did at least stave off privatisation. Nonetheless, increasing commercialisation does not bode well for the independent and minority sector's access to the channel or its charter obligation of multiculturalism.[22]

The commerce–culture divide of British film can be seen at work in the British Film Institute during the decade. At the start of the 1990s, the Institute produced a number of documents arising from a meeting with Margaret Thatcher to discuss the future industry. The plan that emerged was commercial rather than cultural. It attempted to address the shortfall between outgoings and incomings by encouraging industry restructuring, fiscal incentives to invest and additional co-productions, as well as establishing a firm to sell British films internationally.[23] At the same time, Colin MacCabe, BFI Head of Research, claimed that the Institute had demonstrated a 'long-term commitment to a national television and cinema which fully articulates the multitude of cultures that now constitute modern Britain' and claimed Britain as the only European country that had been 'genuinely harnessing the talents of a whole range of communities'.[24] So culturecrat MacCabe claimed a continuing and impressive role for an inclusive film culture, while his commercecrat colleagues proposed a new agenda.

Of course, the dividing line between them is not so great as this might imply, as both were concerned with cinematic specificity and commercial viability. This is clear from the breadth and overlap of their work, from UK Film Initiative pamphlets like *The View From Downing Street*, to the Museum of the Moving Image and *BFI 2000*.[25] The crisis of the left in the 1990s has seen an embrace of the market, while the triumph of the right has seen it needing to heed the demands of minorities, even if it is as niche target consumers rather than as workers and migrants.

Views vary greatly on the merits of British Screen Finance, a quasi-autonomous non-government organisation formed in 1986 to assist commercially oriented films. It has operated through state funds, BSkyB deals, left-over National Film Finance Corporation money, Channel Four and the European Co-production Fund. David Puttnam claims that it has managed to link well with Europe, bring on new talent, and assist unusual projects to secure funding (he lists *Orlando, Scandal* and *The Crying Game* as examples).[26] By contrast, Isaac Julien details instances that suggest black film makers consistently fail to obtain support.[27]

In addition to London-focused bodies, there is vibrant but under-resourced life elsewhere in the UK in the work of production agencies for Wales, Northern Ireland and

Between commerce and culture. Sally Potter's *Orlando* (1992)

Scotland, and in cities such as Sheffield and Glasgow, interested in boosting their cultural credentials (or not: the Liverpool Film Commission elects to advertise itself internationally as 'a lookalike for ... Nazi Germany, and cities of the Eastern bloc'). This work is funded by the BFI, local councils, arts agencies and the Scottish and Welsh Offices.[28] 'Bringing together a range of interests a Glasgow Film Fund was established in 1992 with financial inputs from the Glasgow Development Agency, Glasgow City Council, the European Regional Development Fund and Strathclyde Business Development. This patchwork of sources is typical, as is the decision to combine funds in high-end conventional narrative film-making rather than locally textured, independent, 'edge' cinema.[29] According to David Bruce,

> Location shooting by overseas companies in 1995 ... [was] at a record level and Scotland would be appearing on screen in its own right, or doubling for somewhere else, all over the world. (Someone said that had there been a 1996 Oscar for 'best supporting country' Scotland would have won).[30]

When the various bodies were amalgamated into Scottish Screen in the late 90s, there were accusations that locally-derived Lottery funds were lining the pockets of the English, and outrage when the board, comprised of TV executives and the London Scottish, voted to finance a project by their own Chair.[31]

A Northern Ireland Film Council began in 1989 on a volunteer basis as a forum dedicated to 'the development and understanding of film, television and video in the region'. The Department of Education funded the Council from 1992 and it became a local site for disbursing screen-related Arts Council money and combining disparate funding streams, as well as a public sphere for debating the need to regionalise BBC production.[32] In 1997 it became the Northern Ireland Film Commission, with the task of attracting outside production. Andrew Reid, the Commission's locations officer, reported that: 'Producers come here expecting the place to be rubble.... Instead they end up having a great time. And I can show them mountains, beaches and great scenery. They can't quite believe it'.[33] Five features were shot in Northern Ireland in 1997 – a considerable increase on earlier years.[34]

Much of the money now available to these bodies, both directly and indirectly, comes from the National Lottery, launched in 1995 and now a major source of funds for film production. One idea floated under the Major government was to take £100 million from Lottery funds and match it with £200 million from the City to start a major film studio, complete with share offering. However before Labour's arrival this had been rejected in favour of a franchise system and in 1997 the Arts Council of England nominated DNA, Pathé and the Film Consortium for Lottery franchises and encouraged them to unify production, distribution and sales. The decision was by no means universally popular. One critic complained that under-achieving 'whingeing cultural tsars' had turned into 'greedy moguls' via a system that discouraged diversity and innovation.[35] In December 1998, the government announced that £27 million would be allocated to film from the Lottery, along with £20.8 million in annual direct grants.[36]

Besides measures designed to stimulate film-making, there are other policies which affect the industry. The deregulatory verve of the Conservative government did not apply to questions of public morality in quite the same way that it did to economics. Censorship was increased through the Video Recordings Act in 1984 as part of the moral panic surrounding young people and popular genres, and the Criminal Justice Act of 1994 required censors to address issues of horror, drug use, criminal conduct and violence following the James Bulger murder case.[37] On other fronts, copyright, company incorporation and industrial relations machinery are also parts of state policy that affect film-making, along with general measures designed to stimulate industry, such as the Enterprise Investment Scheme.[38]

Facing the Millennium

There are catastrophic cycles in the history of British film. This is how they run: British movies suddenly become internationally popular; the Americans arrive and buy up everything they can; some years later they pull out; our industry collapses in the wake.

(Sally Hibbin, 1998)[39]

Each new wave of acclamation for British cinema in the 90s was followed by regretful decline, to the point where the triumphs of 1997 and 1998 came to be seen not so much as vital signs but as harbingers of cyclical failure.[40] When it came to power, the Blair government announced its intention of doubling the share of UK box-office for British films. Within its first hundred days the new administration had appointed the country's first official Minister for Film, announced the three Lottery recipients, permitted Channel Four to spend more on film-making, and introduced a hundred per cent tax rebate scheme for production (later problematised by European rules). This was done in the name of 'helping the film industry to develop from a series of small craft businesses into a properly integrated modern industry'.[41] Plans included raising US $24 million annually for development, production and distribution via a voluntary levy on UK film companies, including subsidiaries of US firms, to form an 'All-Industry Fund'. But the idea was ditched toward the end of 1998, when it became clear that both television companies and Hollywood studios were loath to pay for it.[42] The government announced a restructuring of film funding under the umbrella of a new institution to be born from the amalgamation of the BFI, the BFC, and the film section of the Arts Council of England (which administers the Lottery).[43] Meanwhile, four areas of weakness in the local industry were identified by the government's Advisory Committee on Film Policy – training, generic marketing, distribution and development – and industry-government committees were set up to address such matters and provide points of liaison with sources of private finance.[44] Critics of these plans saw them as adding bureaucracy to already strapped institutions; supporters claimed the new arrangements would streamline and co-ordinate the industry. Meanwhile, training had moved toward a corporatist model via Skillset, a tripartite body with David Puttnam as its titular head.[45]

The rhetoric of modernisation was in keeping with the government's broader industrial policy. The move toward import substitution and export-oriented cultural industrialisation showed a preference for large, consolidated entities that work in competition with one another. In the cinema, this has seen a populist, big-budget, apolitical model preferred to an artisanal 'poor' cinema articulated around social issues. According to Puttnam, 'strong cultural resistance can best be built on the basis of a firm understanding of the realities of the marketplace'. He insists on the need to 'get away from relying on cultural defence, and concentrate our energies on industrial success'.[46] Film Minister Tom Clarke argued for films that were 'Made with passion, fuelled by cash', and expressed his enthusiasm for 'large, vertically integrated companies with deep pockets'.[47] But the aim of increasing the proportion of UK film receipts going to British cinema has proved difficult to achieve: market share fell by half in 1998.[48] Outsiders wondered whether direct state intervention via quotas and levies might be the way forward.[49]

Conclusion

Film policy in Britain shares a dilemma in common with that for most other national cinemas – the commerce–culture relationship. There is always a struggle between the desire to build a viable sector of the economy that provides employment, foreign exchange and multiplier effects; and the desire for a representative and local cinema that reflects seriously upon society through drama (as in the work of directors like Derek Jarman, Isaac Julien, Mike Leigh, Peter Greenaway and Sally Potter). Future research and political action by the left into film must avoid cultural reductionism just as keenly as we used to avoid economic reductionism, beware falling for the rhetorics of consumerism and citizenship and require each part of the commerce–culture divide to illustrate the relationship between multinational capital and diversity, the role of the state in consumption, and the place of corporations in culture. Lastly, we must look to minority and multicultural interests. Colin McArthur's requirements of Scottish film could well be read out to whatever remains of the 'sceptred isle': 'a historically specific grappling with the contradictions of the ... past and present, a set of recurrent themes and styles discernibly amounting to a *collectivity*'.[50] The burden of government to address a population in all its life-forms must animate policy.

The future of British cinema? The massive commercial success, *Bean* (1997)

If it does not, we shall see either 'rootless *Titanic*-style movies, free of geography, culture or humour, that play as well in Prague as in Peoria'. That means 'endless Mr Beans and Mr Bonds', but very few Ms Potters or Mr Juliens.[51]

My thanks to Talitha Espiritu for securing materials and to Robert Murphy for editorial comments.

Notes

1 Quoted in Political & Economic Planning, *The British Film Industry* (London: PEP, 1952), p. 12.

2 Colin MacCabe, 'A Post-National European Cinema: A Consideration of Derek Jarman's *The Tempest* and *Edward II*', in Andrew Higson (ed.), *Dissolving Views: Key Writings on British Cinema* (London: Cassell, 1996), p. 192.

3 Toby Miller, *Technologies of Truth: Cultural Citizenship and the Popular Media* (Minneapolis: University of Minnesota Press, 1998), pp. 71–90, 265.

4 Quoted in Victoria de Grazia, 'Mass Culture and Sovereignty: The American Challenge to European Cinemas, 1920–1960', *Journal of Modern History* vol. 61, no. 1, 1989, p. 53.

5 John Hill, 'British Film Policy', in Albert Moran (ed.), *Film Policy* (London: Routledge, 1996), pp. 101–5.

6 Geoffrey Nowell-Smith, prefatory statement, in Lester Friedman (ed.), *Fires Were Started: British Cinema and Thatcherism* (Minneapolis: University of Minnesota Press, 1993), p. vi.

7 Department for Culture, Media and Sport, 'Chris Smith goes to Hollywood', *M2 PressWIRE*, 27 October 1997.

8 Peter Guttridge, 'Our green and profitable land', *Independent*, 11 July 1996, pp. 8–9;

David Bruce, *Scotland the Movie* (Edinburgh: Polygon, 1996), p. vii.

9 Miller, *Technologies*, pp. 171–81; Toby Miller, 'The Crime of Monsieur Lang: GATT, the Screen, and the New International Division of Cultural Labour', in Moran (ed.), *Film Policy*, pp. 72–84.

10 Peter Guttridge, 'Our green and profitable land', pp. 8–9; Paul McCann, 'Hollywood film-makers desert UK', *Independent*, 14 August 1998, p. 7; John Hiscock, 'Hollywood backs British film drive', *Daily Telegraph*, 24 July 1998, p. 19; http://www.britfilmcom.co.uk/content/filming/site.asp.

11 Louise Jury, 'Mission possible: red tape cut to boost film industry', *Independent*, 4 July 1996, p. 3.

12 Marie Woolf, 'Why the next English Patient will be British', *Independent on Sunday*, 20 December 1998, p. 9.

13 Anne Jäckel, 'European Co-Production Strategies: The Case of France and Britain', in Moran (ed.), *Film Policy*, pp. 85–97.

14 Michael Kuhn, 'How can Europe benefit from the digital revolution?', presentation to the European Audiovisual Conference, Birmingham, 6–8 April 1998. Kuhn severed his links with PolyGram at the beginning of 1999.

15 Rupert Murdoch, presentation prepared for the European Audiovisual Conference, Birmingham, 6–8 April 1998.

16 Quoted in Isaac Julien, 'Burning Rubber's Perfume', in June Givanni (ed.), *Remote Control: Dilemmas of Black Intervention in British Film & TV* (London: BFI, 1995), p. 61.

17 John Hill and Martin McLoone, 'Introduction', in John Hill and Martin McLoone (eds), *Big Picture Small Screen: The Relations Between Film and Television* (Luton: John Libby Media, University of Luton Press, 1996), p. 1.

18 Isaac Julien, 'Burning Rubber's Perfume', in Givanni (ed.), *Remote Control*, pp. 56–7.

19 Sarah Street, *British National Cinema* (London and New York: Routledge, 1997), p. 22.

20 John Hill, 'British Television and Film: The Making of a Relationship', in Hill and McLoone (eds), *Big Picture Small Screen*, pp. 160–1.

21 Adam Dawtrey, and Benedict Carver, 'Power trio ink int'l deal', *Daily Variety Gotham*, 1 March 1999, pp. 1, 34.

22 Adam Dawtrey, 'New strategy comes to the 4', *Variety*, 8–14 February 1999, pp. 33, 40.

23 Steve McIntyre, 'Vanishing Point: Feature Film Production in a Small Country', in John Hill, Martin McLoone, and Paul Hainsworth (eds), *Border Crossing: Film in Ireland, Britain and Europe* (Belfast: Institute of Irish Studies/BFI, 1994), p. 103.

24 Colin MacCabe, 'Preface', in Givanni (ed.), *Remote Control*, pp. ix, x.

25 Jane Headland and Simon Relph, *The View From Downing Street* (London: BFI, 1991) was one of a series of pamphlets published under the rubric 'UK Film Initiatives' by the BFI.

26 David Puttnam, with Neil Watson, *Movies and Money* (New York: Alfred A. Knopf, 1998), p. 250.

27 Isaac Julien, 'Burning Rubber's Perfume', in Givanni (ed.), *Remote Control*, p. 60.

28 Stephen Goodwin, 'Screen revival for Scotland's forgotten film collection', *Independent*, 13 August 1998, p. 6; Steve McIntyre, 'Art and Industry: Regional Film and Video Policy in the UK', in Moran (ed.), *Film Policy*, pp. 215–33; http://www.afilm.com/2/01/03/.

29 Colin McArthur, 'The Cultural Necessity of a Poor Celtic Cinema', in Hill, McLoone and Hainsworth (eds), *Border Crossing*, p. 113.

30 David Bruce, *Scotland the Movie*, p. 4.

31 Don Boyd, 'Cowards, liars, cultural despots and subsidized cronies: a portrait of Britain's film industry – from the inside, naturally...', *New Statesman*, 126, 31 October 1997, p. 34.

32 Geraldine Wilkins, 'Film Production in Northern Ireland', in Hill, McLoone and Hainsworth (eds), *Border Crossing*, pp. 141, 143.

33 David Gritten, 'The other Ireland unreels: after watching the Republic become a movie mecca, the Northern Ireland film industry is growing under today's relatively tranquil conditions', *Los Angeles Times*, 1 February 1998, p. 4.

34 Matt Cowan, and Linda Wertheimer, 'Northern Ireland Film Commission', *All Things Considered*, National Public Radio programme, 18 May 1998, transcript; David Gritten, 'The other Ireland unreels', p. 4. See also John Hill, 'Filming in the north', *Cineaste*, vol. xxiv, nos 2/3, 1999, pp. 26–7.

35 Tim Adler, 'A new script to save British film', *Daily Telegraph*, 26 February 1999; Boyd, 'Cowards, liars, cultural despots and subsidized cronies', p. 34.

36 Marie Woolf, 'Why the next English Patient will be British', *Independent on Sunday*, 20 December 1998, p. 9.

37 Jeffrey Richards, 'British Film Censorship', in Robert Murphy (ed.), *The British Cinema Book* (London: BFI, 1997), p. 176; Miller, *Technologies*, pp. 62, 199–200.

38 KPMG, *Film Financing and Television Programming: A Taxation Guide* (Amsterdam: KPMG, 1996), pp. 225–53; Hilary Clarke, 'Hidden tax rises: the making of the movies', *Independent on Sunday*, 7 March 1999, p. 3.

39 Sally Hibbin, 'Britain has a new film establishment and it is leading us towards disaster', *New Statesman*, 127, 27 March 1998, p. 40.

40 Sheila Johnston, 'Was 'British invasion' boon or bane for foreign?', *Variety*, 22–28 February 1999, p. A10.

41 Department for Culture, Media and Sport, 'Chris Smith goes to Hollywood', *M2 PressWIRE*, 27 October 1997.

42 Tim Adler, 'A new script to save British film', *Daily Telegraph*, 26 February 1999.

43 Eric Boehm, 'Mixed reviews on Brit pic fund revise', *Variety*, 15 December 1998, pp. 5, 24.

44 Adam Dawtrey, 'U.K. pols give up plan for film levy', *Daily Variety Gotham*, 1 December 1998, p. 10.

45 'Northern Ireland Film Commission received Skillset training Kitemark from Lord Puttnam', *M2 PressWIRE*, 22 February 1999.

46 Quoted in Boyd Tonkin, 'Will Lottery funding help Mike Leigh or Ken Loach make more and better films? Not if David Puttnam and his friends have anything to do with it', *New Statesman*, 126, 23 May 1997, p. 38 and Angus Finney, *The State of European Cinema: A New Dose of Reality* (London: Cassell, 1996), p. 8.

47 Tom Clarke, 'Made with passion, fuelled by cash', *New Statesman*, 127, 17 April 1998, p. 23. In July 1998 Clarke was replaced as Films Minister by Janet Anderson.

48 *Economist*, 'European film industry: worrying statistix', 350, 6 February 1999.

49 Ian Christie, 'Will Lottery money assure the British film industry? or should Chris Smith be rediscovering the virtues of state intervention?', *New Statesman*, 126, 20 June 1997, p. 38.

50 Colin McArthur, 'The Cultural Necessity of a Poor Celtic Cinema', in Hill, McLoone and Hainsworth (eds), *Border Crossing*, p. 115. For a contradictory view, see Alan Lovell, 'The British Cinema: The Known Cinema?', in Murphy (ed.), *The British Cinema Book*, p. 241.

51 Sally Hibbin, 'Britain has a new film establishment and it is leading us towards disaster', p. 40.

Chapter 5
Spoilt for Choice? Multiplexes in the 90s

Stuart Hanson

The Advent of the Multiplex

The term 'multiplex' was coined by American exhibitor National Amusements for a new generation of purpose-built cinemas with multiple screen facilities. Unlike twinned and tripled redeveloped traditional cinemas, they possessed superior technological features, dedicated car parking, computerised ticketing and shopping and restaurant facilities. The world's first multiplex (the 4-screen 'Metro Plaza') was opened in a shopping mall in Kansas City by American Multi-Cinema (AMC) in 1966. AMC symbolised a new, aggressive form of cinema chain that took advantage not only of relatively low-cost sites and buildings but also of new forms of employment and managerial practices. By the 1980s the multiplex had consolidated its hold over North America and the major chains began to look to the overseas market for new opportunities. As one American exhibitor observed:

> The situation overseas is ripe for a revolution. The theaters in Europe are like the theaters in the States used to be forty years ago: mostly terrible. But give people a reason to go to the movies more often and they will ... especially to American movies.[1]

In November 1985 AMC opened Britain's first multiplex – The Point in Milton Keynes. In addition to its ten screens, which seated 2,046 people, The Point had a restaurant, brasserie bar and social club. The cinema aimed to draw from a catchment area where some 1.5 million people were believed to be within a forty-five minute car journey. The main selling feature was choice, with two or more showings of individual films per evening, at least one screen showing a U-certificated film and the promise of a more flexible screening programme which might include foreign-language films. 'For the first time in my life,' said David Puttnam, 'I'm standing in a UK cinema for the 80s and 90s.'[2]

The building of The Point was a gamble. The BFI's then director, Wilf Stevenson, recalled that 'most of us were convinced they were bonkers ... people thought that video had killed the cinema off.[3] However, after the first year of operation, attendances had exceeded one million and the cinema was generating over 20,000 admissions a week. It seemed that the great experiment was set to work. The Head of the Cinema Exhibitors Association (CEA), John Wilkinson, was in no doubt as to the impact of the new multiplex operators on attendances. Acknowledging that the indigenous cinema owners had begun to recognise that the problems lay with them and not with audiences, he observed that:

> The Point brought together a lot of those ideas in one place, so they were easy to spot and pick up by people who weren't trying them. The multiplexes did stimulate the market, because they made all other exhibitors realise they had to improve.[4]

Since the nadir of cinemagoing in 1984, the number of new multiplexes opened has increased annually as have total cinema admissions. In the same period there has been a small net increase in the amount of cinema sites (660 in 1984 to 747 in 1997) but a much more substantial increase in the number of screens (1,271 in 1984 to 2,383 in 1997).[5] Although multiplexes account for a minority of cinema sites (142 out of 747) they now account for a majority of screens – 1,222 compared with 1,161 in other cinemas.[6]

Inevitably the advent of the multiplex which offers comfort, convenience, high quality facilities and film choice has had an impact on older cinemas which are increasingly seen as unattractive and moribund. Between 1985 and 1991 some eighty independent cinemas closed, which meant that for every multiplex opened another cinema closed.[7] Crucially though, each new multiplex saw an increase in the total number of screens. The 1998 annual admissions figure of 139.5 million adds up to approximately two visits a year per head of population, more than double that of 1985 and there is some evidence to suggest that the boom in cinemagoing has stimulated attendance at cinemas not owned by the big multiplex operators.[8]

Location and Design

Historically, the cinema has been an integral part of the urban landscape. When Milton Keynes was selected for The Point, the mould was cast for the development of a new cinema experience. As in North America, the pattern of multiplex development in Britain was bound up with the shopping centre and in particular the out-of-town shopping centre. The multiplexes constructed in the initial building boom of 1985–90 were primarily sited in out-of-town developments and on former industrial land in major conurbations such as the redeveloped Salford Quays areas of Greater Manchester and the Metro Centre shopping and leisure complex in Gateshead. These were followed by a succession of multiplexes in out-of-town shopping complexes at Crystal Peaks and Meadowhall on the outskirts of Sheffield, Clydebank, Glasgow, Merry Hill, Dudley and in new towns such as Telford, Warrington and Peterborough. Implicit in all these developments was the appeal to the motorist. The construction of the initial wave of larger multiplexes (8–10 screens or more) were dependent on a surrounding population of 500,000–600,000 who lived within a 20 to

Table 5.1   Total annual cinema admissions 1984–97

Calendar Year	Admissions (millions)	Calendar Year	Admissions (millions)
1984	54.00	1991	100.29
1985	72.00	1992	103.64
1986	75.50	1993	114.36
1987	78.50	1994	123.53
1988	84.00	1995	114.56
1989	94.50	1996	123.80
1990	97.37	1997	139.30

Sources: Eddie Dyja (ed.), *BFI Film and Television Handbook 1999*, p. 30 and *Screen Finance*, 2 April 1998.

Table 5.2   Growth in UK multiplex sites 1985–97

Year	Sites	Screens	% of UK Screens
1985	1	10	0.7
1986	4	29	2.2
1987	11	79	6.1
1988	22	186	13.3
1989	38	337	21.8
1990	52	452	27.2
1991	68	565	31.9
1992	78	633	34.4
1993	89	717	38.6
1994	95	772	39.0
1995	103	830	41.4
1996	119	987	45.5
1997	142	1,222	51.2

Source: Screen Finance, 5 February 1998.

25 minute car journey of the site. Commenting on the pattern for out-of-town activities, the *Birmingham Post*'s Terry Grimley observed that:

> The West Midlands has a high proportion of non-city centre cinema seats per head of population, and the reason is not hard to find given the motorway box around Birmingham and the strong regional culture of driving everywhere.[9]

In the period since 1991 there has been a parallel development of smaller multiplex cinemas (5–6 screens) in smaller towns and cities such as Lincoln, Leamington Spa, Mansfield, Shrewsbury and Kettering. These are often operated by smaller domestic exhibitors like ABC and Apollo.

In the short time since the multiplex has appeared five companies – Rank Odeon, National Amusements/Showcase, UCI, Virgin and Warner Village – have come to dominate the multiplex industry and now control 88 per cent of multiplex screens.[10] Although property consultants still claim that 'people find town centres too threatening in the evenings, and they will travel to find everything under one roof', the big five are moving back into the cities.[11] Warner Village, for example, is building a number of 'megaplexes' (cinemas with twenty or more screens) – a 32-screen cinema on the site of London's Battersea Power Station, a 21-screen cinema in Bradford and a 30-screen cinema in Birmingham. But wherever they are built, multiplexes are almost always parts of larger leisure developments. The Star Site in Birmingham, for example, will incorporate a 50,000 square foot shopping and restaurant complex and, though technically in the inner city, it is its proximity to the motorway system that is the attraction to the developers. There are plans for over 2,750 free parking spaces, whilst the prospects for public transport look less promising.

Multiplexes have attempted to re-articulate the cinema as one part, albeit the central part, of a total leisure package set around the notion of a 'whole night out' or even a 'whole

UCI ten-screen multiplex,
Telford Newton, Shropshire,
UK

day out'. The cinema has become not only the best place to see a film but the best place to eat and drink, dance, bowl and swim; all of which you can do after doing the weekly shopping nearby. David Fraser, of design company FITCH, advised multiplex operators to increase the amount of 'experience' their customers got from going to the cinema, adding that 'instead of a product-based decision (going to a particular film) the consumer must be invited to make a lifestyle decision (going for an evening out)'.[12]

Multiplexes are a clue to a process which the American sociologist George Ritzer calls 'McDonaldization' 'by which the principles of the fast-food restaurant are coming to dominate more and more sectors of American society as well as of the rest of the world'.[13] McDonaldization is characteristic of a particular form of capitalist efficiency, in which a large transnational business organisation is run with the smallest possible central organisation and it has been extended beyond the sale of food to encompass other forms of goods and services. It is articulated through the four principles of efficiency, calculability, predictability and control. The proliferation of multiplexes in the UK seems to mirror the adoption and development of these new forms of business and cultural practices not just among US-owned chains but also those owned by non-US companies, such as Virgin or Rank.

Ritzer identifies 'efficiency' as 'streamlining a variety of processes, simplifying goods and services, and using the customer to perform work that paid employees used to do.'[14] Multiplex cinemas utilise economies of scale and new technologies to streamline the process of getting people into the auditoria, showing them the film and getting them out again. Whether the multiplex is 5, 10 or 20 screens the auditoriums share a common car park, box-office, lobby area, toilets and concession area. One or two staff members might check the tickets for cinemagoers entering half the complex's auditoriums, whilst the box-office might be staffed by only two to four people. For those wanting to book seats by credit card (liked by cinema chains since cash is expensive to process and bank) many chains such as UCI have one centralised national booking centre for all their cinemas.[15] Moreover, many cinemas, such as Virgin, have installed machines in the lobby in which customers insert their credit card and details in order to obtain seats, thereby negating the need for the involvement of box-office staff. Multiplexes need only one or two projection staff: computer-controlled projectors perform most of the operations, such as running adverts and trailers, dimming the lights and opening the curtains, without any human intervention. Behind the scenes, cinema chains enjoy the economies of centralised purchasing and have utilised computers to track inventory and prevent spoilage. At its multiplex in Birmingham's Great Park development Virgin has begun to offer a self-serve popcorn and drinks concession stand (selling Virgin's own brand of cola). This has speeded up queues, thus increasing sales, and reduced labour costs since one cashier handles all sales.

'Calculability' is concerned with what Ritzer sees as an emphasis on quantification, on the quantity, rather than the quality, of products and services. Having up to 2,500 cinemagoers buy tickets, popcorn and drinks, move through the lobby and then view up to 20 different films in various auditoria demands some careful calculations. Once the system is organised it becomes easier to predict processes and products. For instance, it is likely that any new Disney cartoon release will generate large numbers of young cinemagoers accompanied by their parents or guardians, who will eat certain foods in certain quantities, come at certain times of the day, need a certain number of visits to the toilet and require more staff to clean the auditoria.

Ritzer claims that what is often operating through an emphasis on calculability is an 'illusion of quantity.'[16] In a visit to a multiplex much of this illusion rests with the concession stand, which has adopted sales practices directly from fast-food restaurants. The 'large' or 'family-sized' popcorn tub is likely to cost upwards of £3, for a product that is ludicrously cheap for the cinema chains who buy it by the metric tonne, but which looks good value as it bulges out of the container. However, the container is likely to be tapered towards the top and striped, giving the illusion of quantity. The fizzy drink will contain large amounts of ice, thus reducing the amount of actual soda, and is bought as syrup, which the cinemas then dilute with carbonated water. Multiplex cinema chains make big profits from concessions (food and drinks) and associated products. According to Peter Dobson, then managing Director of Warner Bros. Theatres in the UK, twenty-five per cent of revenues come from concessions with profits as high as eighty per cent which, unlike box-office receipts, do not have to be shared with the distributor.[17] As one exhibitor observed 'we put people into the theatre to sell them popcorn and soda'.[18] All of the major cinema chains have concentrated heavily on the sales of concessions, and Cinamerica's Charles Goldwater says that his company plans to make concessions 'the focal point of our lobby'.[19]

One of the ways in which McDonaldization is able to maximise efficiency is through 'predictability': an emphasis on things such as discipline, systematisation and routine so that things are the same from one time or place to another. People, it is supposed, like to know what to expect in most settings and at most times – that a Big Mac will taste the same in Exeter as is does in Edinburgh, or indeed in Paris or Sydney. Multiplex cinemas favour predictability because it allows them to make employee behaviour more routine, offer similar or uniform products and create a 'brand' for their particular cinemas in an effort to differentiate themselves from their competitors.

The paradox here for 'branding' is that the appeal of multiplexes, like shopping malls, is based on a certain amount of familiarity and indeed similarity. Companies offer what has come to be identified with the multiplex experience – particular types of seating, certain types of food and drinks, and associated technical features like SurroundSound. For many people the multiplex now offers a similar environment to many others they spend time in, such as supermarkets and bowling alleys. Multiplexes conform to certain styles of design and function to deliver as many people to the film as they can. Implicit in this is the notion of the corporate identity, which sees UCI or Warner Village cinemas, for instance, as broadly similar all over Europe. The drive towards functionalism dictated that The Point's radical pyramid design was not repeated and most multiplexes are concrete boxes superficially glossed over with coloured brick, tiles, glass, chrome and other post modernist adornments. In their efforts to make themselves accessible, multiplexes have surrendered the uniqueness of the cinema as a building. At a multiplex opening in 1989, two distributors commented that they could well have been at an opening for a 'carpet warehouse' rather than a cinema.[20]

Multiplexes try to eliminate uncertainty, through de-skilling a variety of tasks so that anyone can do them. Though they employ many projectionists who would claim justifiably to be skilled in a variety of tasks, such as repairing broken film or 'splicing', much of their role has become subordinate to new technologies which can be mastered with relatively little training. In past times, projectionists would have to run films on two projectors with upwards of three or four reel changes and each change would have to be imperceptible to an audience and therefore called for considerable skill. Nowadays films are spliced together on arrival and put in one continuous reel (a 'platter'), which winds through the projector and is then automatically fed onto another platter ready for the next showing without the necessity for rewinding. Similarly, on the concession counter much of the food arrives pre-prepared, requiring simply re-heating, or is prepared from basic ingredients by machines, thus guaranteeing consistency.

All multiplex companies operate similar regimes with regard to staff behaviour to ensure that their work is predictable. Staff wear uniforms and must work a variety of shift patterns. At UCI and Cine-UK cinemas, staff must know how to work in all sectors of the cinema's operation and work in these various sectors on a cyclical basis: staff may work on the concession counter one day but be cleaning auditoria the next. According to Cine-UK's Operation's Manager, Al Alvarez, this 'gives staff a sense of belonging. If they are multifunctional they can take care of any and every eventuality. It's also a good route to management.'[21] UCI, like other companies, appoints House Managers and Duty Managers from within its organisation, thus ensuring that all managerial staff have experienced all levels of the company's operation. This form of work pattern is an explicit element of a corporate culture that operates a series of incentives, such as promotions and employee awards. Of course, the ultimate form of incentive is the risk of losing one's job and, like their counterparts in the fast-food industries, the US multiplex companies are opposed to trade union membership among their staff. Speaking in 1995 the President of the trade union BECTU, Tony Lennon, observed that 'to this day we have no more than a handful of members in the multiplex sector, and like the rest of the cinema industry, the consequences show in wages and conditions.'[22]

This predictability in manager/staff relations is extended to staff/customer relations through what Ritzer calls 'routinized' or 'scripted interactions'.[23] Like McDonalds, multiplex chains like UCI and Showcase encourage their staff to respond in particular ways to customers, perhaps greeting them in particular ways (saying 'enjoy the film' after handing over tickets) or asking customers if they want a drink if they order food or vice versa. Multiplexes have become sophisticated in the ways they satisfy the customer. At my local UCI in Merry Hill, Dudley, this control begins the moment you enter the car park, with its flashing signs indicating whether and where there are free spaces. As you approach the ticket booths there are channels for queuing above which are indicated the various films and times they are showing. After you purchase your ticket you enter the foyer or lobby area where signs direct you to the appropriate auditoria. However, you have to negotiate the concession counter first, which is similar to many fast-food restaurants in its layout and procedures. Here the task is to help you purchase speedily and make way for others behind you. The lobby has to perform a variety of functions of which the prime one is to provide an invitation to the cinema, through promotions for other films, whilst also doubling as a retail area designed to encourage you to buy food and drink or, in the case of Virgin multiplexes, CDs and videos. However, this space must also be one that moves people through: you must be encouraged only to linger for a moment, which is why many multiplex foyers have no seating. It is especially important that customers do not linger on their way out of the auditoria and that they move speedily to the car park.

Multiplexes manage this complex movement of people through control of start and finish times, which are staggered. The most popular films, often showing on more than one screen at a time, are timed to start before the less popular films, partly to encourage those who arrive to full houses to see another film. Indeed, technological developments in projection mean that multiplexes can control demand for certain films by increasing or decreasing the number of screens showing them. So, when *Titanic* opened at the UCI Dudley it was initially shown on four screens, which decreased in line with reduced demand. This control even extends to the toilets, which have automatic dispensers that give you just enough soap, taps that stay on for a pre-determined time and automatic hand dryers that are designed to give you just enough hot air to dry your hands. Moreover, in the toilets speakers in the ceiling play endless 'muzak' which, presumably, is to discourage customers from staying in there too long!

The Multiplex Cinema Audience and the Myth of Choice

The development of the multiplex has coincided with a steady increase in cinema admissions. The Cinema and Video Industry Audience Research (CAVIAR) 10 survey found that the percentage of people who go to the cinema had risen from thirty-eight per cent in 1984 to sixty-two per cent in 1992, with half of regular cinemagoers visiting a multiplex cinema.[24] Between 1996 and 1998, when multiplexes increased most dramatically, the proportion of adults visiting the cinema increased from fifty-eight to seventy-two per cent.[26] Cinemagoing in Britain is dominated by 15 to 34 year olds, who account for some forty-two per cent of regular cinemagoers but the arrival of the multiplex has seen a broadening of the cinema audience.[26] In 1991 the BFI reported that multiplexes were successfully appealing to those cinemagoers over 35 years old, who made up twenty-seven per cent of the multiplex audience as opposed to nineteen per cent at traditional cinemas.[27] This reflects a more sustained increase in the proportion of over 35s going to the cinema, which has increased every year since the first multiplex opened.[28] According to *Screen Finance*, sixty-one per cent of the audience for *The English Patient* (Anthony Minghella, 1996) was over 35.[29]

The social profile of cinemagoers from the year multiplexes began opening in 1985 up until 1997 shows an increase in the number of ABC1s attending, whilst those classified as C2DEs have decreased as a proportion of the increased audience size generally. The CAVIAR 10 report speculated on the reason for this trend, evident in 1993, citing the impact of video and satellite television on 'lower social grades', the mix of films available, the kinds of cinemas that appealed to those with more disposable income and the greater use of cars to travel to the cinema. [30]

Speaking in 1998 at Cambridge University, Karsten-Peter Grummitt, the Managing Director of Dodona Research, confidently assured delegates that cinema admissions would grow by fifty per cent over the next few years to average three visits a year per person, arguing that: 'More convenient access and more choice will play a large part in encouraging that one extra visit a year'.[31] In the CAVIAR 10 study 'Better choice/Showing right film' was given as a reason for going to the multiplex by thirty-two per cent of respondents and my own survey at the UCI multiplex in Telford revealed that a 'bigger choice of films' was the main attraction for fifty-six per cent of cinemagoers.[32] But the notion of 'choice' needs to be qualified.

A steady supply of films that audiences want to see is crucial to the continued success and growth of multiplexes. During 1997, some 284 films were exhibited in the UK, of which 153 were American and 21 were US/UK joint productions.[33] The distribution of the bulk of the Hollywood films was undertaken by five major distribution companies – UIP, Buena Vista, Twentieth Century Fox, Columbia and Warner Bros. – all of whom are American-owned. The rest of the distribution sector is made up of independent companies that promote most of the British and foreign films and many independent American films. In 1997, over sixty-eight per cent of the films exhibited at Britain's cinemas were American and UK/American co-productions made up another sixteen per cent.[34] A small proportion of major Hollywood studio films receive a disproportionate amount of resources in terms of marketing and screen time. Independent producers and distributors find themselves in the paradoxical position of witnessing an increase in screens at the same time as outlets for their films are diminishing. Heather Stewart, Head of BFI Distribution, argues that there are too few alternative venues for the showing of films, particularly British films. 'It's about time' she argues, 'the Labour Party started thinking about exhibition and cultural diversity, instead of just production.'[35]

The scarcity of outlets for non-Hollywood films is exacerbated by the tendency for multiplexes to hold over some films for successive weeks. Many of the decisions on what films to programme made by the large multiplex chains' central buyers are based on a judgement as to whether they are able to play profitably for a month or more. Giving evidence to the National Heritage Committee, Christopher Hedges, the Managing Director of UCI, described public interest in films as:

> Polarised to a very considerable extent between those they want to see in their droves and those which unfortunately they are less willing to see. The result of that situation is that large numbers of movies lose money, few movies make money.[36]

As far as the multiplexes are concerned these are most likely to be mainstream, big-budget Hollywood films.

Geoff Andrew, Film Editor of *Time Out*, is unambiguous in his criticism of the multi-plexes' policy toward non-Hollywood films, considering them 'responsible for a complete betrayal . . . when they showed up in the late eighties, they promised that one screen would be devoted to arthouse movies. Now they just show *Titanic* on four different screens.'[37] Conversely, many independent cinemas have been unable to compete with the multiplexes and other large cinemas when showing mainstream films because of the attitude of large distributors who place unacceptable conditions upon the showing of their product. Though there are increasing numbers of non-US multiplex chains, they are, according to Simon Perry, Chief Executive of the British Screen Finance Corporation, designed to complete the delivery of blockbuster Hollywood products to a British audience. 'They're temples of American culture, and I don't think they do anything to encourage wider choice.'[38]

In 1996 *Film Magazine* carried an article revealing that at three of Glasgow's cinemas just three films occupied eleven of the twenty-three available screens.[39] This testifies not only to the homogeneity of film exhibition but to the power of the distributors. It is difficult not to be cynical when one considers that many multiplex owners are intimately connected to the distribution of films via their position as either distributors themselves or as part of corporations who own distribution networks.[40] Despite the fact that multiplexes are in a logistical position to programme different films and, by their own admission, have a limited range of 'good product' to choose from amongst the mainstream releases at many times of the year, there has been no commitment to eclecticism in film exhibition or a real faith in the multiplex's ability to transcend perceived public taste. UCI and Virgin do have one-night art house screenings at their cinemas, and films like *Il Postino* (Michael Radford, 1994) have been programmed successfully in multiplexes. But it is difficult to avoid the conviction that film buyers and programmers at the multiplexes are steered toward a narrow range of product from the major distributors. A *Guardian* editorial in 1998 suggested that:

Il Postino (1994) successfully programmed in multiplexes

It must have been a common experience this summer for readers who fancied an evening out at the cinema to run through the list of programmes at the local multiplex and find only those which sensible critics had advised them to keep away from. No use, either, taking the car to the multiplex in the next town or the neighbouring suburb: despite the richness of choice which the move into multi-screen cinemas once promised to bring us, the list there may very well be exactly the same.[41]

The future of the cinema is still uncertain. Audiences are expected to increase for several years and then level out, as the numbers of multiplexes reach saturation point. In the meantime, however, multiplex construction continues unabated and the sizes of complexes get progressively bigger. I will continue to love older cinemas and renew my annual subscription to the Cinema Theatre Association but the future of cinemas as spaces for the public exhibition of moving images looks increasingly tied up with that of the multiplex. It is easy to posit the notion that there is something implicitly good about traditional cinemas: that they should be preserved like working industrial museums, but in examining the faults and limitations of the multiplex – their anonymity and cold efficiency, the illusion of choice – it is important not to forget how they have revived a dying industry.[42] Where a technologically sophisticated multiplex replaces a traditional twinned or tripled cinema plagued by the fatal combination of lack of room, small screens and bad sightlines for audiences or is built in an area where there was no cinema at all, it must surely be welcomed.

Notes

1 Quoted in *Hollywood Reporter*, May 1991, p. S–4.
2 *Screen International*, 30 November 1985, p. 2.
3 Quoted in *Independent on Sunday*, 4 December 1994.
4 *Hollywood Reporter*, May 1991, p. S–19.
5 Eddie Dyja (ed.), *BFI Film and Television Handbook 1999* (London: BFI, 1998), p. 30.
6 Ibid.
7 Andrew Feist and Jeremy Eckstein (eds), *Cultural Trends* (London: Policy Studies Institute, 1991), issue 10, vol. 13, no. 2, p. 29.
8 Figures produced by Dodona Research and cited in *Screen Digest* (May 1996) suggested that admissions to cinemas owned by smaller companies (almost all of which are traditional cinemas) rose from 28.5 million in 1993 to 30.8 million in 1995.
9 *Birmingham Post*, 2 May 1997.
10 *Screen International*, 24 January 1997.
11 Quoted in *Guardian*, 8 October 1995.
12 Quoted by Leslie Felperin, 'Multiplexity', *PACT Magazine*, issue 56, September 1996, p. 17.
13 George Ritzer, *The McDonaldization of Society* (Thousand Oaks: Pine Forge Press, Revised Edition, 1996), p. 1. The theoretical starting point for the McDonaldization thesis was Weber's work on rationalisation. Ritzer claims that his thesis is an attempt to modernise Weber's work, whilst the use of the term McDonaldization reflects his 'conviction that the fast-food restaurant, rather than Weber's bureaucracy (and the process of bureaucratisation), is a better paradigm for that process in the contemporary world'. George Ritzer, *The McDonaldization Thesis: Explorations and Extensions* (London: Sage, 1998) p. 2.
14 Ritzer, *The McDonaldization of Society*, 1996, p. 58.

15 UCI says that each telephone transaction takes on average 64 seconds.

16 Ritzer, *The McDonaldization of Society*, 1996, p. 78.

17 Cited in *Independent on Sunday*, 4 December 1994. According to Cineplex Odeon's 1995 Annual Report, Cineplex Odeon's revenue from concessions was in excess of US$126 million as opposed to cost of concessions, which was some US$22 million.

18 *Screen International*, 1 January 1996, p. 20.

19 Ibid.

20 Quoted in *Producer*, Issue 12, Summer 1990, p. 21.

21 Quoted by Leslie Felperin, 'Multiplexity', p. 19.

22 *Stage, Screen and Radio*, October 1995.

23 Ritzer, 1996, p. 81.

24 Cinema Advertisers Association (CAA), *Cinema and Video Industry Audience Research (CAVIAR) Number 10*, 1993, published by the CAA, 127 Wardour Street, London W1V 4AD. The survey was based upon a sample of 2,800 people interviewed face-to-face during October and November 1992. Regular cinemagoers are defined as those attending once a month or more.

25 *Observer*, 27 October 1998.

26 CAA, *Cinema and Video Industry Audience Research (CAVIAR) Number 15*, 1998. The survey was based upon a sample of 3,000 people interviewed face-to-face during October and November 1997.

27 David Leafe (ed.), *BFI Film and Television Handbook 1992*, (London: BFI, 1991), p. 39.

28 CAA, *CAVIAR 15*.

29 *Screen Finance*, 19 March 1998.

30 CAA, *CAVIAR 15*, p. 22.

31 Dodona Research (1997), 'Coming soon – A cinema near you?', presentation given at Jesus College, Cambridge, September 1997, URL: http://www.dodona.co.uk/somethingtoread.html.

32 CAA, *CAVIAR 10*; Stuart Hanson, *The development and growth of the multiplex cinema: 1985–1992*, unpublished undergraduate dissertation, July 1992, Department of Cultural Studies, University of Birmingham. The research consisted of face-to-face interviews with 50 people in the foyer of the UCI cinema in Telford (25 men and 25 women) during January 1992.

33 Eddie Dyja (ed.), *BFI Film and Television Handbook 1999*, p. 35.

34 Ibid.

35 Quoted in the *Guardian*, 26 September 1998.

36 National Heritage Committee, *The British Film Industry, Vol. 1: Report and Minutes of Proceedings* (London: HMSO, 1995), p. vi; *A Policy Document, Incorporating the Government's Response to the House of Commons National Heritage Select Committee, The British Film Industry* (London: HMSO, 1995), p. xvi.

37 Quoted in the *Guardian*, 26 September 1998.

38 Quoted in the *Observer*, 18 August 1996.

39 Cited in the *Guardian*, 19 May 1998.

40 For instance, Universal Studios, itself part of MCA Communications, is part owner of UIP Distributors. Along with Paramount Studios, Universal is also part owner of UCI, the largest multiplex cinema chain in Britain. Moreover, UIP is a leading film distributor in the UK (and the largest with an interest in exhibition) with some 21 per cent of the market, worth over £82.4 million in 1997 (*BFI Film and Television Handbook 1999*).

Time-Warner, the biggest media company in the world, owns Warner Bros. Studios and Warner Film Distributors, whilst its chain of cinemas under the Warner Village brand is one of the major multiplex operators in the UK.

41 *Guardian*, 27 August 1998.

42 For discussion of the decline of cinema prior to the development of the multiplex see Simon Blanchard, 'Cinema-going, going, gone?', *Screen*, vol. 24, nos 4–5, July–October 1983, pp. 109–13; David Docherty, David Morrison and Michael Tracey, *The Last Picture Show: Britain's Changing Film Audience* (London BFI: 1987); and Wally Olins, 'The best place to see a film?', *Sight and Sound*, Autumn 1985, pp. 241–4.

Chapter 6
Pathways into the Industry

Kate Ogborn

What kind of people made films in the 1990s? Where did they come from? How many of them were successful? What kinds of films did they want to make? In researching this chapter I discovered that very few of the organisations engaged in funding new talent keep information on the educational and professional backgrounds of the people applying to them for money. What follows is therefore a personal survey drawing on my experience of executive producing the BFI's and Channel Four's New Directors scheme during the 90s.

New Directors was started as a production fund for short films in 1987 by BFI Production and Channel Four Television. The intention was twofold: first, to nurture and promote the art of the short film, making it accessible to cinema and television audiences; and second, to provide the writers and directors with a calling card to help them develop their film-making careers. The scheme funded drama, animation, experimental and avant-garde work as well as documentaries, and there were no rules about length, subject matter or format. The budget ceiling was initially £20,000 per film and this has now doubled to £40,000. From the start New Directors focused on developing film-makers in an industry that in the late 80s had developed mostly writers. In the first year, the slate of film-makers included directors who had been to art school and film school, but also some whose main experience had been in theatre, visual art or writing.

In 1995 we gathered information on the background of all the applicants to the scheme: twenty-six per cent of applicants had a degree in film or television production; fifteen per cent had a background of working in television; twenty-four per cent had a degree in fine art; thirty-five per cent had gained professional experience and training through funding schemes via regional arts boards. We also began tracking the career developments of film-makers commissioned through New Directors. Since 1988, fourteen film-makers have completed their first features and many more have gone on to direct further short films.

When discussing shorts it is important to recognise that it is not just a matter of writers and directors using them as a way into the industry. Shorts can be a way of testing out collaborations, finding the people you can trust and work with, and developing your skills and expertise. Many people get their first break from their experience on shorts: Seamus McGarvey, for example, whose first film as a director of photography was a short for the BFI and Channel 4, has gone on to shoot features with directors such as Michael Winterbottom, Tim Roth and Stephen Frears.

Routes into the industry for those wishing to be producers are different, though still extremely varied: from production assistant to production manager to associate producer, for example; or from script development or the music promos and commercials world. As Alison Owen, producer of the Oscar-nominated *Elizabeth* recently said:

People are always asking me, how do they become a film producer, and I tell them you just have to say that's what you are and get on and do it ... You find a script you like, a director you can work with and start trying to raise the money. Hey presto, you're a film producer.[1]

In looking at the types of career development New Directors has been able to support and nurture, it is important to bear in mind where the scheme is located within the industry and what kinds of film-makers it will therefore attract. Raising money for a film – whether a short or a feature – is not an objective exercise. You can't divorce yourself from the agenda, remit or personalities of the organisations and individuals with the money. Film-makers go to the places and people they feel will be sympathetic to them: there needs to be some common ground in aspirations between film-makers and financiers.

New Directors was initiated by two organisations with clearly stated public remits: the BFI, a publicly funded organisation with a commitment to encouraging the arts of film and television, and Channel Four Television, whose mission at its inception was to provide 'television with a difference' for audiences and programme-makers not traditionally catered for by the main broadcasting channels. Both organisations shared a strong interest in supporting and developing voices from the margins and in exploring what the medium of film could do. It is significant, though, that the New Directors scheme was initiated at a time when Channel Four was withdrawing most of the funding it had provided to the independent workshop sector, an indication of the switch away from infrastructure funding to production financing for one-off films.

In the late 1990s there were fundamental changes in government funding for film. In 1999 the government undertook a spending review of all the film organisations it funded and announced its intention to create a unitary body to deliver a comprehensive and coherent strategy for the development of film culture and the film industry. This new body, the Film Council will incorporate the funding for features and short films currently administered by the Lottery Films Department at the Arts Council and BFI Production, and will have a close relationship with British Screen. It is important to bear in mind that government-funded organisations like the BFI have always had the dual remit of supporting and nurturing a distinctive film culture (sustaining film-makers such as Derek Jarman and Terence Davies) as well as developing new talent. Once New Directors had become established as an on-going scheme in the mid-1990s, it was increasingly seen as part of the research and development work of BFI Production, finding those film makers whose voices will challenge and enrich the mainstream. It is hoped that the Film Council will continue to provide space for this sort of risk-taking which does not necessarily bring immediate returns for the industry.

The 1990s have seen major changes within the film industry, some of which have had an impact on the way in which film-makers can kick-start and then sustain their careers. There has been a massive proliferation of schemes around the country that fund short films. Most of the regional arts boards, the media development agencies, the local broadcasters, the national broadcasters and the national funders have such schemes, all with a brief to 'talent spot'. Shorts are the firmly established way in which the feature film-makers of the future are spotted and developed. For example, *10×10*, the production series for shorts run by BBC2, now in its twelfth series, has long been a way into both television and cinema and has supported film-makers from the most eclectic range of backgrounds.

10×10 comes out of BBC Features at BBC Bristol, a department which is primarily concerned with commissioning documentaries and animation. The first series exclusively commissioned documentaries by students at film schools, providing them with a bridge into the BBC. The second series were all in-house documentaries. From series 3 on, *10×10* has attracted a mixture of film school graduates, BBC staff and freelancers (editors, designers, cinematographers) wishing to move into directing, and directors who have been cutting their teeth on commercials and promos. According to Jeremy Howe, the series producer:

> The series mixes fiction and non-fiction and the directors of the two genres often have very different backgrounds. In order to apply the directors must submit a showreel, so the applicants need a high degree of visual literacy, and tend to come from within the ranks of the film and tv industry or from film schools. The most common CV of a *10×10* director is someone who is two or three years out of film school or someone wanting to change career direction.[2]

We can see similar patterns emerging elsewhere. The majority of film-makers who have received funding have done degrees in film production and have typically gone on to free-lance production work, documentaries and short films. They often begin their own authored work on microscopic budgets and then move up the funding and budget ladders to the national schemes which offer larger budgets.

The speed at which a film-maker can progress from graduation film to short to feature has accelerated enormously over the last few years, perhaps widening the gap between those that make it and those that don't. An interesting case study is the Scottish film-maker Lynne Ramsey, whose debut feature, *Ratcatcher*, was released at the end of 1999. Lynne Ramsey trained at the National Film and Television School as a cinematographer. In her final year she persuaded the head of the school to allow her to direct and shoot her graduation film, *Small Deaths* (1996) which attracted the attention of Gavin Emerson, the producer of a number of high-budget advertising campaigns, including work for the Italian fashion design company, Prada. *Small Deaths* was selected to be screened at the Cannes Film Festival in 1996 where it won the Critics' Prize. Ramsey then went on to direct another two shorts: *Kill the Day* (1997) for the BFI and Channel Four, and *Gasman* for Scottish Screen and the BBC. *Gasman* was screened at Cannes in 1997 where it won the Jury Prize. Meanwhile the then Head of Drama at BBC Scotland, Andrea Calderwood, had commissioned Ramsey to develop a feature. When Andrea Calderwood left the BBC to become Head of Production at Pathé (which had won a successful bid for one of the three Lottery-funded franchises), she continued her involvement with the feature and it eventually went into production in 1998 funded by the BBC, Pathé and Lazennec (a French company who had previously invested in Ramsey's shorts). What Lynne Ramsey's journey from film school to feature illustrates is, aside from extraordinary talent, her faith in her own vision, and the role played by producers who shared that faith.[3]

As shorts increasingly get tied into the development route to features, their role as a forum for purely visual and avant-garde work is in danger of disappearing. Simon Beaufoy, writer of *The Full Monty* (Peter Cattaneo, 1997), and his co-directing partner, Bille Eltringham agree that 'a short is not merely a mini-feature but something that expresses a fleeting and intangible emotion, a cinematic poem.'[4] Prior to writing *The Full Monty*, Beaufoy and Eltringham co-wrote and co-directed two short films: *Yellow* (1996), which starred Ray Winstone and was funded through the New Directors scheme and *Closer* (1998) which was funded by the BBC and Channel 4's 'Brief Encounters' scheme.[5] Shorts have their own

'New Director', Jim Gillespie's *I Know What You Did Last Summer* (1997)

language and disciplines and can be extremely difficult to get right. At their best, such as in the work of Jamie Thraves, Andrew Kotting and Lynne Ramsey, they can be satisfying self-contained works of startling insight, humour and emotional resonance. It seems somewhat ironic that shorts have become the training ground for features. They can and should be more than vehicles for film-makers out to prove they can tell a story, know where to put the camera, and blag a lot of favours to make the film look as if it cost more than it did.

There is a chicken and egg cycle at work here. The BFI has funded less and less purely experimental pieces and therefore receives fewer and fewer applications for that kind of work. It could be that more and more people want to tell stories now. Maybe more and more people want to go to Hollywood and are inspired for example, by Jim Gillespie, whose New Directors short led to a feature film, *I Know What You Did Last Summer* (1997) and the Sylvester Stallone blockbuster, *Detox* (1999). However, the Artists Film and Video Department at the Arts Council has concentrated on funding work by artist film-makers, who have managed to maintain a professional profile through work for broadcasters keen to encourage collaborations between different art forms in series such as BBC2's *Sound on Film* and *Dance on Film*. With the rapidly growing new media technologies, perhaps the spaces to experiment are happening outside the reach of the film institutions and broadcasters. Adam Barker, the Commissioning Editor for Independent Film and Video at Channel Four, said recently

> The department was invented as a bridge between independent cinema culture and television and a lot of interesting work came out of those two rubbing up against each other. Today, if you asked me how you create a department of formal innovation and where the interface is, I'd say it's more about television and the web and new media interacting with each other.[6]

Artists such as Douglas Gordon, Steve McQueen, Gillian Wearing have been incorporating film into their work using film as another tool, a found object to be sampled and reworked without reverence for its status. The major London art school, Central St Martins is in the process of redevising their film course, a course which has produced interesting film-makers such as John Maybury and Isaac Julien. The school is shifting the focus of their BA away from film-makers who wish to make films for the cinema towards students who wish to use film in their work, but whose context is the gallery space. Many of the film-makers supported by the BFI and the Arts Council have come from a fine art background and have then moved via the cultural organisations into the industry, but future graduates might be more likely to approach Saatchi or the Jerwood Foundation than the BFI, Channel 4 or the BBC for funding.

During the last decade there has been a proliferation of film and television production courses. Alongside the academic and practical courses offered by a number of universities around the country, there has been a growth in postgraduate degrees in screenwriting, such as those offered by the Northern School of Film and Television, the National School of Film and Television and the London College of Printing. There are also a number of workshops, short courses and training programmes, predominantly aimed at aspiring and more experienced screenwriters, and all contributing to growing numbers of aspirant film-makers in an increasingly competitive market.

In discussions about access there is a tendency – particularly within organisations with a primarily cultural remit – to argue for an egalitarian approach and to encourage access to the industry for those people who for reasons of gender, race, sexuality, disability, or even where they live, have been denied access to the mainstream industry. The BFI – among many other organisations – has contributed to these cultural remits, trying to ensure that the most diverse range of voices are heard by the widest range of people. While acknowledging the need to loosen the stranglehold of the white middle class male-dominated industry, it is also important to recognise the need for talent. Where the cultural organisations have been most successful is in recognising that a film-maker has a genuine voice before the mainstream industry is ready to hear what he or she has to say. Film-makers as diverse as Sally Potter, John Maybury and Carine Adler come to mind. Carine Adler, a graduate of the National School of Film and Television in the 1980s, had spent a number of years developing screenplays for the BBC, the BFI and British Screen but none had progressed to production. Deciding in 1994 to return to the short film, she was commissioned by the BFI and Channel Four to write and direct a short, *Fever* starring Katrin Cartlidge, for the New Directors scheme. At the time of this film's completion the BFI and Channel Four were actively looking for women writers and directors for their joint development fund, having decided to address proactively the lack of women feature film-makers in the UK (by contrast with a much healthier scene in the US and Australia). Carine Adler was commissioned to write a feature script, which became *Under the Skin*, which went into production in 1996, funded by the BFI, Channel Four, the Merseyside Production Fund and Rouge Films. It was released in the UK in 1997, having won the Michael Powell Award for Best British Feature at that year's Edinburgh Film Festival and the Critic's Prize at the Toronto Film Festival. For Carine Adler, making a low-budget feature was an opportunity to take risks both in the story she told and the way in which she told it.

It has always been difficult for the more uncompromisingly art house, or politically conscious, film-makers to sustain a career within Britain. Most, such as Ken Loach and Peter Greenaway, have relied on funding from Europe and Japan, and have often found it difficult to gain serious recognition in the United States. For those film-makers who eschew the art house movie and are more interested in aiming their films at a multiplex audience, the role models and the routes have been different, with seemingly self-taught film-makers such as Tarantino and Rodriguez providing vital influences. Guy Ritchie, the director of *Lock Stock and Two Smoking Barrels* (1998), had no formal training, left school at fifteen and went to work at Island Records. He then spent several years travelling and doing menial jobs, before at the age of twenty-five getting his first job as a runner. By shooting promos for German rave bands, he learnt enough about the technical side of film-making and earnt enough money to make a short film, *The Hard Case*, which was the springboard to *Lock Stock and Two Smoking Barrels*.

The most common route into the industry now appears to be: a degree in film or media followed by work as a freelancer within the corporate, commercial or television industry, paralleled by film-making on microscopic budgets, the achievement of a higher profile through a television broadcast or a festival screening, and then, hopefully, the 'lucky break'. But it is a route that is often short-circuited or deviated from. Peter Carlton of Nottingham film workshop, Intermedia, described Shane Meadows, whose first feature film *Twenty-FourSeven* was released in 1998, as an 'immaculate conception' – a film-maker who came from nowhere, who proved that you didn't need to go to film school, that all you needed was a strong enough desire to make films and the gift of the gab. Meadows began by using the facilities at Intermedia to enable him to make micro-budget films shot in and around the Nottingham area and mostly utilising the talents of his friends. He then had a low-budget short, *Where's the Money Ronnie?* (1995) commissioned through a broadcaster's new talent scheme, which was followed by a very low-budget feature, *Smalltime* (1997) which was initially resourced by ingenuity and then found money from BFI Production to complete its post-production and transfer it from video to film. It was selected to be screened at the Edinburgh International Film Festival, a key platform for launching new talent in the UK, where it created a huge buzz.

Though he has been marketed as the maverick outsider who begged, stole and borrowed to get his films made, a lot of people were involved in his 'immaculate conception': Robin Gutch, then Commissioning Editor for Independent Film and Video at Channel 4, invited him to direct a documentary, *The Gypsy's Tale* (1995); Steve Brookes at BFI Production put crucial completion money into *Smalltime*; Steve Woolley, on the jury which awarded *Where's the Money Ronnie?* the Channel One short film prize, encouraged him to develop the feature which became *TwentyFourSeven*, which was produced by Woolley's company, Scala. The interesting aspect to Meadows' progression and development as a film-maker is that he paid no attention to the kinds of films he was supposed to make, and didn't waste time trying to second guess the successful formula for getting funding. Instead he concentrated on the resources that were available to him on his doorstep, and on telling the stories he and his friends wanted to hear.

In this he might be seen as a harbinger of those film-makers who will take advantage of the explosion in digital technology. Next Wave Films, an independent company which has set up a completion fund for ultra low-budget features funded by the Independent Film Channel in the US, provides assistance in marketing and selling as well as production capital. According to Peter Broderick, who runs the company, ultra low-budget production is:

> the most independent form of feature film-making. It allows directors greater creative control than they may ever have again.... Film-makers on the cutting edge are shooting

New manifestos for film-making. Dogme 95 director Thomas Vinterberg's *Festen* (1998)

with digital video cameras, recording sound with DAT recorders, and using the latest software to edit, create special effects and mix on home computers. Each of these elements are key links in a new digital production process that enables film-makers to make films in a radically different way. For the first time, many independents will be able to own a camera that captures high-quality images and uses low-cost stock that doesn't require expensive processing.[7]

There have also been breakthroughs in the quality of transfers from video to film and the quality of video projection. This enables the films to be shot on video, post-produced digitally and transferred to 35mm for theatrical distribution. For Broderick, the implications of these digital breakthroughs are very significant. Not only do they make the means of production far more accessible to far more people, but also:

> At this budget level, someone can afford to make a first feature and if it isn't good enough to show as a debut film, then make another. Digital video will enable directors to make features more frequently, allowing them to practice their craft, take new risks and keep improving. Instead of making a feature on film every three years as is typical today, film-makers may be able to make a movie a year.[8]

Nick Roddick argues that, whilst the British film industry is commercially healthier than it has been in decades, the film culture it has grown out of is dangerously narrow and derivative. 'Didn't other sorts of cinema used to be rewarding, even enjoyable? Didn't they inspire young film-makers to make their own films and, in the long run, change the language of the mainstream?'[9] The key point here is in where today's – and future generations – of young film-makers will be finding their inspiration. Will their only model be what can be marketed and sold? Will the talent spotters fall into the trap of lessening the risks associated with new talent by looking for those film-makers who appear fresh but who are simply singing the same old song?

A number of contradictions seem to be emerging; alongside the drift away from the avant-garde and art house cinema, and a growing crisis in distribution which makes it harder and harder for certain kinds of non-commercial films to reach audiences, the technological changes and the expansion of funding schemes mean that there are more and more ways and opportunities to make low-budget, and personal films. In the late 90s, a manifesto for a new style of film-making which emerged from a group of Danish film-makers, including Lars Von Trier and Thomas Vintenberg caught the imagination of the press, financiers and the public. Partly a fantastic prank, partly a serious critique of the overblown excesses of the Hollywood machine, Dogme 95 has already resulted in some very interesting films including Vintenberg's award-winning *Festen* (1999). The Dogme 95 collective created their manifesto in reaction to their perception of an increasing superficiality in films. They argue that the technological revolution, as identified by Peter Broderick, is making cinema far more accessible and proselytise for a more disciplined form of film-making in which film-makers sign up to a 'vow of chastity' and abandon the technological excesses of high-budget productions. This 'vow of chastity' prohibits studio shooting, use of non-diegetic music, opticals, cranes and dollies, widescreen formats and directorial credits. Whilst seeming to poke fun at both the director as auteur and the director as studio plaything, Dogme 95 has successfully reinvigorated debates around the ways in which low-budget film-making can take advantage of the available technology to encourage financiers and film-makers to take risks, with their content and their form. As an alternative to aping Hollywood, it could be seen as a useful model for the development of indigenous cinema.

Notes

1 *Guardian*, 16 March 1999, p. 6.
2 From an interview with the author.
3 Ramsey's *Gasman* is a brilliant example of what can be achieved, visually and emotionally, in a short.
4 From an interview with the author.
5 'Brief Encounters' was a joint production scheme between the two broadcasters which for two years replaced Channel 4's 'Short 'n' Curlies' scheme. This unusual collaboration between two broadcasters came out of the arrangements put in place after the death of Dennis Potter whereby the two broadcasters collaborated on the funding and broadcasting of his last two screenplays.
6 *Broadcast*, 12 February 1999, p. 22 .
7 *Movie Maker*, September 1998, p. 46.
8 Ibid.
9 Nick Roddick, 'Show me the culture!', *Sight and Sound*, December 1998, p. 24.

Chapter 7

As Others See Us: British Film-making and Europe in the 90s

Ian Christie

En réalité *Brassed Off*, le titre original des *Virtuoses*, dissimule un jeu de mots: 'brass' signifie les cuivres d'un orchestre, et l'expression 'to be brassed off' peut être lue comme l'équivalent de notre locution 'en avoir ras-le-bol'.

(Dossier pédagogique sur *Les Virtuoses*)[1]

What do we mean by 'British cinema and Europe'? Fear of invasion by the subsidy-bloated Europuddings? An appreciative market for all those worthy British films that no-one wants to see in Britain ('they just *love* Ken Loach')? Forcing audiences to watch quotas of certified European films, instead of the Hollywood movies they really crave? Brussels bureaucracy . . . French intransigence . . . British – well, British *what*? The statistical record shows that in 1998, of all European film screenings in specialist cinemas throughout the European Union, a quarter were 'British', according to some definition while in Britain the number of films from other European countries achieving distribution had dropped to its lowest level ever.[2] A case of populist British films becoming the *lingua franca* of European cinema, while British audiences are cut off from all but a tiny proportion of other European films?

There are a number of factors that need to be considered before drawing any firm conclusions. The most basic of these is the actual availability of cinemas for minority-interest films, which is what almost all European productions inevitably are. The UK has about 2,000 screens, of which fewer than 200 show any 'non-national' (i.e. other than British) European films. By comparison, France, with a similar population, has some 4,000 screens, with approximately 800 of these regularly showing European films.[3] Quite apart from attendance levels, this means that there are more than twice as many opportunities to see non-national European films in France, and a similar pattern is repeated in Italy, Germany and Spain. With a larger market place, there is more incentive for distributors in these countries to risk acquiring European films, to invest in dubbing or subtitling these – given that more prints will be justified – and in promoting them.

Thus a virtuous cycle can develop, with films from other European countries at least paying their way in distribution and exhibition, and a few breaking through to much greater profitability. By contrast, French, Italian or German films in Britain are the exclusive preserve of a small (and diminishing) number of severely undercapitalised distributors, who will typically release between two and ten prints (compared with the many hundreds of prints used for a major release of a Hollywood studio film). In this vicious cycle, levels of publicity-spending and the period of time that such films can play at any one cinema are correspondingly reduced, so that even if a 'foreign' film proves popular, there is rarely a chance to capitalise on this success. Typically, Roberto Benigni's *Life is Beautiful*, immediately after its Academy Awards triumph in early 1999, was only showing in a handful of smaller London screens, which were regularly sold out, while many regional cinemas were forced to take if off to make way for subsequent foreign-language releases. Nor did a belated multiplex release achieve anything like the scale of attendances elsewhere in Europe, where the film attracted half a million admissions in the second half of 1998 alone.

Such underlying determinants are all too often ignored in discussion of the relative strengths and weaknesses of the European market. The fact that the UK has made remarkable progress from its lowest level of cinema admissions in 1984–5, and an equivalent low level of feature production, should not disguise the nature of these twin recoveries. The doubling of attendances owes much to a programme of multiplex building which began in the mid-80s; and the multiplexes have little interest in showing foreign films. Their identity and publicity are firmly geared to a mass audience in search of pre-sold studio fare, accompanied by popcorn and cola. This ambience has served some of the new British films of the 90s well, from *Four Weddings and a Funeral* (Mike Newell, 1994) and *Trainspotting* (Danny Boyle, 1996) to *The Full Monty* (Peter Cattaneo, 1997) and *Shakespeare in Love* (John Madden, 1999). But the multiplexes have ignored many more, and more challenging, domestic productions, while proving almost wholly unsuited to foreign-language films (whether dubbed or subtitled).

Elsewhere in Europe, the structure of exhibition has remained less polarised, with specialised or 'art' cinemas forming a larger proportion of the total, with many of these well-placed to promote non-national European films more equally alongside Hollywood blockbusters. Hence the often impressive box-office figures for films by such directors as Ken Loach, Sally Potter, Mike Leigh and Peter Greenaway, which have remained niche products in the UK. As an example, across the 3,000 screens belonging to the Europa Cinemas network, Loach's typically uncompromising *My Name is Joe* (1998) achieved over 8,000 screenings and nearly 350,000 admissions in the second half of 1998. In Britain, it managed just over 200,000, based on box-office takings.[4]

Depressing though this contrast is, it needs to be seen in several other contexts that are characteristic of the 90s. One is the increasingly active role that UK television now takes in producing films intended to have a cinema launch. Another is the growing network of Europe-wide support structures that are attempting to make a reality of that chimera, 'European cinema', in which the UK is involved. And yet another, which may be the most difficult for Britons to assess, is the extent to which 'British' films have proved genuinely popular throughout much of Europe, seeming to bridge the gulf between vernacular and art cinema that has bedevilled many of Europe's national cinemas, and introducing themes and characters which many find missing in their own productions. The films of Loach, Leigh and latterly Mark Herman are particularly appreciated in this respect, for their portrayal of working class characters and of work itself in a time of often painful transition.[5]

It is easy to forget that before the advent of Channel Four in the early 80s British television played virtually no part in producing films intended for theatrical release, unlike public-sector networks elsewhere in Europe. There were isolated experiments, such as Peter Hall's *Akenfield* (1974), financed by London Weekend Television and tentatively offered to cinemas; and the BBC's seemingly almost accidental investment in Hans-Jürgen

Syberberg's massive *Hitler, a Film from Germany* (1977).[6] However, it was more common for British independent film-makers to get seed funding from German or French television, than to find support at home. Such films as Steve Dwoskin's *Behindert* (1974) and *Silent Cry* (1976), both dealing with disability in unusually avant-garde ways, were largely financed by France's Institut National de l'Audiovisuel (INA) and West Germany's Zweites Deutsches Fernsehen (ZDF).[7] Ron Peck and Paul Hallam's intentionally low-key 'coming out' drama *Nighthawks* (1978) also benefited from ZDF support and Chris Petit's *Radio On* (1979), responsible for getting the BFI into 35mm production, drew on German television funding through its co-producer Wim Wenders' Road Movies company.

The significance of such support was greater than its low level – typically less than £10,000 and effectively a pre-purchase of transmission rights. Having even a small amount guaranteed up front helped to raise other funding and it enabled film-makers to tackle subjects and forms which did not then find favour with either commercial backers or cultural agencies in Britain. It also left film-makers free to arrange whatever form of distribution they wanted in Britain, although this was rarely more than a brief London art house launch followed by scattered screenings at BFI-supported regional film theatres. Even this, however, was better than the limbo into which a film financed entirely by UK television could fall. Because television and cinema production offered quite different terms to actors and musicians at this time, a film made under 'TV contracts' was effectively barred from cinema release by the threat of union sanctions, unless the producers had had the foresight (and budget) to negotiate this in advance. Of three enterprising features produced by ITC's Black Lion subsidiary at the turn of the 80s, only John Mackenzie's *The Long Good Friday* (1980) reached cinema screens, and that only after the intervention of George Harrison's HandMade Films, while Stephen Frears' *Bloody Kids* (1979) and Ken Loach's *Looks and Smiles* (1981) appeared only on television in the UK until they were later granted a limited BFI-sponsored release.

Jeremy Isaacs' first commitment as founding chief executive of Channel Four was to the substantial financing of features, at least some of which were to be allowed a full theatrical release before transmission. This novel policy reflected Channel Four's mandate to act as a publisher rather than in-house producer, but was also directly inspired by the impact that especially French and German television funding had made on European cinema in the 70s. From the outset, however, it exposed a fundamental tension between the priorities of television scheduling and the risk inherent in theatrical release. One of the first Film on Four commissions was a debut feature from Neil Jordan, then known only as a literary writer. When *Angel* (1982) was perceived to have theatrical potential, after a triumphant Edinburgh Festival premiere, Channel Four initially rejected the idea of delaying its transmission to allow for a cinema release, and only intensive lobbying secured a reprieve, without which Jordan's directorial career would have been damaged, if not aborted.

Without a legislative framework (as in France), suitable distributors and exhibitors and, perhaps most important, a culture which *values* cinema exhibition, the course of British television's involvement in supporting an 'amphibious' production economy has remained fraught. After relatively few Film on Four productions had reached the cinema during the 80s, the new decade began with another controversy over whether a C4-funded film, this time by Loach, should be released theatrically. Again, intensive lobbying secured a limited 'window' for *Riff-Raff* (1990) and makeshift distribution was started by the BFI, before being taken over by Palace Pictures. Given the limited scale of release in Britain, the results were encouraging rather than commercially viable. But elsewhere in Europe, this modest and often ruefully humorous portrait of a motley group of building workers – latter-day descendants of Robert Tressell's *Ragged Trousered Philanthropists* – struck a deeper chord.[8] Given a full-scale theatrical release in most countries, the film achieved impressive box-office results and went on to win the newly instituted European Film Award in 1992.

The fact that *Riff-Raff* enjoyed greater success in Europe than in Britain underlined the continuing structural weakness of UK exhibition and distribution, polarised between blockbusters and severely restricted 'art house' releases. A radical yet populist film such as *Riff-Raff* stands little chance of reaching a mass audience in Britain, but even when dubbed or subtitled can still be shown widely in other European countries. Some UK reviewers claimed that the film's regional and ethnic accents, naturalistically recorded, were hard to understand – a class-related charge that has dogged Loach ever since *Kes* (1969) – and, with some irony, it could be argued that this disincentive for at least some UK audiences was avoided elsewhere in Europe by dubbing or subtitling.

Language, of course, remains a contentious issue across Europe, with the continent divided between countries which prefer dubbing or subtitling for foreign-language films.[9] The underlying reality, however, is that for *all* European territories except the UK, the majority of films shown are 'foreign-language', since they're American. This simple fact may go some way towards explaining why the UK seems to stand alone among its neighbours in regarding all continental European films as 'specialised'. Given the UK's traditional antipathy towards dubbing, compounded by the lack of an economic base for high-quality dubbing into 'British' English, no foreign-language film has the opportunity to be shown as a mass-audience release. To the amazement of French observers, even the popular time-travel farce *Les Visiteurs* (Jean-Marc Poiré, 1993) became a kind of art film *manqué* in the UK, subtitled and given a censor's certificate which would have excluded the bulk of the film's vast youth audience in France. Equally, *Riff-Raff* could only be perceived as a kind of art film, presenting characters and situations more usually seen in television drama, but lacking the positive exoticism of foreignness.

Channel Four wanted to transmit *Riff-Raff* as a television premiere, no doubt influenced by the memory of Loach as a pioneer of British television's distinctive genre of dramadoc, with his Wednesday Plays of the 60s, *Up the Junction* (1965) and *Cathy Come Home* (1965). Another important circumstantial factor was the film's completion within months of the fall of Margaret Thatcher. For some, Loach and his writer Bill Jesse reflected a class antagonism which already seemed dated: better to show it quickly on television. They were not alone in failing to realise that *Riff-Raff* might appeal to audiences throughout Europe, who could easily recognise the casualised, multicultural building site as a microcosm of their experience, with cut-price urban 'regeneration' to benefit profiteers, and youthful optimism eroded by readily available hard drugs; and who would respond to the bawdy humour of Ricky Tomlinson's militant navvy, and to the vivid metaphor of rats being hunted on the site of a hospital being turned into luxury flats.

With hindsight, *Riff-Raff* can be seen as pioneering what would become British cinema's most successful genre of the 90s, the tragi-comedy of urban survival, which includes Loach's subsequent *Raining Stones* (1993), Mike Leigh's *Naked* (1993), Danny Boyle's *Trainspotting* (1996), *Brassed Off* (Mark Herman, 1996) and *The Full Monty* (1997). Loach's own cinema career also revived in the wake of *Riff-Raff*'s recognition. After the somewhat strained conspiratorial politics of *Fatherland* (1986) and *Hidden Agenda* (1990), he was able to return to an apparent simplicity and emotional directness which would culminate in *Land and Freedom* (1995), a truly European film in all respects and a convincing refutation of the belief that co-productions are inevitably compromised. The core of Jim Allen's script is similar to George Orwell's classic memoir of the Spanish Civil War, *Homage to Catalonia*: an idealistic journey from England to defend democratic socialism against fascism, which leads to the bitter discovery that antagonisms within the left are even more treacherous, and ultimately doom the Republic. Allen and Loach's protagonist, however, is not the traditional leftist 30s intellectual, but an unemployed English worker inspired to volunteer by a political meeting complete with propaganda film.

Loach's budget of £3m (his largest to date) for *Land and Freedom* was absurdly low for any conventional treatment of a large-scale period subject, but it matched his inclination to treat the civil war as a series of informal miniatures – in the front-line trenches, in a village experiencing political awakening and in a city divided by cross-fire. Dealing with a conflict that attracted volunteers from around the world encouraged an internationalism in casting and a naturalistic portrayal of language difference: within the film characters translate for each other, speak in their own languages and are subtitled when necessary. This all contributes to a vivid sense of the civil war's contemporary impact, and is framed by present-day scenes that combine pathos and Loach's distinctive defiance.

Nothing could be less like a 'heritage' film – this is far removed from the strenuous period reconstruction of such 'history from beneath' epics as Hugh Hudson's *Revolution* (1985) or Claude Berri's *Germinal* (1993) – and, perhaps surprisingly, it filled what had been a void in European popular memory, particularly in Spain itself, where it was widely

Land and Freedom (1995)
– a truly European film

seen and appreciated by youthful audiences. Appropriately, the film's complex financing reflected this wide spectrum of interest. A three-way co-production between the UK, Spain and Germany, it relied upon broadcasters in all three countries making a substantial contribution.[10] As a sign of the changing times, the Spanish television participation was split between the main state broadcaster, Television Española, and the Spanish branch of the French-based cable company, Canal Plus; while in Britain it was backed by BBC Films. Two public subsidy organisations also took part: Germany's Filmstiftung Nordhrein-Westfalen, one of the largest such investors in Europe; and in the UK, British Screen and the European Co-production Fund which it administers. A vital further level of support was provided by the pan-European Eurimages Fund, which had by the mid-90s, become an important new option for British film-makers.

To understand how these new kinds of alliance between television and cinema, and between private and public funding, have developed, it is necessary to look back to their origins in the 80s. What Channel Four introduced to the UK was a principle already well established in France and Italy, whereby broadcasters part-fund a rolling portfolio of films intended for cinema release, which then become available for transmission after – in France's case – a statutory period. Film on Four made C4's Drama Department the co-producer, not only of a growing proportion of UK-based films, but increasingly of international productions with more obvious cultural than commercial intent.[11] Thus, for example, Wim Wenders' *Paris, Texas* (1984) was a West German-French-UK co-production, with twenty-two per cent of its budget of £1.16m covered by £250,000 from C4 and in the same year, another leading European auteur, Theo Angelopoulos, drew fourteen per cent, or £50,000, of the more modest budget of his *Voyage to Cythera* from the same source, combining this with funding from Greek, German and Italian television. Two years later, and even more improbably, C4 invested £275,000 in what would prove to be Andrei Tarkovsky's last film, *The Sacrifice*, a latter day mystical apocalypse made in Sweden with private and state support from France. The fact that these films could all now be considered in some sense 'British' is an important sign of the changing definition of cultural identity in Europe.

But they were also French, and the fact that France has remained the most active co-producer also means that French values and attitudes to cinema have been widely diffused through the new pan-European structures and schemes. The French cinema support system is undoubtedly the most developed in Europe, relying upon a network of institutions to manage the provision of public funding in the form of advances, concessions and quality subsidies. Its declared aim is to ensure that indigenous production remains at a viable level to supply a significant proportion of cinema releases and television productions – in short, to maintain 'French cinema' as a going concern in the face of ever-increasing Hollywood hegemony. Hence the stand taken by France in the 1993–4 GATT negotiations, to secure a 'cultural exception' for cinema, a position which many in Britain openly derided, while remaining grateful that the European case was being made. In doing so, French administrators (and ultimately politicians) have long realised that indirect means are often more effective than direct promotion. To support the Cannes Festival, for instance, as the world's leading focus for cinema as both culture and commerce helps to maintain the image of France as, in some sense, cinema's homeland. Similarly, to promote European co production and the very concept of 'European cinema' is ultimately beneficial to France, since French cinema remains the most widely distributed and respected of all European national cinemas beyond its own frontiers.

Both of the new pan-European cinema schemes which appeared at the beginning of the 90s had a distinctly French character. Chronologically, the first of these was Eurimages, a co-production funding agency established by the Council of Europe in 1989 (and based at their headquarters in Strasbourg), with a budget of some £6m and twelve founder members. Given France's record of over twenty bilateral co-production treaties, compared with the UK's five, it is possible to see this as the traditional French postwar approach writ large. The creator of Eurimages, however, was the Italian Gaetano Adinolfi, who patiently lobbied each potential member country, and its first chief executive was a Dutchman, Ryclef Rienstra. Despite subsequent modifications, the fund continues to offer essentially completion or 'end' funding, to projects with producers in at least three member countries, up to a maximum of twenty per cent of the original budget or £600,000, which is recouped from the producers' net receipts. It also provides support for cross-border distribution and exhibition with the aim of ensuring that European films achieve wider exposure in Europe itself.

Whatever doubts they might have about Eurimages bureaucracy, British film-makers could only look on in envy, since the UK government initially refused to join. In the xenophobic anti-European climate of 1989–91 (at the time of the Maastricht Treaty negotiations), there was little chance of a Conservative government agreeing to support a pan-European production fund, when domestic production funding had been sharply reduced and the limited tax incentives of the mid-80s withdrawn. However, by April 1993, the Major government succumbed to industry pressure and Britain joined what was now a group of twenty-four countries with around £18m available to fund more than seventy projects annually. During 1994–5 it has been estimated that one third of all British films, totalling over fifty features and long documentaries, received Eurimages funding.[12] Apart from *Land and Freedom*, these included Mark Peploe's £8.6m Joseph Conrad adaptation, *Victory* (1994), a low-budget debut feature by Benjamin Ross, *The Young Poisoner's Handbook* (1994) and Peter Greenaway's *The Pillow Book* (1995). Then, abruptly, in 1996 Britain's membership of Eurimages was cancelled by a government apparently more concerned with saving the subscription than with its image throughout Europe. The newly appointed British chief executive of Eurimages, Barrie Ellis Jones, had to resign and the UK returned to temporary isolationism, until the new Labour government pledged re-entry.

If Britain's intermittent relationship with Eurimages has disappointed film-makers wanting a link with the Anglophone world, the European Union's MEDIA programme has at least offered continuity throughout the 90s. MEDIA, however, is not concerned with direct support for production, but with 'developing the audio-visual industries'. In this sense, it was intended to be complementary to Eurimages, seeking to promote a culture of cross-border co-operation through specific inducements and also to promote greater 'professionalism' among European film- and programme-makers by stressing development, training and marketing, rather than mere 'creativity'. Launched in 1991 after a pilot phase, the first five year programme grew Topsy-like to a total of nineteen individual schemes, some of which seemed little more than personal fiefdoms for ambitious international operators. But the total funds involved were very small, compared with most EU programmes, and some MEDIA schemes quickly became central to an increasingly interdependent industry. Britain took an early lead in espousing the cause of pre-production development by establishing the European Script Fund, which offered funding to bring together potential writer–producer–director teams.

Inevitably, many more projects were supported than ever reached the screen and most that did achieved little more than the average European low-budget film. But even those who were sceptical about the Script Fund's missionary belief in well-structured scripts – seeing in this a capitulation to Hollywood screenplay norms – could scarcely deny that many promising European projects were distinctly vulnerable during the early development phase. A good example of a film that owed much to Script Fund support during its long gestation was Sally Potter's *Orlando* (1992). Indeed, the very possibility of bringing Virginia Woolf's fantasia on gender and history to the screen, and in a form in which it could achieve a similar scale of success to that of Greenaway's *The Draughtsman's Contract* a decade earlier, says much about the climate of internationalism surrounding MEDIA. The elaborate production credits of *Orlando* record a project which capitalised on a wide array of resources – traditional studio and costume facilities, as well as winter landscape, through Lenfilm in Russia, Dutch production design, from collaborators already associated with Greenaway, French and Italian funding, supplemented by money from British Screen and the European Co-production Fund. And after the film's successful launch at the Venice Festival in 1992, three other strands of the MEDIA programme played a part in ensuring its wide diffusion. EFDO, the European Film Distribution Office based in Hamburg, offered advances to distributors to encourage them to promote European films more competitively. A video support scheme, EVE (Espace vidéo européene), with offices in Brussels and Dublin, offered similar support to the emergent video publishers willing to handle specialised material. And the Paris-based Europa Cinemas network, funded jointly by MEDIA and Eurimages, sought to increase by means of incentives the number of prime cinemas across the continent willing to devote half or more of their screen time to European films.

The question of identity has acquired a new economic significance in the 90s, since deciding what counts as a 'national' or a European film affects the availability of production funding and eligibility for quotas. *Prospero's Books* (Peter Greenaway, 1991), for example, could benefit from Eurimages at a time when the UK did not belong because it was officially a Dutch–French–Italian co-production, with only a minor contribution from Channel Four. Similarly, *Orlando* had three Eurimages members among its five co-producing states. Two criteria have been laid down by the MEDIA committee: one requiring at least fifty per cent of financing from an EU member state; and the other awarding points to all the main production personnel, in order to establish whether a film is 'creatively' European. Many British films, in particular, have been classified as 'non-European' because the bulk of their financing is American, including such quintessentially 'English' narratives as *Sense and Sensibility* (Ang Lee, 1996), *Shadowlands* (Richard Attenborough, 1993), *The English Patient* (Anthony Minghella, 1996) and *The Full Monty*. However, the introduction of a new 'automatic' support scheme for distribution in 1996, under the MEDIA II programme, has led to these criteria being adjusted to offer more scope for co-productions with non-EU partners.[13] As a result, British films of sharply differing kinds have dominated recent MEDIA popularity listings. The single most popular European film in all EU cinemas in 1997 was *Bean*, with nearly 15 million admissions, followed by *The English Patient* at 9 million and, in fourth place, Mike Leigh's *Secrets and Lies*, with a total of 2.4 million admissions over two years.[14] Four other UK films make the 1997 Top Ten: *Brassed Off*, *Spice World – The Movie*, *A Life Less Ordinary* and *Career Girls*, all with 500,000 to 750,000 admissions.

The automatic distribution aid scheme is one of the main planks of MEDIA II, running from 1996–2000, which marked a shift away from the decentralised networking of the first

John Gielgud in Peter
Greenaway's *Prospero's Books*
(1991) – a consciously
Europeanised Dutch–French–
Italian (and British)
co-production

programme, towards fewer and more economically focused schemes. One of its architects
was David Puttnam, who has since published a detailed study of the political economy of
cinema, in which he observes that:

> Europe has traditionally concentrated nearly all of its energies on one part of the industry
> – production – and largely ignored changes to the marketing, distribution and exhibition
> networks which could possibly have put more indigenous films on the screen and achieved
> a higher level of box-office popularity.[15]

The thrust of MEDIA II is towards development, distribution and training, and after a mid-
term European Audiovisual Conference, held in Birmingham in April 1998 during the UK's
presidency, the economic theme was intensified, with proposals under consideration to
extend the automatic support scheme into video and television, to introduce a central
European Guarantee Fund (long mired in dispute) and to attract more private capital into
production. Under MEDIA's development strand, loans are currently available to support
company development and the formation of groups aiming to move beyond the cottage
industry level. Such funding has been given to The Film Consortium, a group that includes
Scala Productions and Parallax Pictures, responsible for many of Jordan's and Loach's films
respectively, and which is also a beneficiary of part of the UK's £100 million Lottery

Consortium funding, introduced in 1997. However welcome this may be in view of the UK's lack of production support compared with other European countries, I have argued elsewhere that the allocation of such largesse to what are essentially production groups, despite the inclusion of token distributors and exhibitors, perpetuates an historic fallacy in British state support for cinema.[16] Until there is sustained and substantial investment in new exhibition spaces in the UK – miniplexes to balance the rash of multiplexes; cinemas within new residential and leisure districts; colleges, museums, galleries and libraries – it is futile to provide more production funding, or expect new distributors to enter a market that lacks realistic retail capacity.

Meanwhile, in the brave new world of MEDIA II, British cinema rules. But is this a cinema with which we – whoever 'we' are – can identify? Most discussion of modern British cinema has taken place within quite narrow culturalist assumptions. Jarman v. Greenaway or Loach v. Leigh are familiar and acceptable choices while the Beatles films and even the *Carry On* films have been sanctified by the passage of time and nostalgia. But Mr Bean and the Spice Girls as British entries in Europe's Top Ten? Before rushing to dismiss these as aberrations of marketing, it is worth pausing to consider how a European dimension has already helped transform the 'Britishness' of British cinema. In the first place, it has broadened and consolidated the social cinema that withered after the 60s (or rather disappeared into television). It was European recognition, initially through festivals and then with funding, that allowed not only Loach to re-emerge, but also Leigh to develop as a film-maker, with his suburban odyssey *Secrets and Lies* largely funded by France's CiBy 2000. Again, European recognition and support has encouraged the diversification of a British realism that was once essentially English into Welsh, Irish and especially Scottish strands. In a 'Europe of regions', there is a ready audience for the differences between these sub-national cinemas and as Murray Smith argues in his account of *Trainspotting*'s 'black magic realism', that film's 'expansive and confident aesthetic ... may be taken as emblematic of the way in which British cinema as a whole has diversified in the 80s and 90s.'[17]

Unsurprisingly, British cinema's other revitalised genre, the Elizabethan romance, owes even more to foreign popularity and support. *Elizabeth* (1998), Shekhar Kapur's intelligent and innovative contribution, received MEDIA development support and registered healthy attendances throughout Europe and in the United States. In many ways, it can be seen as carrying forward and popularising the subversive, anachronistic tendency first staked out by Derek Jarman's (unsubsidised) *Jubilee* (1978) and continued in *Orlando*. The Elizabethan romance, of course, intersects with Shakespeare adaptations, which have also become a staple of modern British cinema. Again, Jarman was seminal, with his pop-hermetic version of *The Tempest* (1979), while Greenaway consciously Europeanised *Prospero's Books*, and *Shakespeare in Love* (1998) ingeniously combines these traditions. There is more in the pipeline. Among projects listed in MEDIA development are *Shakespeare, King of Naples* and *Mary, Queen of Scots*. And here there is considerable scope for ambivalence, given how central Shakespeare and the Tudor era are to the UK tourist industry. But as recent writers on Shakespeare such as Barbara Hodgdon and Jonathan Bate have shown, the Shakespeare heritage business is an important way in which *we* rethink our attitudes to gender, ethnicity, race and class and, ultimately, Englishness – as well as earning our keep.[18]

There is one further area in which the current 'professionalisation' of MEDIA and Eurimages should give cause for concern, and this is the field of experimental work. In the 70s and 80s, a considerable number of British avant-garde film-makers, of whom

Greenaway and Jarman are only the best known, won support from festivals or small-scale funders elsewhere in Europe before they were recognised at home. Through the patronage of maverick public-service television executives, festival directors, distributors and curators (and often with the discreet support of the British Council) their distinctive identity as film-makers was nourished, and they in turn inspired younger artists around Europe. Now the climate has changed. With Channel Four's abandonment of its original commitment to experimental programming (except in animation), the continued reduction of funding for BFI Production and the closure of the Arts Council's Film and Video Department in 1998, there are few obvious domestic sponsors for the paradigm-shifting new image-makers of the future. Can the current government be persuaded that this is vital for our industry as well as our culture in the next millennium, or must we lobby for MEDIA III to support innovation as well as sound business principles?

British film-making has a long-standing inferiority complex, hence its attachment to Truffaut's notorious put-down, duly quoted and refuted by Stephen Frears in his cente-nary of cinema documentary.[19] It has an equally long-standing, largely unrequited admiration for American cinema, which is sometimes expressed in terms of wanting to compete, but more often in terms of abject worship and surrender. The idea that it is a 'European cinema' for better and ill – meaning that it needs support, protection and what-ever strength there is in unity – has been as slow to make headway as the wider European political idea. But we're getting there.

Notes

1 Vinciane Fonck, *Les Virtuoses/Brassed Off: un film de Mark Herman* (Liège: Le Centre Culturel les Grignoux, 1998), p. 5.

2 Eddie Dyja (ed.), *BFI Film and Television Handbook 1999* (London: BFI, 1998), p. 39.

3 Comparison figures from presentations by Jonathan Davis and Michel Humbert, Summary Report, Europa Cinemas Exhibitors' Conference 1996.

4 A C Nielsen EDI Ltd, 1999.

5 The *dossier pédagogique* on *Brassed Off*, quoted above, proposes a series of five analytical frameworks, ranging from the political to the musical, which take the film considerably more seriously than any UK criticism that I know.

6 *Hitler* was a three-way co-production between WDR Cologne, INA and the BBC.

7 For background on France and Germany, see Jill Forbes (ed.), *INA: French for Innovation* (London: BFI, 1984) and Richard Collins and Vincent Porter, *WDR and the Arbeiterfilm: Fassbinder, Ziewer and Others* (London: BFI, 1981).

8 Tressell's autobiographical novel, about the exploitation and gullibility of building trade workers, was first published posthumously in 1914 and became a classic of the English labour movement.

9 France, Germany and Italy, the so-called 'FIG' countries, generally favour dubbing for wide releases, with subtitled 'original versions' sometimes also released simultaneously. Northern and smaller European countries generally subtitle all films.

10 See my article, 'Film for a Spanish republic', *Sight and Sound*, October 1995, pp. 36–7.

11 Information on C4 investment and budgets which follows is from John Pym, *Film on Four, 1981–1992: A Survey* (London: BFI, 1992).

12 Angus Finney, *The State of European Cinema* (London: Cassell, 1996), p. 110.

13 The Automatic Support Scheme awards money to distributors in proportion to admissions

achieved, which must be reinvested within a fixed period in acquiring and/or promoting new European films.

14 Source: *Media*, the Media Programme Newsletter no. 17, October 1998, p. 5.

15 David Puttnam with Neil Watson, *The Undeclared War: The Struggle for Control of the World's Film Industry* (London: HarperCollins, 1997), p. 345.

16 Ian Christie, 'Will Lottery money assure the British film industry? Or should Chris Smith be rediscovering the virtues of state intervention?', *New Statesman*, 20 June 1997, pp. 38–9.

17 Murray Smith, 'Transnational Trainspotting', in Murray Smith, Jane Stokes and Anna Reading (eds) *The Media in Britain: Current Debates and Developments* (London: Macmillan, 1999), pp. 219–27.

18 Barbara Hodgdon, *The Shakespeare Trade* (Philadelphia, PA: University of Pennsylvania Press, 1998); Jonathan Bate, *The Genius of Shakespeare* (London: Picador, 1997).

19 The opening narration of Frears' film, *Typically British*, produced by BFI Television for Channel Four, 1995 runs: 'The great French film director, François Truffaut, once famously said there was a certain incompatibility between the term "cinema" and "Britain". Well... bollocks to Truffaut.'

Chapter 8
Hollywood UK

Neil Watson

In the 1990s the British film industry displayed new-found energy, confidence and optimism. This was spurred by such international successes as *Four Weddings and a Funeral* (Mike Newell, 1994), *The Full Monty* (Peter Cattaneo, 1997) and *Shooting Fish* (Stefan Schwartz, 1997), the emergence of a new generation of entrepreneurial, commercially-aware producers and increasing cinema admissions. As a result, the share of national box-office held by British films which averaged around eleven per cent for most of the decade, jumped to twenty-three per cent in 1997.[1]

Meantime, driven by the construction of a new generation of multiplex cinemas, admissions rose. After hitting a post-war low of 54 million in 1984, they climbed back up to 100 million by 1991, and had reached 139.3 million in 1997, a figure which would have been unthinkable just a few years earlier.[2]

Investment in production also rose dramatically. In 1989, annual investment in UK production (including US productions shot at British studios) was a meagre £104 million. By 1996, this figure had soared to £741 million.[3] But although the indigenous film industry showed renewed signs of health and prosperity over the decade – particularly by contrast with the late 1970s and early 1980s – much of this reversal of fortune could be ascribed to the impact of Hollywood on the British industry.

Indeed, if the recovery of the 1990s was indicative of anything, it was that the fortunes of the British industry were still heavily dependent on investment by the major US studios and their subsidiaries. The influence of Hollywood was apparent right across the British industry from development and production through to distribution and exhibition. While such American investment was almost universally welcomed by the British film community, it served to underline the fragility of much of the indigenous industry.

Production

While investment in UK-based film production jumped sharply during the 1990s, much of it came from the US studios, with high-budget American-financed movies accounting for as much as ninety per cent of inward investment in the UK in some years. This was part of a phenomenon known as 'runaway production', which first became a major issue in the 1960s when the success of American-financed films such as *Tom Jones* (Tony Richardson, 1963) and the James Bond films, persuaded Hollywood companies to set up British subsidiaries. Although a spate of box-office disasters led them to scale back their activities, Hollywood production has become increasingly 'portable' due to the improvement in studio facilities elsewhere in the world, and the increased availability of overseas tax incentives.

The UK has been a particular beneficiary of this. During the 1990s Hollywood companies such as Warner Bros., Paramount and Universal invested significant amounts of money in productions such as the £30 million *Interview with a Vampire* (Neil Jordan, 1994) and the £50 million *Judge Dredd* (Danny Cannon, 1995) while their specialist subsidiaries such as Miramax (now owned by Disney) and Fine Line (now part of Time-Warner), invested in medium-budget films like *The Wings of the Dove* (Iain Softley, 1997) and *Little Voice* (Mark Herman, 1999), budgeted at £8.7 and £4.2 million, and in low-budget films such as *The Full Monty* (Peter Cattaneo, 1997) and *Sliding Doors* (Peter Howitt, 1998) which were both made for under £2 million. US investment in the UK film industry easily outstripped that of Europe, despite the growth in co-productions (notably with France and Germany) and financing from European broadcasters.[4]

The level of US production investment in the UK is partly dictated by exchange rate fluctuations; so long as the pound remains below $1.70, there is a significant cost advantage to US producers wishing to shoot in the UK, with some producers suggesting that the UK is up to thirty per cent cheaper than the US. Equally, the availability of fiscal incentives for the industry – in the form of tax write-offs for production expenditure – can also help to attract US producers to the UK.

However, by comparison with such countries as Australia, Canada and Ireland which introduced a raft of new measures during the 1990s aimed at attracting big-budget American pictures, the UK's fiscal incentives remained rather limited. In 1997, the Labour administration introduced a new first-year hundred per cent write-off to complement the

Little Voice (1999) – benefited from US finance

existing three year write-off on production expenditure. But the benefits were restricted to films budgeted up to £15 million – to the dismay of the American studios, most of whose films are budgeted at a higher level because of the cost of 'A' list stars or special effects.

The reputation of British studios, particularly Pinewood and Shepperton, together with the quality of technicians, continued to play a major part in attracting the Americans to the UK, but other factors – such as the need to use British locations or the desire of key talent (Steven Spielberg, George Lucas, Stanley Kubrick) to work in Britain – also played their part in boosting the number of Hollywood films made in the UK.

Such big-budget films benefit the industry in a variety of ways. Films like *Tomorrow Never Dies* (Roger Spottiswoode, 1997) and *The Fifth Element* (Luc Besson, 1997), with their high production values, inevitably demand the highest standards from technicians, creative and craft personnel, And pictures which are heavily dependent on special effects such as *Mission Impossible* (Brian De Palma, 1996) and *Event Horizon* (Paul Anderson, 1997) stimulate the development of the technical support structure – digital technologies, computer-based film editing, computer-driven video and film special effects – and help to make London the world's leading centre for post-production outside of Hollywood.

This sort of investment also brings economic benefits to other areas beyond the feature film business: it is generally assumed that for every job created on a film, a further 1.7 jobs are created indirectly. Insurance companies, hotels, transport firms and catering outfits all profit from film production. However, it is clear that a viable, long-term industry in the UK cannot be built solely by relying on inward investment or the vicissitudes of the international currency markets.

It was worrying therefore that throughout the 1990s much of the indigenous production and distribution industry remained highly fragmented, made up of a large number of small independent production companies, ill-equipped to compete with the US studios with their large capital base and their international marketing networks. This underdeveloped nature of the British industry inevitably meant that most domestic film production took place on a one-off basis in a financially volatile environment. Many British producers continued to push their films into production before the script had been fully developed in order to secure the production fees which are their financial lifeline, and which are only payable once the cameras start turning. Needless to say, this often damages the commercial prospects of the film. These difficulties were exacerbated by the almost complete absence of indigenous, vertically-integrated companies. British film-makers are largely divorced from those sectors which market their work, whether through cinema exhibition or on video. This made it almost impossible for producers to secure consistent sources of investment finance and to establish long-term arrangements for the distribution and exhibition of their films.

Much of the industry remained dependent on finance from television broadcasters, principally the BBC and Channel 4, who are only able to afford low-budget films. It could be argued that this diminished the ambitions of British film-makers and placed an artificial ceiling on the competitiveness of British product. Companies such as Thorn-EMI, Virgin, HandMade and Goldcrest which played a crucial role in helping to nurture some of the finest British films of the 1980s have subsequently wound down their film-making activities. It is hoped that the three franchises (The Film Consortium, Pathé Pictures and DNA) to which the National Lottery Fund has apportioned £90 million will fill the gap, but corporate and equity finance for the UK film production industry continues to be thin on the ground and most production companies operating in the sector remain hopelessly under-capitalised.

The fragmentation of the production sector was countered throughout most of the 90s by PolyGram Filmed Entertainment which provided finance for many UK producers and a distribution operation which served as an alternative to the American studios. A subsidiary of the international music group, PolyGram, eighty per cent owned by the Dutch electronics giant, Philips, PFE had an ambitious plan to become the first European film company truly able to compete with Hollywood since J. Arthur Rank's doomed attempt in the late 40s. The success of *Four Weddings and a Funeral* in 1994, which was produced by PFE's subsidiary Working Title, was largely responsible for igniting the firestorm in UK film production, which continued to burn through the rest of the decade.

In 1997, at the peak of 'Cool Britannia', PFE was by far the biggest UK-based investor in British films. It poured more than £50 million into fourteen productions and earned plaudits from Tony Blair's new youth-friendly government. The company's international chief Stewart Till was even appointed co-chairman of the government's Film Policy Review Group. In 1997 PFE financed three of the top five British films at the UK box-office – *Bean* (Mel Smith), *Spiceworld* (Bob Spiers) and *The Borrowers* (Peter Hewitt) – and all three were internationally successful, *Bean* taking over £198 million world-wide.

PFE also set out to create its own film and video distribution companies from scratch in various countries around the world. The final plank in the gameplan was to be an American distribution company, producing and releasing its own movies in the US, which represents forty-five per cent of the world market. Unfortunately, the ambitions of Poly-Gram's management, led by Michael Kuhn, were thwarted by the decision made by Philips in 1998 to sell the company to Seagram, the drinks company which was also the owner of Universal, in a deal worth US $10.6 billion. Like Korda and Rank before it, PFE's dream of building a British-based film company which could compete with Hollywood in its home market eventually collapsed.

While its losses often counterbalanced its profits, PFE undoubtedly reinvigorated the whole European film industry by proving that Europe could produce global hits to rival the Americans. But instead of achieving a Hollywood ending the company has ended up as part of the Hollywood locomotive it set out to derail. PolyGram acted as a standard bearer for the British production industry. With its demise, the possibility of building a strong, well-capitalised indigenous alternative to the Hollywood studios seemed more remote than ever.

Distribution

Throughout the decade, Hollywood also continued to dominate the UK distribution market. In the 1980s, a producer looking to secure a distribution deal could choose between mid-size companies like Rank and Virgin and a range of smaller, feisty independents like Enterprise. But as the cost of prints and advertising (P&A) rose ever-higher, many of them fell by the wayside. Although distributors are notoriously reluctant to release figures about P&A costs, even for relatively modest campaigns they can now reach £400,000 to £500,000, while in the case of very wide releases, with 400 prints or more, the costs of advertising might well be pushed over £1 million in the UK alone.

As a consequence, if a company wishes to succeed in the UK distribution market it must have access to significant amounts of capital. By the end of the 1990s only a handful of smaller UK companies were active in mainstream distribution, of whom the most notable were Entertainment Film and Film Four. A number of specialist companies including Artificial Eye and Electric Pictures continued to serve niche audiences but the way was left clear for the Hollywood studios to dominate UK distribution. They have a number of key strategic advantages. Firstly, the fact that they have an international distribution network enables them to co-ordinate aspects of the marketing and promotion of a film across a large number of countries. This can be particularly important, for example, with regard to co-ordinating tours of the stars so that they undertake promotional visits to several European territories in rapid succession. Secondly, they are able to utilise the expert knowledge and contacts of their local office in each particular country to maximise the commercial potential of a film in that territory.

However, it's not just the amount of money spent by the US studios on the marketing campaign for a film that's important. It's also the fact that they go to considerable and increasingly sophisticated lengths to test the audience response to a film prior to its release using specialist research groups such as the National Research Group, which recruits representative sample audiences to view films. This provides them with the opportunity to both amend the actual elements of the film and to revise the marketing and distribution campaign for the picture in order to adjust consumer perception.

Film distribution, like film production, is a high risk activity, since just a handful of titles will enjoy substantial profits, while most pictures lose money in theatrical release. According to most industry estimates, seven out of ten pictures made in Hollywood will fail to recoup their costs from theatrical exhibition – in many cases even their distribution costs. Companies like Warner Bros., Columbia Tri-Star and UIP (a joint venture between Paramount, Universal and MGM) are vertically-integrated with interests spanning development, production, and in some cases exhibition, as well as distribution so they have been able to spread their risk against a guaranteed and relatively consistent output of films. Such security of supply is vital in an industry where huge upfront commitments are being made to fund production. Since indigenous distribution companies do not have the financial resources available to the vertically-integrated US studios, their ability to provide British films with a wide release is severely restricted. Far fewer prints are made of most British films released in the UK than are made for US films.

While this reflects the relatively meagre ambitions of some British film-makers, the problem is ultimately circular, the poverty of resources prevents films from breaking out to wider audiences, and this reinforces the limited aspirations of British film-makers. At one extreme, a British independent film such as *Hear My Song* (Peter Chelsom, 1991), was released with only eight prints and earned £740,000 (a relative success given its low budget and the fate of less popular British films) while, at the other end of the market, a major US film would be released with upwards of 350 prints and might earn up to £20 million. But the US majors invest far more in prints and advertising at all levels of the market; both *Sliding Doors* and *The Full Monty* benefited from clever – and well-funded – marketing campaigns. The evidence suggests that a British independent film handled by a US major will be released with up to four times the number of prints a UK distributor would allocate for a similar type of picture.

Some British films received comparatively wider distribution in other countries than they did in the UK. *The Crying Game* (Neil Jordan, 1992) was released in Britain with only twelve prints and earned about £2 million at the box office, an average of £169,000 a print. The film's US distributor decided to invest in a release which was (even allowing for the larger size of the American market) very much larger – 500 prints. The strategy paid off handsomely – the film earned around £39.9 million at the box-office, an average of £798,000 per print. In most cases, however, the UK distribution and exhibition sector tends

Four Weddings and a Funeral
(1994) – advertised as
'America's No. 1 Smash Hit
Comedy'

to take its lead from the US and British screens are dominated by films which have already proved to be hits across the Atlantic. One example would be *Four Weddings and a Funeral* which was initially released in the US, then advertised in the UK as 'America's No.1 Smash Hit Comedy!"

Exhibition

The investment in multiplex cinemas which revolutionised cinemagoing in the UK was also largely financed by American companies – and it is they who have reaped the benefits. Though they represent thirty-seven per cent of total UK screens, they account for over fifty per cent of revenues. Despite the increase in the number of available screens, it sometimes proves difficult to hold-over a film that is performing relatively well for more than a few weeks simply because of the sheer volume of product jostling for space in the marketplace. Every week four to eight new movies are released to compete for finite screen space.

Many of the early multiplexes consist of five to eight screens which only allowed the exhibitor to play a handful of top titles. In these cases, there is simply no space for films with a more limited appeal. In the larger complexes, where there is space, popular block-busters often occupy three or even four of the available screens. This means that a greater number of screens are continually accruing to a smaller number of films. And while most

British films eventually receive a cinema release of some sort, they represent only a small proportion of the total number shown and a much smaller proportion of tickets sold. The UK continues to be under-screened in general and in particular in respect of art house cinemas. This has acted as a constraint to the effective release of British films, many of which play well at specialist locations yet fail to attract audiences when they play at out-of-town multiplexes.

The multiplexes meanwhile are dominated by a small number of high profile films. Big-budget US films continue to be released in the UK with an ever-increasing number of prints. Even though, on the bigger films, multiplexes can use one print for two or more screens, it is believed that the next generation of megaplexes wish to use separate prints for the biggest releases, thus offering staggered start times for those titles. As the volume of new titles coming into the market increases, distributors will be tempted to open films as widely and as early as possible because of the pressure of product coming up behind. These changes will tend to benefit the American majors more than anyone else, since their distribution subsidiaries dominate the UK.

The Future

The Hollywood majors continue to play a vital role in all aspects of the UK film industry and have helped revitalise and sustain it during the 1990s. However, the failure to develop a stable mainstream industry means that the UK continues to suffer from a talent-drain as stars, directors, technicians and others flee to Hollywood, which offers the long-term work opportunities they crave. This applies not only to high profile directors like Michael Apted, Mike Figgis and Danny Cannon but to technicians and craftspeople. Indeed, it's estimated that as many as two-thirds of the designers, and a third of the editors working at the very top in Hollywood are British.

As the revenues which accrue from film and related benefits grow, many argue that we should be doing more to ensure that a greater proportion of these revenues remain in the UK, and that they should be recycled as capital to support the future development of the British film industry. In the long run, it is likely that the only way of creating a truly flourishing indigenous industry which delivers real benefits to the national economy is to encourage the creation of fully integrated companies, capable of producing both films and television programmes on a consistent basis, and able to exploit aggressively the markets opened up by the increasing convergence between the television, computer and telecommunications industries.

For today's movies are really 'brand names'. Every single film put out by the Hollywood studios is, in a way, its own brand which, when successful, becomes a locomotive dragging behind it many other sectors of the economy, everything from fashion to fast-food chains, books and video games.

While Hollywood's support continues to provide vital nourishment for the British industry, over-dependence on investment from the US ultimately makes British cinema vulnerable to the boom and bust cycle which has plagued the industry throughout the twentieth century. The challenge for the twenty-first century is to capitalise on the real strengths of the British industry – the depth of talent, the quality of technicians and film studios, and rising cinema admissions – and to create a truly sustainable industry driven by four or five well-capitalised companies which can weather the hard times, and which can compete with Hollywood for a share of a growing global business.

Notes

1 *A Bigger Picture – The Report of the Film Policy Review Group* (London: DCMS, 1998).

2 Eddie Dyja (ed.), *BFI Film and Television Handbook 1999* (London: BFI, 1998), p. 42.

3 Ibid., p. 17.

4 Ibid., pp. 22–4. In 1997 the value of the fourteen predominantly American-financed films made in Britain added up to £259.2 million. The combined value of the twelve predominantly European-financed films was £52.96 million, though there was minority European (and Canadian and Japanese) investment in a further fifteen British films with a combined budget of £48.43 million.

Chapter 9
Image and Nation in 1990s British Cinema

Moya Luckett

During the 1990s, British national identity has become increasingly fraught, threatened by European federalisation and the imminent break up of the United Kingdom. Ironically this same period has seen British cinema enter one of its upward cycles, seemingly thriving as films like *Four Weddings and a Funeral* (Mike Newell, 1994), *Shallow Grave* (Danny Boyle, 1994), *Secrets and Lies* (Mike Leigh, 1996), *Trainspotting* (Danny Boyle, 1996), *The Full Monty* (Peter Cattaneo, 1997), *Spice World* (Bob Spiers, 1997), *Sliding Doors* (Peter Howitt, 1998), *Elizabeth* (Shekhar Kapur, 1998) and *Shakespeare in Love* (John Madden, 1999) received a combination of critical and box office success at home and overseas.[1] Despite their differences, these films suggest that a recognisable but diverse set of characteristics readily identify the 'Britishness' of the nation's film productions, albeit in the absence of a national consensus as to what 'Britain' itself might mean in the late 1990s.

This increased demand for British films suggests a changed relationship between the British public and its national cinema, hinting at these films' capacity to express otherwise ineffable dimensions of national identity and a spectatorial desire to see this identity expressed on screen. This can be seen in the formation of a new British film canon that counters traditional heritage-centred ideas of British cinema. Spearheaded by mass-circulation popular magazines like *loaded*, this 'alternative canon' focuses on violence, style and sexuality as well as more traditionally reified traditions of British horror and comedy. British cinema is 'redefined' with the rediscovery of films like *The Long Good Friday* (John Mackenzie, 1980) the *Confessions* series of the 70s, *Quadrophenia* (Franc Roddam, 1979), *Get Carter* (Mike Hodges, 1971) and *Performance* (Donald Cammell, Nicholas Roeg, 1970) and the new image is played out in recent hits like *Lock Stock and Two Smoking Barrels* (Guy Ritchie, 1998). Such films inspire fashion spreads that testify to their continued impact on British style, sexuality and youth culture.[2] Articles on older films indicate the formation of an 'alternative heritage' that expresses the energy, style and sexuality of British culture, an image fiercely counterposed both to the gentility and restraint of Merchant-Ivory films and to Hollywood. An essay recalling the continued impact of *Quadrophenia*, for instance, ends with the following comment:

> The Americans had *Grease* but we had and still have *Quadrophenia* and at the end of the day, would you rather be poncing round to 'Greased Lightning' going 'Well-a-well-a-well-ooo' or would you rather be driving through Sussex on a scooter with no helmet on knowing you're going to have it off with Lesley Ash in Brighton?[3]

This discourse suggests that British cinema is characterised by an emphasis on appearance and representation that stylises and re-imagines everyday life in ways Hollywood and European Art Cinema cannot. This conjunction of the stylistic and the realistic engages British

Quadrophenia (1979) – an example of 'alternative heritage'

cinema's two supposedly divergent characteristics, suggesting that it is precisely their inter-action within texts, not their opposition across discrete films and genres, that creates the dialectic that characterises British cinema in the 1990s. During this decade, public relations has also been used to reposition the interactions between image and 'reality,' establishing a set of practices that cinema draws upon and intersects with, adapting PR's strategies of producing images to promote unity (in the service of dominant powers) by eroding class-based conflicts and radicalism. Peter Mandelson's role in promoting New Labour is perhaps the most famous instance of PR being mapped onto government, an intersection that once again results in a primary concern with images of nation.

Although the events of 1997 (the election of New Labour, the death of Princess Diana) have been hyped as the most pivotal moments of changing national identity, these shifts merely capture and repackage earlier trends. Nonetheless, 1997 afforded the media the opportunity to ponder the question of British national identity and, in particular, to offset definitions of the nation rooted exclusively in its past, evidenced most strongly in the broadly ridiculed attempts to rebrand the state 'Cool Britannia.'[4] In 1998, Tony Blair con-vened Panel 2000, consisting largely of young media entrepreneurs like Waheed Ali and designers like Stella McCartney, to:

> convey an accurate, constructive picture of modern Britain.... Some still see Britain as it
> was two decades ago: in decline; others as no more than a relic of the past, a theme park of
> castles and villages. We do not reject our heritage, but we also need to be a forward-
> looking country.... Our task is to replace a myth of an old Britain with the reality of the
> modern Britain.[5]

Benedict Anderson has argued that national consciousness is fundamentally representa-tional, requiring literacy and mass media to create the 'simultaneity' that is the nation's time.[6] A sense of nation requires an awareness of the diversity of experiences that bind the people together, constituting an awareness of shared space and generating a sense of culture. But a level of self-consciousness needs to be added to Anderson's taxonomy because media also create a nation's *international* identity, a move that involves overcoming previous representations generated at home and overseas that might mitigate any currently favoured discourses of nation and thus erode the national agenda these serve at home and elsewhere. During the 90s, Britain has had to face the challenge of re-imagining itself as ultra-modern while simultaneously being renowned for its history, replacing and reconfiguring Thatcherism's combination of economic 'modernity' and veneration of 'heritage'. Tony Blair offered one possible solution in a Design Council report on 'Creative Britain': 'I am determined that we use *the strengths of our history* and our character and build on them for the future – *not discarding tradition, but building on it*'.[7] This necessarily invokes selective recollection while concepts of building on tradition suggest at best a dialectical concept of the past. Indeed, Blair's 'strengths of our history' might find parallels in the 'selective amnesia' that Benedict Anderson links to the writing of national history in the nineteenth century.[8]

These strategies – the emphasis on the image and selective recollection – mark post-1997 British history films like *Elizabeth*. With its combination of highly authentic pictorial detail (most major characters closely resemble surviving portraits) and scant respect for actuality, *Elizabeth* underlines how history can be marketed more easily when few viewers are aware of historical events and their consequences. Audiences familiar with Elizabeth's portraits are unlikely to know much more about her reign than a vague connection with Sir Walter Raleigh, Mary Queen of Scots and the Spanish Armada. Thus the images of the Queen that book-end the narrative are based on portraits, foregrounding their authenticity. Elizabeth's appearance at her coronation is closely modelled on the National Portrait Gallery's copy of a painting of 1559 that shows her in a gold dress and ermine robe with a crown over her long, reddish-blonde hair.[9] Even more familiar is the representation of a white-faced, bewigged Elizabeth in an enormous, white, jewel-studded dress that ends the film. This was based on the largest portrait painted of Elizabeth, and is sufficiently monumental to authorise the film's conclusion, despite dating from decades later.[10]

The life of the young Queen is represented in terms of a lavish and anachronistic 'girl power' as young Elizabeth flirts and dresses up to preserve her power and manipulate a highly patriarchal court and parliament. Her appearance provides her with pleasure, as does her active display of her body through dance. Throughout the film, such 'feminine' codes as her costume, hairstyling and make-up index her increased or diminished power, simultaneously playing with the viewers' knowledge of her, not as a young and vital girl, but as a heavily-upholstered dowager. The details of Elizabeth's appearance thus tease spectators with their diversion from the well-known image, culminating in the final, devastating scenes of her (historically incorrect) destruction of her beauty and her ascension to autocracy.

Locations and settings further authorise this presentation of Elizabeth's story as we glimpse her walking between pillars, dwarfed by monumental ceilings, or hear her feet echo across stone floors like footfalls in a very large church. The darkness of the film's settings is offset by its lavish costumes and the light of candles, producing an alternate vision of 'heritage' for a contemporary nation. While images of the countryside and its castles nod toward heritage films' more romanticised versions of the national past, they are peppered by the dead or bleeding bodies of untrained soldiers. This dystopic vision is reinforced

through graphic images of the Tower of London, where torture and the cries of individu-
alised figures are represented in intimate close-ups. Such cruelties are ameliorated through
the figure of Elizabeth, her renunciation of sensual beauty and her transformation into a
combination of Protestant martyr, Virgin Mary, supreme monarch, living portrait and
bride of England. This new orientation of heritage purports to reveal both sides of the
images we have inherited from history – from the cruelties inside castles to the visage of
Elizabeth herself – and it demonstrates how suffering was ultimately in the service of the
grander cause of preserving national borders and establishing a national identity – the cause
for which Elizabeth sacrificed herself.

Elizabeth thus narrates a new history, one that reinforces the power of images over
archival knowledge, and thereby legitimises a similar strategy for more contemporary narratives. The film might be seen in the context of Tony Blair's attempts to update the
monarchy by demonstrating how the *image* of a monarch might produce national renown
even in the face of very real domestic problems and their potential threat to nationhood.
Elizabeth suggests, then, how a reconceived history – both as a discipline and as a specific
narrative – might have practical efficacy in pre-millennial Britain. If 'authentic images'
replace contested facticity, then the nation might find its identity again.[11]

Discussions of contemporary national identity cannot, however, escape the monumental nature of constitutional changes deriving from a devolved UK with closer links to the
European Union. As Paul Willeman points out, traditionally an 'identification with the
British state is in fact English nationalism, as opposed to Welsh, Cornish or Scottish nation-
alisms.'[12] Given this structure, devolution threatens to change both the physical shape of
the nation and the emotional allegiances and expressions of nationalism. Nineties films
articulate this awareness of a national identity in flux, producing multiple visions of the
nation for an increasingly regionalised home market. Besides envisioning nation and space
from multiple and often irreconcilable perspectives, production itself has also become
increasingly localised with the emergence of film production companies yoked to the
regional television companies and Lottery grants. This increased regionalism has even
inflected Hollywood-funded British films like *The Full Monty* and *Brassed Off* (Mark Herman, 1996) that question ideals of unified national tradition. Furthermore, historical
pictures like *Braveheart* (Mel Gibson, 1995, USA), *Michael Collins* (Neil Jordan, 1996) and
even *Elizabeth* remind viewers that the 'national unity' of the United Kingdom is a relatively recent phenomenon, legitimising considerations of its demise.

Recent policies on devolution and the imminent institution of an elected mayor for London further emphasise the marginal, the exceptional and the culturally distinct aspects of
the United Kingdom. As political scientist, William L. Miller, observes, popular identity
negotiates myriad allegiances, including local and national, making it more productive to
consider questions of devolution and regionalism dialectically rather than as a clash of
opposing identities. Furthermore, such an approach will also illuminate the non-
monolithic nature of Scottish, Welsh and other regional affiliations:

> Except in the eyes of romantic nationalists [Scotland] is not united. Many outside the
> central belt look upon Glasgow and Edinburgh with almost as much suspicion as they do
> London. In the 1979 referendum on a Scottish assembly... there were serious threats that
> Orkney and Shetland would defect from Scotland and establish a new direct relationship
> with London, taking their claims to North Sea Oil with them.[13]

While Scotland was united in the 1997 referendum, its national allegiances are neither as homogeneous, nor as antagonistic to London or England, as Hollywood visions like *Braveheart* might suggest. *Braveheart* authenticates its Hollywood version of history by placing both Scotland and the US as similarly colonised victims of imperial Britain. In practice, however, Scottish films rarely have such a unified view of the nation, as regional and cultural differences are expressed through religious, football, town and country divides, and the distinct characters of major cities.

Recent Scottish hits like *Trainspotting* and *Shallow Grave* foreground this fragmented national Scottish identity. *Trainspotting* undermines tourist images of Edinburgh as a 'heritage' city of castles and arts festivals, inserting the kinds of drug, rave, youth culture associated more with Glasgow (or larger English cities like Manchester and London). As John Hill notes, it

> plays with the inherited imagery of England and Scotland. Thus when the film's main character, Mark Renton ... arrives in London, the film cheerfully evokes the most clichéd images of London in an ironic inversion of the touristic imagery which commonly accompanies the arrival of an English character in Scotland. In a similarly iconoclastic manner, the film accompanies its main characters to the Scottish countryside, not to invoke the 'romantic' beauty of the Scottish landscape but to provide Renton with the occasion for a swingeing attack on 'being Scottish'.[14]

After Renton has started to work in London, *Trainspotting* undermines this tourist gaze, producing images of its sordid, dark and over-priced flats as we follow Renton on his job for an estate agent. Despite his new be-suited, professional identity, we see that Renton's life in London is no less squalid than his drug-fuelled existence in Edinburgh. This further suggests that there is less difference between both large cities than there is between Edinburgh and the same Scottish countryside that angers and stifles Renton.

Boyle's previous feature, *Shallow Grave*, has a similarly playful attitude towards Scottish iconography and cultural traditions. After dismembering and burying a corpse, the three principals, Alex, Juliet and David, attend a charity ball. Everybody wears tartan, even the young and boisterous Alex, who is juxtaposed with the staid, elderly doctors and his old-fashioned flatmate, David. As Alex heckles the toastmaster, shouting out 'where did they dig him up?' we expect him to disrupt the ball and undermine its cultural heritage, yet he rushes to dance, revealing how modern Scots respect their culture and tradition but are not defined or limited by it. The diversity of the culture is further emphasised as scenes of a mobster being locked in a freezer to die, are intercut with the ball.

Most notably, *Shallow Grave*'s representation of Edinburgh departs from the kind of long-shot, bird's eye view iconography commonly used to introduce cities in the cinema. At the start of the film, a camera, apparently underneath a car, speeds past crescents of imposing, gothic, terraced stone houses accompanied by techno music. Highly visible edits underline this stylisation as the movement pulls us further into the city. This stylistic choice enhances the stature of the architecture while imbuing it with a new energy and modernity, highlighting Scotland's urban sophistication and producing an emphasis on the surface that continues with the presentation of the main characters' impossibly large and beautiful flat. Image-consciousness is reinforced throughout the film as the frame is adorned with candles and cascades of fruit to resemble still-life paintings. We are invited to judge these characters on their appearance and, as none are particularly glamorous, their image-consciousness is all the more unnerving, demonstrating that cruel superficiality exists everywhere.

Heralded as a 'Welsh *Trainspotting*', *Twin Town* (Kevin Allen, 1997) displays another series of conflicting British relationships, this time between England and Wales. Like *Trainspotting*, it views English and Welsh identity as intertwined, sharing contempt for both cultures, England for dominating and diluting Welsh culture and Wales for acquiescing to British imperialism. The *mise en scène* interrogates questions of national identity and local pride as in the scene where two characters (one of them leaning against a statue of Noddy, a symbol of imperialist English children's culture) are waiting outside Swansea Station and see 'Ambition is critical' inscribed in the pavement. The older one tells his friend that this is a response to Dylan Thomas's edict that Swansea is 'the graveyard of ambition', but he is a Scot and hasn't heard of Dylan Thomas. Visible behind them is a bilingual British Rail sign with the English text (in darker letters) placed above the Welsh, suggesting the hegemony of British identity while highlighting Wales' linguistic difference and its battle for bilingual public signs.

Twin Town plays with the idea that sound might represent national specificity, with its use of the Welsh language, its reference to Dylan Thomas and the Male Voice Choir so loved by the twins' father. Sound is generally regarded as secondary in its power and importance in visual media like film, but as *Twin Town* reminds us, it is also infinitely pervasive and affective. Similarly, *Brassed Off* and *The Full Monty* link sound to regional identity, using the brass band to suggest local pride and the centrality of masculinity, both phenomena eroded by a southern hegemony equated with consumerism and an obsession with image. In *Brassed Off*, for instance, Gary describes the local brass band as 'only thing left going here'. Sound – particularly music – comes to stand for a regional refusal to acquiesce to imperial or metropolitan power. At the end of *Twin Town,* the twins' father's funeral is

Twin Town (1997) – Welsh and English identities intertwined

accompanied by a large choir, and a Welsh flag draped on his coffin as a testament to national pride. Associated with loss, these sounds locate Welsh nationalism as an almost bygone tradition that, despite all the odds, refuses to die.

This old Wales, defined through its subordinate relation to Westminster and its absorption into the United Kingdom, is about to become a relic itself. Nonetheless, as Miller reminds us, devolution does not mean absolute separation from Westminster and the creation of independent new nations. Instead, it involves the redefinition of the UK as a 'multinational state, a voluntary organisation linking together fundamentally different peoples and countries'.[15] Consequently difference is dispersed across the state (the United Kingdom) rather than along national boundaries, highlighting that cultural differences are not co-extensive with either land or race.[16] This is not to deny the existence of regionally-specific economic, political and social conditions that, in turn, produce distinct local cultures. For example, the much heralded boom of the mid-to-late 1990s and the development of media archetypes like 'Cool Britannia' for some only underscored the poverty of the margins and their exclusion from dominant ideas of the nation, a premise foregrounded in *Brassed Off, My Name is Joe* (Ken Loach, 1998) and *The Full Monty*.

Indeed, many 90s films stabilise their representations of regional difference within the UK by articulating the north/south divide in terms borrowed from 1960s cinema. While the 1960s also witnessed changing and uncertain national identity, the passage of three decades has reshaped its images to connote a distinct, recognisable, image of nation. Films like *Spice World*, for example, self-consciously recall 'Swinging London' while *The Full Monty* and *Brassed Off* borrow the shots of 'our town from that hill' from the realist/New Wave films with equal awareness.[17] This return to earlier traditions of local representation invites a critical examination of the dialectic between past and present, memory and current experience, economic power and disadvantage. The opening of *The Full Monty* foregrounds the relationships between history, representations and social reality by opening with a short promotional film from the mid-1970s, *Sheffield: City on the Move*. Matted

The Full Monty (1997) – 'our town from that hill'

into the centre of the screen, its status is clearly that of representation not diegetic reality. Against a jaunty canned music track, a southern, male voice-over narrates the joys of Sheffield, emphasising its leisure amenities built upon an infrastructure of steel. The film presents a sunny city with fountains, indoor shopping centres, football, colourful, almost tropical parks, pools, the bright lights and neon signs of Sheffield's nightlife and shots of steel foundries. After a title, '25 years later', we see the contemporary city – exemplified by the ruined inside of an industrial building. As *The Full Monty* systematically explores how nearly two decades of Conservative policies have eroded the city's prosperity and its steel industry, it also undermines the truth of any image presented in this promotional film – images of a leisure-oriented, sub-tropical Sheffield cannot be reconciled with any image of the urban north.

The Full Monty positions itself within the tradition of the Angry Young Men films of the late 1950s and early 1960s. The dialectic between the corruption of 1960s consumerism and the present is accentuated as Serge Gainsbourg and Jane Birkin's 'Je t'aime' plays over shots of ruined foundries and the derelict city centre, segueing into a desperate middle-aged steel-worker's vain audition for Gary's troupe of male strippers. In a series of gender-based reversals, male strip shows have become the town's sole growth industry, staged inside working men's clubs where women enter men's toilets, talk about sex and copy the way men urinate. As Gary laments, 'men are dinosaurs... yesterday's news', their extinction induced by economic developments that create a feminised society. Even if they are not personally responsible for causing recession, women generally exacerbate men's plight while maintaining their own status and jobs. While Gary steals steel girders to pay maintenance for his son, his ex-wife lives in a modern, detached house with her new middle-class husband. In turn, Gerald's wife's lust for consumer goods prompts him to hide his unemployment while she books ski-ing holidays and shops with credit cards.

The loss of work also deprives men of a public, homosocial space, feminising them and turning their interests towards their bodies. Concerned that his overweight body cannot live up to feminine ideals, Dave's depression nearly ends his marriage. Horse, the black member of the troupe who catalyses Dave's self-doubt, has a bad hip and resorts to using a pump in a vain attempt to live up to the bawdy connotations of his name. As the motif of stripping makes clear, male body-consciousness is the product of the new feminine social order – itself the consequence of a combination of Thatcherism, southern influence and the shrewish, upwardly-mobile femininity of the likes of Gerald and Gary's ex-wives. As in *Saturday Night and Sunday Morning* (Karel Reisz, 1960), *The Loneliness of the Long Distance Runner* (Tony Richardson, 1962) and *This Sporting Life* (Lindsay Anderson, 1963), *The Full Monty* constructs a dialectic between prosperity and loss across lines of sexual difference to point to the inauthenticity of feminine culture and its corruption of regional identity. In the more recent films, however, sexuality itself is increasingly corrupted as the vivid masculine force of the body, represented perhaps most prominently in Albert Finney's forceful, muscular physique in *Saturday Night and Sunday Morning*, is physically undermined, transmuted into the scrawniness of Robert Carlyle as Gary in *The Full Monty* or Stevie in *Riff-Raff* (Ken Loach 1990). The continued success of consumerism in the absence of any real work in 90s films produces male melodramas where this reconfigured male body articulates a loss of authenticity and the demise of a judicious social order.

The explicit anti-Thatcherism of 1996's *Brassed Off* is touted both in its opening titles and its treatment of the alternately dying, impoverished and isolated male body. The narrative starts with the imminent closure of Grimley Colliery, one of the few Yorkshire pits

to survive the 1980s. The arrival of a young female Coal Board surveyor, Gloria, causes suspicion because she is a middle-class member of management. While her local credentials
are impeccable – she even plays her grandfather's fluegelhorn in the colliery band – her
appearance and gender alienate many locals (she dresses like a 1980s business woman,
recalling the spectre of Thatcherism). When she finally discovers what the miners knew all
along – that her report will not be considered, that it is simply a public relations gesture –
she resigns, making her a loyal and suitable partner for Andy, her now unemployed miner
lover. Her knowledge, gleaned from a university education, is thus more useless than the
local men's folk wisdom that leads them to predict a future they cannot change. Meanwhile,
Danny, the conductor of the colliery's brass band, persists in following his dream of winning a national championship, even though he is deathly ill with lung disease. Although the
band finally proceeds against the odds to win the national championship at the Albert Hall,
Danny realises that this is a hollow triumph, renounces the award and addresses the crowd
about the emptiness of working-class culture and ceremonies in a world without mining
jobs.

This renunciation of Thatcherism represents another defining element of late 90s politics and culture. Elizabeth Wilson has observed that the public mourning for Princess Diana
'may have been – as some suggested – a generalised regret for eighteen years of Thatcherism'.[18] Mapping political failures onto narratives of entertainment and male bodies
circumvents the history of Thatcher's public support while retaining the pleasures of affective regret. Although *Brassed Off* ultimately exposes the Marxist truism that culture has no
value without an economic infrastructure, it leaves its protagonists in abeyance and in tran-
sit in the carnivalesque world of London's nightlife. In contrast, *The Full Monty* produces
reconciliation and resolution, celebrating the men's performance and its promised wind-
falls. Its logic is that of the Lottery, with its promise of miraculous wealth derived as 'divine'
retribution for unfair struggles.

Like the Lottery, both the story of *The Full Monty* and its huge success in the international market provides a national narrative that managed to unite the nation across very
real differences (as seen in Prince Charles' much-reported staging of the dole queue scene
at one of his many fiftieth birthday parties). This idea of unity across difference, whether
regional, class or ethnic, also offers a way to approach questions of the nation's precise identity through the trope of multiculturalism. Contemporary mainstream British film-making
is, perhaps, too eager to subsume cultural difference, highlighting the presence of Afro-
Caribbean or Asian actors in otherwise ethnically unmarked supporting roles. This strategy
of inclusion extends and updates the nation, while simultaneously suggesting both the
authenticity of its representations and the exoticism of home. This produces a proliferation of black and Asian characters with strong regional accents, like Mel B/Scary Spice in
Spice World and Horse (Paul Barber) in *Monty*. During its self-reflexive credit sequence,
Spice World foregrounds multiculturalism's spread outside the capital when Mel B suggests
that her character develops the catchphrase 'I'm not from London, you know'. The composition of the Spice Girls testifies to this superficial multiculturalism – black and white
girls from the north and south, posh and working-class, from London, Liverpool, Leeds
and Hertfordshire are all unified under the Union Jack, reproduced on their double-decker
bus, mini-dresses, platform boots and T-shirts. *The Full Monty*'s multiculturalism similarly
exists solely at the level of the unifying image. In a city where class and gender relations are
still marked by conflict, racial interactions are quite utopian. Horse is completely assimi-
lated; the conductor of the brass band, the most 'authentic' aspect of local culture, is black;

and the end of the film hints at a potential future interracial and multigenerational relationship. Horse's niece is strongly attracted to the middle-aged Gerald, and a shot-reverse shot sequence during the men's strip show hints at a future empowering romance.

This multiculturalism evacuates ethnic difference, transforming it into taste or style. Hence in *Twin Town*, characters can comfortably order a curry with 'half rice, half chips', reinforcing Paul Willeman's observations that multicultural practices and policies finally ghettoise the 'authentic' immigrant cultures within their midst. 'And in that way, the host culture can reaffirm its own imaginary unity and the illusion of its specialness and authenticity.'[19] Ironically, films like *Twin Town, Shallow Grave*, and *Trainspotting* position Welsh and Scottish national difference as more complex and 'authentic' than any ethnic or racial difference. Regional difference is thus increasingly included as an important part of British multiculturalism, as the following example from *High Life*, British Airways in-flight magazine illustrates:

> A hundred years ago, Britain presided over the largest empire the world has ever known.... Now that diversity is concentrated within its own shores. One of the points of this series is to glean some evidence about the nature of multiculturalism in 1999. We begin this month in the West Country – land of rocks and rolling hills.[20]

This version of multiculturalism conflates regional and ethnic difference with discourses of empire to produce another set of hierarchies that suggest distance and marginality. Minorities, especially ethnic minorities, are used to authenticate the affective, melodramatic component of contemporary narratives. This is most strikingly demonstrated in the discourse around the death of Princess Diana. Commenting on media representations of the mourners in the Mall, Sara Maitland observes:

> A remarkable amount of attention was given... to anyone who could display 'suffering'. In the absence of very many sick people, any outsider would do: the very young, the very old, ethnic or sexual minorities... A mysterious *we* emerged... (In the light of this, the number of black people chosen for vox pops was quite extraordinary in a country where, *pace* New Labour, old racism still thrives).[21]

Part of the drama (and 'realism') of Mike Leigh's *Secrets and Lies* is in its inversion of this set of assumptions. After her adoptive mother dies, Hortense Cumberbatch, an unemotional and repressed middle-class young black woman decides to search for her birth mother. She reacts passively to a series of increasingly bizarre events, including the discovery that her mother, Cynthia, is white, lonely, poor and uneducated, and has convoluted and explosive relationships with her daughter, Roxanne, and brother, Maurice. In contrast to her daughter, Cynthia is volatile, hyper-emotional and needy, inverting stereotypical images of racial difference. This is further underscored in their social positions. Cynthia is marginalised at every level; her poverty and lack of education prevents her full participation in London life and she has been largely abandoned by her family. In contrast, Hortense lives in a centrally-located flat, decorated with white, impractical upholstery that indicates her own investment in images, appearances and style. Clearly, these representations contrast strongly with late 90s discourses on race and ethnicity that, for example, reveal systematic racial discrimination by the police (in the Metropolitan Police's investigation of the murder of Stephen Lawrence for example). Like 'history' and 'heritage,' then, *Secrets and Lies* both articulates and critiques a 'multiculturalism' that tends more towards image than substance at the expense of the specificities of ethnic and racial identity and the disequilibriums of power across race relations.

Like New Labour, then, it seems that much 90s mainstream cinema aspires to public relations, erasing conflict through the creation of images designed to create the illusion of direct communication with the public. This slickness marks one of 1998's biggest hits, *Sliding Doors*, distinguished from other British hits through its more American mode of production which involved PR tactics like public and industry previews.[22] *Sliding Doors* itself incarnates this PR emphasis on the all-unifying image that speaks to public desires, telling the fairy-tale story (or stories) of Helen, a public relations executive, fired for stealing vodka from work. Her life splits in two as she alternately catches or misses the tube home. One Helen dyes her hair blonde and establishes her own successful PR company, underlining that image is everything; while the other flounders, taking on two menial jobs. The death of blonde Helen at the end suggests a return to authenticity, but the film inverts this, strongly hinting that brunette Helen's life will follow the same trajectory trail-blazed by her blonde counterpart. In the final scene, she meets James, her doppelgänger's love interest, in precisely the same way as 'before,' getting into a lift with him and accidentally dropping her earring on the floor. This gesture suggests the magical resolution of image and real life, while successfully erasing the spectre of her impossible other. It also reconciles two economic and social experiences, effacing class through images and illusions.

Together, then, 90s films suggest a set of problems around the representation of nation and national identity that cannot be easily reconciled. As *The Full Monty* demonstrates, some regional identities are on the verge of possible extinction precisely because of the erosion of the industrialised, masculine culture on which they are based. This, in turn, threatens to destroy associations between land, environment, economy, society and culture that have produced the conceptions of regional identity that are a fundamental part of the nation. Even *Sliding Doors* indicates that national identity requires some 'authenticity', despite its ultimate endorsement of glamour, the superficial and the magical. After all, Gwyneth Paltrow is American, and despite her appearances in films like *Emma* (Douglas McGrath, 1996) and *Shakespeare in Love* as the 'quintessentially British' heroine, her star image undermines her authenticity. Consequently, *Sliding Doors'* attempts to find the truth of the nation rest on supporting characters who all have strong regional identities (James is Scottish; Helen's best friend, Anna, is Irish; and her two-timing fiancé, Jerry, is played by Irishman, John Lynch). This leaves a vacuum at the centre of the nation: in a London where there are no native Londoners. This suggests that national identity is always elsewhere, a paradox that seems to be echoed in the current efforts of audiences to find the nation in the images of British cinema.

Notes

1 See, for example, Dan Glaister, '*Full Monty* adds spice as UK film industry doubles box office takings', the *Guardian* 15 December 1997, (www.guardian.co.uk). As with all other periods of success for the British film industry, though, the figures hardly indicate national dominance, even at home.

2 See, for example, 'Enhanced performance', *loaded*, September 1998, pp. 132–41 – a tribute to *Performance* that is also used to market the video.

3 Michael Holden, 'Great moments in life: Watching *Quadrophenia*', *loaded*, September 1995, p. 16.

4 The *Guardian* points out that this was initially the name given to an American brand of ice cream manufactured by Ben and Jerry's. For a more detailed critique and history of 'Cool Britannia', see Andy Beckett, 'The myth of the cool', *Guardian, G2* section, pp. 1–3, 5 May 1998.

5 'Britannia's committee for cool', BBC News, UK, Website (www.news.bbc.co.uk), 1 April 1998; 'Panel 2000: Towards a 'Cool Britannia', Greenwich 2000 website.

6 Benedict Anderson, *Imagined Communities: Reflections on the Origin and Spread of Nationalism*, revised edn (London: Verso, 1991), p. 26.

7 Quoted in 'Britannia's committee for cool,' *BBC News* (www.news.bbc.co.uk), 1 April 1998, n.p. Emphasis mine.

8 Anderson, *Imagined Communities*, pp. 192–201.

9 This picture is reproduced as a frontispiece in Rosalind K. Marshall, *Elizabeth I* (London: HMSO in association with the National Portrait Gallery, 1991), p. iv.

10 Ibid., p. 136.

11 While also based on the demands of trade and the economics of the free market, recent Labour government interventions into the film industry suggest a similar logic at work. 'Managing the mini boom,' *Sight and Sound*, October 1998, p. 19.

12 Paul Willemen, *Looks and Frictions: Essays in Cultural Studies and Film Theory* (London: BFI, 1994), p. 210.

13 William L. Miller, 'The Periphery and its Paradoxes', in Hugh Berrington (ed.), *Britain in the Nineties: The Politics of Paradox* (London: Frank Cass, 1998), pp. 179, 180.

14 John Hill, 'British Cinema as National Cinema', in Robert Murphy (ed.) *The British Cinema Book* (London: BFI, 1997), p. 252.

15 Miller, 'The Periphery and its Paradoxes', p. 184.

16 Ibid., p. 171.

17 See Terry Lovell, 'Landscapes and stories in 1960s British realism', *Screen* vol. 31, n.4, 1990.

18 Elizabeth Wilson, 'The Unbearable Lightness of Diana' in Mandy Merck (ed.), *After Diana: Irreverent Elegies* (London: Verso, 1998), p. 119.

19 Willeman, *Looks and Frictions*, p. 207.

20 Mark Jones, 'The Britain files', *High Life*, January 1999, p. 3.

21 Sara Maitland, 'The Secular Saint', in Mandy Merck (ed.), *After Diana: Irreverent Elegies*, pp. 64–5.

22 Peter Howitt, 'Lose the tube train, cut the leading man – and by the way, *who wrote that script*', *Guardian Saturday section*, 2 May 1998, p. 4.

Chapter 10

Here and Then: Space, Place and Nostalgia in British Youth Cinema of the 1990s

Karen Lury

A discussion concerning British youth cinema in the 1990s might be expected to offer points of connection to other aspects of British popular culture. For example, 'Cool Britannia' and the rise of Brit-pop; the continuing extension and development of the dance scene; yoof television (from *The Word* to *TFI Friday*); books for and about youth (*Generation X, Trainspotting* and *The Beach*) could all be used to demonstrate the way in which British youth was addressed and represented in the 1990s.[1] Within such a context, a range of British films – including *Shopping* (Paul Anderson, 1994), *Shallow Grave* (Danny Boyle, 1994), *Blue Juice* (Carl Prechnezer, 1995) *Trainspotting* (Danny Boyle, 1996) and *Small Faces* (Gillies MacKinnon, 1996) – appear, in terms of their content and style, to reproduce and incorporate developments within popular culture generally.

While not wishing to deny the interaction between these aspects of popular culture and youth films, there are other qualities and activities – the presence of nostalgia, the particular character of consumption in the 1990s – which reveal interesting commonalties and significant distinctions between youth films of the 1990s and earlier films for, or about, youth. The focus of my argument will concern two films in particular – *Shopping* and *Trainspotting* – which usefully illustrate how key features addressing youth were employed in the 1990s. While the success of *Trainspotting* can be related to its fortuitous appearance in conjunction with some of the developments already indicated, it was its emergence as a *brand,* that granted the film a specific identity and authority in terms of its relationship and representation of British youth.

That successful films became brands in the 1990s will be understood not simply as a commercial imperative, but as a response to a particular cultural context, where the integration of different media and media forms – music, television, publishing, even clothing – became increasingly important as the decade progressed, and particularly so in relation to the youth market. *Trainspotting* can be compared to *Shopping* which attempted to address the same audience and in many ways reproduced a similar version of youth and contemporary experience but failed to establish itself, either at the box-office, or in terms of its cultural profile, as representative of 1990s youth. This failure stemmed from the uneasy marriage of certain stylistic features within the film which frustrated the ambition of the film's makers to position the film as an attractive commodity for, rather than a commentary on, youth.

'British' incorporates a diverse array of strong regional and national identities. In addition to the relatively clearcut national distinctions between Scotland, Wales, Northern Ireland and England, there are also regional variations within the category 'English' relating to communities who are distinct from one another, and which include identities relating to specific geographical areas such as, for example, Northerners or Londoners. Certain aspects of youth culture in the 1990s worked to highlight these distinctions, notably the Brit-pop battle between two rock groups: Blur (Essex/London, middle-class, art school) and Oasis (Manchester/Northern, working-class). Different youth films, whether it was the Cornish-based *Blue Juice*, the Scottish aspects of *Shallow Grave, Trainspotting* and *Small Faces*, or the implied London-centred action of *Shopping* also attempted to incorporate and articulate these distinctions – different national/regional accents, locations and activities being used to imply authenticity. The importance of the peer group and local affiliations (whether to a particular town, a local hang-out, a football team, a musical band or to a particular fashion) have been well documented in relation to youth culture in Britain and it is therefore unsurprising that films attempting to reach or represent this audience should wish to draw on such a recognisable series of cultural signs.[2]

However, in many youth films, the representation of such identities and locations is ambiguous. For example, in *Blue Juice* the characters and the action are located in an exclusive insider culture that is literally isolated and distant from London: a surfing sub-culture based in Cornwall. The film does this by constructing a specific culture and identity, incorporating aspects of the Cornish landscape (beaches, the sea and rocky cliffs) and climate (bleak winters and summer sunshine). The quality of work within the region/culture is also significant; work within the community is presented as being organic and appropriate to the geography of the place and to local needs. The only industry referred to is fishing (although this work is never seen), and the main characters are seen teaching surfing, working in a café, or as craftsmen in a workshop dedicated to the making of surfboards. Into this carefully constructed idyll the characters Josh (Steven Mackintosh) and Dean (Ewan McGregor) are introduced – as, respectively, a cynical record producer and a drug dealer. They are both clearly identified as London-based, as well as apparently disenchanted and/or corrupt.

The representation of a particular community by the film is therefore designed to construct a somewhat idealised local culture as a place outwith, and literally distant from, the commercial taint and inauthenticity represented by London. However, the insertion into the film of a local radio station featuring two heavily-accented and older DJs, whose commentary alternatively narrates or provides a counter-point to the action, allows the film to locate its characters as being both within and without the community. While Josh, in particular, is made conscious of his own inauthenticity (and thus locates the cause of his personal dissatisfaction) through his encounter with certain aspects of local culture, the exaggerated yokel qualities and quaintness represented by the voices of the two DJs (the only Cornish accents present in the film) establish a distance between the characters from some potentially less credible aspects of Cornishness that are also part of the local culture. The same strategy is evoked in *Trainspotting*; the famous 'Scotland is shite' speech similarly enables Renton and his peers to be both contained within, and remain resistant to, the dominating stereotypes and other supposed characteristics inherent within representations of their local landscape and culture. This ambivalence serves to articulate the tension between staying and going, a feature of nearly all the youth films of this period and one which resonates with many young people's own ambivalent feelings about growing up and leaving home.

National and regional identities are also important in establishing the films, and the youth represented on screen, as part of an emerging cultural and economic dynamic played out between local and global cultures. Indeed, in many of these films, it is the relationship between a local culture (a region, a town, a peer group) and the global culture which demonstrates the particular 1990s character of these films. While not exclusive to youth cultures, or youth experience, the dynamic opened up by the interaction between local and global cultures and the emphasis on cultural hybridity became increasingly significant to the understanding of the experience and identities of young people in the 1990s. Doreen Massey explains:

> The spatial openness of youth cultures in many if not all parts of the world is clear. Across the world even the poorest of young people strive to buy into an international cultural reference system; the right trainers, a T-shirt with a Western logo, a baseball cap with the right slogan. Music draws on a host of references which are fused, rearticulated and played back. Anti-roads protesters and young ecologists link up via the Internet with environmental battles world-wide (internationalism can mean interconnection without implying sameness). The youngest generations of diaspora societies wrestle constantly to find an enabling interlocking of the different 'cultures' in which they find themselves; it is a struggle indeed to build another – 'hybrid' – culture.[3]

Although youth culture in Britain, like other youth cultures, has long been characterised by 'spatial openness', revealed by its willingness to embrace other cultures – American or Afro-Caribbean music for example – hybridity as a defining quality or practice within British youth culture became increasingly self-conscious in the 1990s.[4] Notable developments were the growth and success of rap, hip hop and sampling as musical forms which embrace a hybrid aesthetic as part of their musical practice; global clothing franchises, such as Benetton; global brands such as Nike, as well as the spread of global youth media such as MTV. All these musical forms, products and brands, are incorporated into youth cultures in ways that are peculiar to local practices and histories and a distinction can be made between the way in which these elements were used by British youth in the 1990s, and the way in which the interaction between external and indigenous cultural practices were experienced by young people in previous decades.

Earlier generations of youth had been thought of as new and original in the way in which they experimented with fashions, music and other products (such as scooters and cars, drugs and alcohol). Despite borrowing from other cultures and relying on the impure activity of consumption, mods, hippies and punks were often presented as untainted by commercial manipulation.[5] In fact punk presented itself as the last authentic youth rebellion precisely because it demonstrated that its own figureheads were already 'sold out' and openly inauthentic. It was a sentiment encapsulated by the title of the Sex Pistols' film *The Great Rock'n'Roll Swindle* (Julian Temple, 1979). The youth sub-cultures emerging after punk's demise were therefore informed by the cynicism of punk, but grew up in a context in which the market and popular culture became an increasingly important part of social life and individual identity. Nineties youth knew that everything had been done before, whether it was fashions (flares, the mini-skirt), or music (the Beatles-like guitar rock of Oasis). Frequently, nostalgia accrued doubly: since earlier youth fashions had already often exaggerated or parodied other earlier cultural trends, a nostalgia attached both to the initial source and to the youth fashions and music which celebrated this source. For example, *Velvet Goldmine* (Todd Haynes, 1998) pays homage to the glam rock era of the 1970s, yet this particular musical scene was already indebted to, and celebrated, the rock-'n'roll era of the late 1950s, through its use of straightforward rock'n'roll rhythms and outlandish performers. The knowing-ness this practice implied can also be seen in the way in which the transience of particular cultural practices, icons or crazes was openly understood to be connected not only to the practice of young people themselves, to enable them to be different or new, but also to the crass and commercially-inspired machinations of the market.[6]

Despite this, particular commodities and fads remained an integral part of growing up. The contradictory and ambivalent relationship towards such commodities and icons was a significant element within films: in *Shopping* for example, the detritus of Billy's childhood and teenage years – his *Star Wars* scrap book, his skateboard and drainpipe jeans – are ridiculed by his peers (as 'so 80s') whilst elsewhere in the film, another antique commodity, the 'Krazy Cars' computer game, is valued according to its status as an original, and thereby celebrated by the characters.[7] *Trainspotting* too, with its use of 1970s music and its loose representation of 1980s urban youth culture, and even Renton's ability to find a job in a London property firm, establishes a nostalgic context for its narrative and the characters, which while representative of youth experience, also prevents the film from acting as a commentary on the activities of the young audience who are watching the film.[8]

Thus far, I have implied that youth films are about youth. All the films I have mentioned involve young characters and their specific problems and lifestyles, and all are clearly constructed to attract a young audience. But films, like other products and texts, do not necessarily appeal only to those markets or audiences they seem designed to attract. The extent of *Trainspotting*'s box-office success indicates that its audience extended beyond young people. Equally, the relative openness of the film text will mean that films not intended or addressed to a young audience will also be attractive to them. The near total penetration of the VCR in Britain, and the growth of video rental outlets enables young people to select and enjoy films from both the past and present, suggesting that this generation's experience and connection with films is not restricted to those films currently in distribution. In 1998, a film tour orchestrated to appeal to the youth audience – 'Primal Screen: essential cult films as they should be seen' – included in its line-up several films that clearly did not address young people exclusively; neither *The Wicker Man* (Robin Hardy, 1973), *Dr. Strangelove* (Stanley Kubrick, 1964), *Paths of Glory* (Stanley Kubrick, 1957) nor *Delicatessen* (Jean-Pierre Jeunet, 1991) feature youth or young people centrally. Yet by association, the tour established a link between these films and a series of films which very clearly did, such as *Fast Times at Ridgemont High* (Amy Heckerling, 1982), *Ferris Bueller's Day Off* (John Hughes, 1986) and *The Warriors* (Walter Hill, 1979). The tour's promoters and organisers clearly felt that a youth audience would not find this association problematic.[9]

The films' categorisation as 'cult' was significant here: the young film audience is often understood to be particularly susceptible to, or active in, the instigation of a cult around a specific film text, or, as implied by the tour's relatively extensive play list, around a series of different film texts. Indeed, there is a temptation to blur the categories 'youth' with 'cult', to connect the aesthetic qualities of the films with a particular audience. Such blurring could draw upon many of the films' independent or art house looks and controversial subject matter; and be related to an audience who respond to the films in such a way as to distinguish themselves, both in their pleasure and in their viewing habits, from the mainstream audience for cinema. And young people do watch films in a specific, and cultish manner; Primal Screen's premiere was a forty-eight hour film marathon in the Prince Charles cinema in London, and the inclusion of 'trash' films in the tour, such as *Beyond the*

Valley of the Dolls (Russ Meyer, 1970) is indicative of a viewing culture which takes pleasure in films that are 'so bad they're good'.[10]

Unfortunately, there are two problems which undermine this association. Firstly, since, in the 1990s, young people made up the largest share of the mainstream cinemagoing audience in the UK, it could be argued that they were not as selective in their choice of films, or as specialised in their viewing practices, as the category 'cult' necessarily implies.[11] Secondly, the cult film audience, while often associated with youth, is not necessarily, demographically speaking, young.

This latter point leads me back to another difficulty in defining what is meant by 'youth', and what segment of the viewing population are 'young'? Are young people understood to be between fifteen and twenty-four years in age or eighteen to thirty-four? Should all teenagers, and therefore, thirteen and fourteen year olds also be included? In terms of their tastes, expectations and common areas of identification and understanding, most thirty-four year olds are clearly very different to most fifteen year olds. In addition, for the young film audience, the continued existence of film classification in Britain restricts access to certain films in relation to age and breaks up this population into different audiences.[12] If it is impossible to be clear as to what age they are, and therefore to be certain about who 'youth' are, how can this audience be satisfactorily appealed to, and/or represented? One way of evading this problem is to follow a strategy common to many youth films: place the film and its characters firmly in the past, and thereby avoid alienating any particular contingent of those viewers who consider that they, rather than anyone else, are 'youth'. Earlier British films, such as *Quadrophenia* (Franc Roddam, 1979), which concerned the mod sub-culture in the 1960s, and *Absolute Beginners* (Julian Temple, 1986), which was set in 1950s London, had applied this strategy with differing degrees of success. In the 1990s, *Backbeat* (Ian Softley, 1993) a biopic of the 'fifth Beatle', Stuart Sutcliffe, continued this trend.

Authenticity in terms of location and period detail were significant factors in each film's success. Whilst the artificial London created by *Absolute Beginners* failed to engage its audience, the effective use of real locations (Hamburg and Liverpool) contributed to the success of *Backbeat*. But *Backbeat* was also successful because, unlike *Absolute Beginners*, its soundtrack managed to integrate the authentic sound of the past (the early Beatles' music – such as cover versions of 1960s girl group songs like 'Please, Mr. Postman') with a veneer of credibility from the contemporary music scene. Although mimed by the actors portraying The Beatles, the songs in the film and soundtrack album were actually performed by an 'all-star' band, including REM's Mike Mills, Soul Asylum's David Pirner and Nirvana's Dave Grohl; produced by Don Was, the grunge and alternative rock credentials of these performers established a doubly authentic feel for the music and the film. In contrast, David Bowie's title song for the film, 'Absolute Beginners', did well in the charts at the time but failed to connect to, or resonate with the period supposedly reproduced in the film and did little to help it at the box-office. Although the film's plot was concerned with the business behind the inauthentic creation of teen idols and their manufactured sound, the film had, in pre-publicity suggested that it would contrast this with the look and feel of the authentic sound of the London jazz scene in the 1950s. The marginalisation of this more credible musical scene contributed to the film's failure to connect with the contemporary youth audience.

The presence and the influence of the past continues to be important in many youth films. *Trainspotting*'s subtle incorporation of the past contributed to its success. Surprisingly, considering its association with the contemporary zeitgeist, the film makes little reference to the cultural events, music and performers of the 1990s, and instead refers to past heroes and icons: its reference to the 1978 World Cup Goal by Scotland's Archie Gemmill, Sick Boy's obsession with Sean Connery and his James Bond films. Furthermore, the music in *Trainspotting* – which includes contemporary music as well as music from the 1970s and 1980s – is integrated sensitively and is used almost entirely in a non-diegetic way, enabling it to comment on, but not periodise the events taking place. In contrast to this, *Shopping* rejects the past in order to project an immediacy and a strictly contemporary relevance for its characters; this is confirmed, for example, by the rather stage-managed appearance of 'DJ Tim' in the film, as well as pert post-modern observations by the characters, such as 'Everyone's on TV'. *Shopping*'s continual attempts to portray the characters' obsession with labels and brands also indicates its awkward attempt to both comment on, and represent, British youth, who were, as Massey suggests, learning to manage a hybrid culture, and struggling to make local meanings from global brands. *Shopping* is also considerably less subtle in its use of music and is particularly heavy-handed in the way in which it distinguishes the music of contemporary youth from 1980s yuppie music. In one scene, Jo (Sadie Frost) throws a series of cassettes (Whitney Houston, Billy Joel and Dire Straits – all emblematic of 80s easy listening music) at a pursuing police car.

Furthermore, while *Shopping* is relentlessly present tense, in *Trainspotting*, Renton's voice-over functions as another way of detaching the film from the contemporary. As the voice-over comments upon, links or narrates particular scenes, the story is made both present and absent. On the one hand, the flow of speech promotes an impression of immediacy, while on the other hand its presence necessarily sets the events of the film in the past. In addition, this cinematic device also serves to associate the film with a period genre, and acts in the same way as the unreliable narrator found in film noir.[13] These elements, and the film's anti-realist style, ensure that *Trainspotting* cannot be seen as social commentary and it avoids, despite its subject matter, any direct or explicit observation of the contemporary youth scene. By contrast, *Shopping* was reportedly pitched to its

Shopping (1994) – social commentary and critique

financiers with the assistance of a video montage of surveillance camera footage showing ram-raiders in action.[14] The completed film displays a tendency towards social commentary and critique which inform both the script, and in certain sequences, its visual aesthetic. For, although the visual style of *Shopping* is clearly indebted to Luc Besson's *Subway* (1985), it can also be seen to conform to the visual conventions of British social realism. Familiar images of social decay, such as graffiti, rubbish and an imposing tower block feature prominently, and interactions between the characters, a few high angles not withstanding, are conventionally choreographed, replicating the look and feel of British television drama. In contrast, the licence that the voice-over apparently gives *Trainspotting* often enables its characters to be framed unconventionally and subjectively while many of the scenes are designed and lit in such a way that they become artificially flattened. This is particularly obvious in the sequence in which Spud attends a job interview; his warped perspective is mirrored in the way that the interview is presented – through a heady mix of fish-eyed lens shots, long shots and extreme close-ups – and the garish tropical beach scene that apparently covers one side of the interview room is typical of the way in which backgrounds are used throughout the film to flatten scenes and accentuate their comic strip quality.

The distinction between *Shopping* and *Trainspotting* is quite clear: *Shopping* straightforwardly critiques the hybrid culture where the commodity and the brand have become a fundamental part of youth culture, and its response is bleak and pessimistic; evident throughout the film, this perspective is confirmed by the final sequence in which both the main characters die. *Trainspotting*, rather than a commentary becomes a brand itself, offering a distinctive visual aesthetic, its extension into the market of posters, T-shirts, video sales and CDs supported by two key promotional campaigns. Firstly, a television campaign excerpted Renton's now famous monologue 'choose life' and thus explicitly mimicked and parodied the language by which brands are established. Secondly, a poster campaign featured the main characters photographed in black and white, apparently lined up against a

Trainspotting (1995) – a distinctive visual aesthetic

white background, and since they were not actually in shot together, seemingly 'pasted' side by side, conjured up the 'micro-media' of youth-flyposters and images ripped from magazines. Each of the characters were numbered, and to one side, or across the top of these images (depending on the version), and superimposed over a block of orange colour, the title 'Trainspotting' appeared vertically or horizontally, as if on the spine of a book or CD. The film's posters and publicity thereby recalled the original book and not just because later editions featured this image. The use of this signature image to brand the film also incorporated the soundtrack CD; a natural and inevitable brand extension to the film. Numbering the characters emphasised their status as commodities, recalling the practice of collecting cigarette cards of football players or film stars. It also mirrored the basic, own-brand packaging used by many British supermarkets, and referred to the distinctive logo and typesetting used on the cover of the youth magazine *The Face*. By drawing on all these associations, the film was able to establish itself as a youth brand, but at the same time to parody (by being the lowest kind of brand) the whole concept of branding. While those involved with *Shopping* had also played with the notion of constructing the film as a brand, and certain products (key rings, T-shirts and posters) were proposed which were to feature a '$' (as in $hopping), this was never fully realised, possibly because of the American associations tied to the '$' and the lack of response to the film overall.

In another way, the two films also responded to the 'commodity culture' of the 1990s in an apparently similar fashion. *Trainspotting* presents its characters as 'poachers': Renton and his peers live by pilfering, stealing and adapting to a landscape of which they are a part, but which they do not own, and cannot control.[15] Superficially, this position makes them akin to the characters in *Shopping*: like Billy, they are thieves who steal commodities from the wider culture; unlike Billy, however, *Trainspotting*'s characters steal to support their own private economy – the drug economy and their heroin sub-culture – rather than aiming to subvert or rebel against the status quo. Poachers are marginal figures, incorporated within rather than resistant to the world they inhabit, whereas Billy, modelled in the image of James Dean, is clearly a rebel. In *Trainspotting*, the majority of the characters are confident in their ability to learn and adapt within the wider culture and economy if they so choose. Examples of this are numerous and include rituals such as Sick Boy's method for coming off heroin, Renton's scam, which enables Spud to fail his job interview while still meeting the guidelines to retain his benefits, Sick Boy's encyclopaedic knowledge of the Bond genre, and Renton's ability to get a job – all tactics that are about surviving, accommodating and coping with society rather than representing a complete rejection or rebellion. It is significant however, that such tactics are not unambiguously successful; although Renton does escape with the proceeds a of a drug deal we do not know his final destination, and Tommy, the most vulnerable of the characters, succumbs to disease and death. Yet the success of *Trainspotting* depends upon this ambiguity and its refusal to offer a consistent morality. As a commodity which critiques but also takes part in a culture increasingly defined by the character and power of the brand, the film engineers an ambivalence which resonates with the particular qualities of British youth in the 1990s. Whether the investment in such tactics is uniquely British is a moot point; indeed it may be that *Trainspotting* achieved both international and domestic success primarily because it was not about its apparent subject matter – British youth – but was made to appeal to the youth of a global, hybrid culture, where the ambivalent play, negotiation and celebration of the commodity was unavoidable in the making and understanding of identity.[16]

Notes

1 Douglas Coupland, *Generation X: Tales for an Accelerated Culture* (London: Abacus, 1991); Irvine Welsh, *Trainspotting* (London: Secker & Warburg, 1993); Alex Garland, *The Beach* (London: Viking, 1996).

2 See, for example, Stuart Hall and Tony Jefferson (eds), *Resistance through Rituals: Youth Sub-cultures in Post-War Britain* (London: Unwin Hyman, 1976); Paul Willis, *Profane Culture* (London: Routledge & Kegan Paul, 1978); and particularly, Dick Hebdige, *Subculture; The Meaning of Style* (London: Methuen, 1979).

3 Doreen Massey, 'The Spatial Construction of Youth Cultures' in Tracey Skelton and Gill Valentine (eds), *Cool Places: Geographies of Youth Cultures* (London: Routledge, 1998), p. 122.

4 Dick Hebdige, *Cut'n'Mix: Culture, Identity and Caribbean Music* (London: Comedia, 1987).

5 See Sarah Thornton, *Club Cultures: Music, Media and Subcultural Capital* (Cambridge: Polity Press, 1995), for an elaboration of this argument.

6 For example, the Spice Girls, like Madonna before them, were celebrated as much for their canny marketing as their music or talent. Even the supposedly purer arena of guitar rock was not immune – U2's 'Zoo TV' (1992) tour openly played with, and acknowledged the commercial and commodity aspects of their music and image - it was a parody and critique of the 'stadium tour'. It was also massively successful.

7 Computer games were one of the few media forms with which this generation of young people could claim a privileged relationship or knowledge.

8 The characters' clothes and hair-cuts all call up aspects of early 1980s fashion, and thus refer to the period in which the original book is set and not to contemporary 1990s culture, although this time-slip is never made explicit in the book or film.

9 Sponsored by Stella Artois and the *Guardian* newspaper, the 'Primal Screen' tour covered most of the UK playing at different independent cinemas. The tour's publicity and advertising clearly indicated that the selected cult films being screened were targeted at a youth audience, with prominent double page spreads in youth publications such as *Neon*, *i-D* and *The Face*.

10 See Jeffrey Sconce, 'Trashing the academy: taste, excess and an emerging politics of cinematic style' in *Screen* vol. 36, no. 4, 1995, pp. 371–94. Quentin Tarantino's much-publicised love of 'trash' movies also played a part in establishing the legitimacy of this kind of film viewing, as well as its particular connection to young people.

11 See Andrew Pulver, 'Bard to worse at the multiplex', the *Guardian*, February 5, 1999, p. 19.

12 Although the less rigorous policing of the audience in video stores may well restore these divisions they are still important, particularly in terms of how individual films are perceived by this audience.

13 Renton's voice-over refers most obviously to the narrators of Billy Wilder's *Double Indemnity* (1944) and *Sunset Boulevard* (1950). A more contemporary example would be the voice of Henry Hill (Ray Liotta) in Martin Scorsese's *Goodfellas* (1990); it is surely not coincidental that this film too refers to a period and place that is past.

14 See Xan Brooks, *Choose Life: Ewan McGregor and the British Film Revival* (London: Chameleon Books, 1998), pp. 30–1.

15 This term is borrowed from, and is elaborated by Michel de Certeau in *The Practice of Everyday Life* (Berkeley, Los Angeles, London: University of California Press, 1988).

16 This argument is taken up in greater depth in Karen Lury, *British Youth Television: Cynicism and Enchantment* (Oxford: Oxford University Press, forthcoming).

Chapter 11
Black British Cinema in the 90s:
Going Going Gone

Karen Alexander

> ... the habit of ignoring race is understood to be a graceful, even generous, liberal
> gesture. To notice is to recognise an already discredited difference. To enforce its
> invisibility through silence is to allow the black body a shadowless participation in the
> dominant cultural body.
>
> (Toni Morrison)[1]

Institutional racism was the phrase on everyone's lips following the publication in March
1999 of the Macpherson Report on the handling of the Stephen Lawrence murder. Cited
in the first instance in relation to the police, the boys in blue and other public bodies were
forced to examine their race relations policies and practices and found themselves wanting. If a writer had submitted the Stephen Lawrence story for script development, chances
are that it would have been refused on the grounds that it was too far-fetched, that it put
the police in a bad light, and that as a society we have moved on from the racial antagonism of the 70s and 80s. But fact is stranger than fiction and a few weeks later the nail bombs
planted in Brixton, Brick Lane and Soho came as a bleak reminder that the more things
change the more they stay the same. The murder of a young architecture student made the
country as a whole sit up and take notice of the issues of race and race hatred, but this only
came after years of ceaseless campaigning, and an unshakeable resolve from the Lawrence
family and their supporters. If this is what it takes to deal with the truth, what resolve and
persistence is then required to produce a fictional version of the management of the everyday? And, if these fictions are thought to be unnecessary or unimportant to society as a
whole, what will it mean for our collective imaginations if the primary audience for our
national cinema continues to be positioned as white?

When, in the wake of the 1980s uprisings, black film-makers began to talk about working collectively and set up workshops, they had their sights on a very particular prize. Theirs
was an idea of cinema that would be about transgression, imagination, illumination and
pleasure, words up until that point never associated with immigrant groups and arts practice. The minority ethnic communities had been almost uniformly constructed as
problem-ridden, undesirable and most of all invisible. The 'work' of black film-makers in
the 80s was explicitly cultural and aesthetic. Their practice was about autonomy and
complexity, only in this way could they work from within the institution of cinema,
and against it. As Kobena Mercer has written: 'the 1980s were lived as a relentless vertigo

of displacement'.[2] Along with the then new Channel Four and the Greater London Council, black film workshops like Black Audio Film Collective, Sankofa and other radical
cultural workers recognised that British cultural identity could be, and should be re-con-
structed and rewritten in their own image. Black film-makers seized the moment to
produce films like *Territories* (Sankofa Film and Video, 1986), *The Passion of Remembrance*
(Maureen Blackwood/Isaac Julien, 1986), *Handsworth Songs* (John Akomfrah, 1986), *Looking For Langston* (Isaac Julien, 1986), *My Beautiful Laundrette* (Stephen Frears, 1985),
Dreaming Rivers (Martina Attille, 1988), and *Twilight City* (Reece Auguiste, 1989). These
films mapped out a possibility of Britishness that could contain and engage with diversi-
ties of race, gender, sexuality and class in a meaningful and often poetic way. These films
challenged what British film-making is all about; they were made by young black Britons
who despite being British were rooted in another culture, be it African, Caribbean, Pak-
istani or Indian. As one film-maker reminds us: 'blackness as a sign is never enough. What
does that black subject do, how does it act, how does it think politically?'[3]

Hanif Kureishi, the writer of *My Beautiful Laundrette, Sammie and Rosie Get Laid*
(Stephen Frears, 1987), *London Kills Me* (Hanif Kureishi, 1991) and *My Son the Fanatic*
(Udayan Prasad, 1997) has managed to show a version of British culture that is both familiar yet unknown from an insider/outsider point of view. In a discussion at London's
National Film Theatre in April 1999, Kureishi talked about how black writers have a
responsibility to their own imaginations and of how he sought to show London as a play-
ground for immigrant communities, the place where they could try things out.

Kureishi would be the first to point out that he got into film-making by luck rather than
design; Asian voices were being sought at the time, and being seen as a writer had its advantages. Other respected writers like St. Kitts-born Caryl Phillips, writer of the bittersweet
Playing Away (Horace Ové, 1985), didn't attract quite so much attention. *Playing Away*, a
very different film to *Laundrette*, moved away from urban centres and looked at racism in
the English countryside using cricket as a metaphor. It drew criticism because writer and
director – both black – were trying to say something about white people, race and racism
from a black point of view.

*A Fuller Picture: The Commercial Impact of Six British Films with Black Themes in the
1990s* looks at *Baby Mother* (Julien Henriques, 1998)), *Bhaji on the Beach* (Gurinder
Chadha, 1994), *The Crying Game* (Neil Jordan, 1992), *Dancehall Queen* (Don Letts, 1997),
Secrets and Lies (Mike Leigh, 1996) and *Welcome to the Terrordome* (Ngosi Onwurrah,
1995) as a reflection of the diversity of product around that is called black, and concludes
that there are as many markets for black audiences as there are for white audiences.[4] This
points to a problem in how race is looked at in Britain. To quote Julien, 'being black isn't
really good enough for me: I want to know what your cultural politics are'.[5] The film-
making practice of Sankofa and Black Audio was intended to illuminate the everyday and
challenge the taken-for-granted. Seeing *The Crying Game* or *Secrets and Lies* as black-
themed films is to miss the point. The stories are not told from a black point of view and
the fact that they have interesting black characters does not make the films black. This is
not to say that only black film-makers or writers can do this, but the work has to provide,
as the writer 'bell hooks' suggests, a 'concrete interrogative evidence that it was not so much
the color of the person who made images that was crucial but the perspective, the standpoint, the politics'.[6]

A Fuller Picture sets out to challenge the idea of cultural film-making and fails to see that
film can be both commercial and cultural. Perceptive remarks made by Stuart Hall and

Isaac Julien about film as a cultural product are dismissed and the authors fall into the trap of thinking market forces and box-office decisions tell a 'fuller' story. However, the interviews included in the report give an insight into how decisions are made.

Steve Woolley, the producer of *Mona Lisa* (Neil Jordan, 1986), the all black *A Rage in Harlem* (Bill Duke, 1991) and *The Crying Game*, cites growing up in a multicultural Islington as giving him his main insight into race and the maltreatment of black people. *The Crying Game* was not aimed at the black community even though it has black characters, and the IRA content put off the white British audience. The film's success was in America, where due to clever marketing and its 'queer' subtext it made $62 million. Woolley talks about his problems with Equity over casting the American, Forrest Whitaker as one of the leads in *The Crying Game*. He claims he was unable to find a suitable actor in the UK, but the main reason was probably that casting Whitaker – who had established an international reputation by playing Charlie Parker in Clint Eastwood's *Bird* (1988) – made it easier to raise money outside the UK. This gives bad signals to young black British talent and it is not surprising that actors like Thandie Newton who starred as one of the three leads in *Beloved* and Adrian Lester who worked alongside John Travolta in *Primary Colours* look to Hollywood for work. In Mike Leigh's *Secrets and Lies* (1996) Hortense (Marianne Jean-Baptiste) 'is the catalyst who makes the rest of the characters face up to their secrets and lies' but as Geoffrey Macnab points out, Leigh 'spends precious little time sketching in her background' and 'skims over the black experience of "Englishness"'.[7] Many black people weren't convinced by Marianne Jean-Baptiste's performance because her mixed race character came over as phenotypically unconvincing – she didn't look right. But few would deny her talent and her contribution to the success of the film, or regret the fact that she has been subsequently neglected. She was not invited by British Screen to participate in a new talent showcase held at the Cannes Film Festival, and her only major screen role since then has been playing Doreen Lawrence in the 1999 made-for-TV special about the murder of Stephen Lawrence.

Marianne Jean-Baptiste as Hortense with Brenda Blethyn (Cynthia) in *Secrets and Lies* (1996)

Black contributions to British cultural life are more and more evident: from Chris Ofili winning the Turner prize to Steve McQueen's exhibition at the ICA (the only solo black artist to be honoured in this way to date). Both artists' engagement with race is cutting and playful, revelling in the contradictions that being black and British throw up. With this in mind it is interesting to reflect on the relative absence of this side of British culture in the increasing number of British films being made. A Massive Attack remix of a Nusrat Fateh Ali Khan devotional song or the dance tunes of the Asian Dub Foundation display a comfort with the inevitable fusion or 'post-colonial hybridity' that living in the United Kingdom is all about, but British cinema has failed to reflect this hybridisation so evident in other areas of British cultural life. The roll call of black-themed, -penned, -directed and theatrically released films in the 90s – *Smack and Thistle* (Tunde Ikoli, 1990), *Ama* (Kwesi Owusu/(Kwate-Nii Owoo, 1991), *Blue Notes and Exiled Voices* (Imruh Bakari, 1991), *Who Needs A Heart* (John Akomfrah 1991), *London Kills Me, Young Soul Rebels* (Isaac Julien, 1992), *Wild West* (David Attwood, 1992), *Bhaji on the Beach, Welcome to the Terrordome, My Son the Fanatic, Dancehall Queen, Franz Fanon: Black Skin White Masks* (Isaac Julien, 1997) and *Baby Mother* – is lamentably low.

Of these films, only two – *Welcome to the Terrordome* and *Bhaji on the Beach* were made by women. *Bhaji*'s co-writer and director, Gurinder Chadha, traces her interest in film-making back to seeing *My Beautiful Laundrette*. Chadha, a journalist at the time, felt film-making was the best way to tell the stories she wanted to hear. What engaged critics and audiences alike was the opportunity of seeing and hearing from a section of the community so often constructed as silent. Refreshing and important as *Bhaji* was, Chadha has yet to be given the opportunity to make another film. Unfortunately this is often the case with black women directors, even in the United States where Julie Dash (*Daughters of the Dust*, 1991), Darnel Martin (*I Like It Like That*, 1994), Cheryl Dunye (*Watermelon Woman*, 1997) have been unable to establish themselves despite critical or even box-office success,

Gurinder Chadha's *Bhaji on the Beach* (1994) – a community presumed to be silent

though hopefully, Kasi Lemmon's *Eve's Bayou* – the highest grossing independent film in the US for 1997 – will make her an exception to this rule.

The 90s has been the site of cultural struggle for the arts as a whole. The systematic dismantling of public sector organisations and groups which started with the demise of the GLC really hit home in the early 90s, and led to the commodification of almost every popular art practice. Although there is a renaissance in British cinema – backed by millions of pounds of Lottery money – the Britain that is being disseminated on cinema screens around the world is steeped in heritage, literary culture, and conventional ideas of class relations. It is also overwhelmingly white, in sharp contrast to our workplaces, high streets and bedrooms which tell a very different story. British cinema is the place where ideas of nationality are played out, but – as *Four Weddings and a Funeral* (Mike Newell, 1994), *The Full Monty* (Peter Cannateo, 1997), *Elizabeth* (Shekhar Kapur, 1998) and *Shakespeare in Love* (John Madden, 1999) bear witness – it is a narrow and nostalgic view of Britain which is presented.[8]

The 1990s started off well for people like Isaac Julien whose prize-winning film *Young Soul Rebels* 'challenged with passion and beauty the previous static order' by inscribing a black presence and a black gay presence to a period of British cultural history popularly remembered for punk's social challenge and the Queen's Silver Jubilee.[9] As with so much of British cultural history the black contribution had been underwritten or completely eroded. The film's release came at a time when people who were encouraged to think of themselves as cultural film-makers were suddenly being judged on their engagement with the market. Ideas of culture and experimentation were paid lip-service to, as funding was systematically withdrawn and the infrastructure needed to sustain any meaningful alternative film-making activity run down.

What differentiates black British culture from what goes on in the United States under the banner of black culture is the 'post-colonial hybridisation' of British culture. It is precisely this mix that makes Britain, and particularly London, the cultural capital of the world. As Salman Rushdie has said '*The Satanic Verses* is for change by fusion, change by conjoining. It's a love-song to our mongrel selves'; and an ethnically-mixed band such as the Afrocelts can produce a CD which fuses African rhythms with traditional Celtic music.[10] In the same way this fusion which is missing from our cinema screens flourishes in our clubs and on our radio stations via the music of people like Natacha Atlas, Talvin Singh, Roni Size and Nitin Sawhney. It seems ironic that the complexities of black British culture can be encapsulated in a love song or a dance track but fail to find articulation in one of the most modern of art forms, cinema.

I would argue that the failure of any sustained development in the last decade, of the work that black film-makers began in the late 1980s, has much to do with the on-going crisis that Britishness has with itself as it shifts and transforms with each generation. Cinema for the white people in charge has become a site of struggle: this is where Englishness and Britishness gets written and re-written. It is not by chance that an idea which had all black male leads ended up with just one black male character and went on to become one of the most successful British films ever made.[11] In the UK, cinema is a powerful weapon of both culture and commerce, but it is being transformed into an industry, where the market calls all the shots.

What has to be looked at is precisely what do we want British to mean and who has the purchase on these definitions? Race is a minefield: in America the issue is tip-toed over and around at every opportunity, but the one thing the various immigrant groups can agree on is that they are American with all the problems that brings with it. Until Cool Britannia can acknowledge the visibility of others and think about inclusivity instead of exclusivity on a broad institutional and cultural level, the idea that the nation has of itself, namely that Britishness is something to aspire to, is under threat. The lesson the black film-makers from the 1980s taught is that, while they might be creating from a position of being black they are not talking exclusively for black people. If they are ever allowed a chance to speak again, audiences will find their messages are for everyone. We want our cinema to be different, but not too different, we want to be celebrated not dismissed.

Notes

1 Toni Morrison, *Playing in the Dark: Whiteness and the Literary Imagination* (London: Picador, 1992), p. 5. Toni Morrison makes a heartfelt argument that American literature needs to take account of the presence of black people in the United States and that 'the contemplation of this black presence is central to any understanding of our national literature and should not be permitted to hover at the margins of the literary imagination' (p.9–10). Although applied to literature I feel the sentiments and issues raised in the book are as applicable to the moving image.

2 Kobena Mercer, *Welcome to the Jungle: New Positions in Black Cultural Studies* (London: Routledge, 1994).

3 Quoted in bell hooks, *Reel To Real: Race, Sex, and Class at the Movies* (London: Routledge, 1996), p. 6.

4 Onyekachi Wambu and Kevin Arnold, *A Fuller Picture: The Commercial Impact of Six British Films with Black Themes in the 1990s* (London: BFI, 1999).

5 Quoted in bell hooks, *Reel To Real: Race, Sex, and Class at the Movies*, p. 6.

6 bell hooks, *Reel to Real: Race, Sex, and Class at the Movies*, p. 7.

7 *Sight and Sound*, June 1996, p. 51.

8 Paul Gilroy makes the point that although *Elizabeth* had an Asian director, Shekhar Kapur, and a black director of photography, Remi Adefarasin, neither here, nor in the obviously anachronistic *Shakespeare in Love* is there any attempt to register the fact that there was a black presence in Britain during Elizabethan times. 'Key note address' at the New Futures for Black Cinema conference, National Film Theatre, October 1998. See also, Peter Fryer, *Staying Power: The History of Black People in Britain* (London: Pluto Press, 1984).

9 Quoted in Kobena Mercer, *Welcome to the Jungle*, p. 16.

10 Ibid, p. 28.

11 *The Full Monty* (Peter Cattaneo, 1997). Monika Baker, 'The Missing Monty', *black filmmaker*, vol. 1, no. 2, 1998, p. 14.

Chapter 12

Fewer Weddings and More Funerals: Changes in the Heritage Film

Pamela Church Gibson

> When the real is no longer what it used to be, nostalgia assumes its full meaning.
>
> (Jean Baudrillard)[1]

In the last year of the decade, it seems that two of its most successful British films will be *Elizabeth* (Shekhar Kapur, 1998) and *Shakespeare in Love* (John Madden, 1999). Both have been critically acclaimed and commercially triumphant, rewarded with Golden Globes, Oscars and BAFTA awards. *Elizabeth* is an extraordinary mixture of epic film, grand opera and grand guignol; *Shakespeare in Love* is a multi-faceted flit around a number of filmic and televisual forms, switching seamlessly between slapstick and passion, near-tragedy and farce, characterised throughout by post-modern jokiness, different modes of self-referentiality and the gleeful use of anachronism. Both films have quirky casting, which involves much extra-diegetic information and further levels of intertextuality; both feed the still insatiable appetite for spectacle, period costume and picturesque setting. Neither is exactly a heritage film, and yet neither would be so popular were it not for the preceding two decades of heritage film and television. Both films are generic hybrids, working to subvert heritage cinema while conspicuously deploying its conventions and simultaneously drawing on other generic traditions.

Critical studies of heritage cinema have explored the links between the success of the films and the growth of the 'heritage industry'. Some writers have dismissed such films as reactionary, finding them overly nostalgic and selective in their presentation of the past. Others have claimed that they provide a critique of social repression and sexual politics which can be seen as progressive.[2]

In the last ten years, there has been some analysis of the specific pleasures provided by these films. Richard Dyer writes of the 'sensuousness' of the 'fixtures and fittings' which need the 'skilled decoding ... of the female spectator'.[3] Stella Bruzzi engages with and explores the role of costume itself within the films and examines 'the fetishistic value of history and historical clothes'. She raises, too, the 'crucial issue ... whether to look at or through the clothes'.[4]

A second area of academic interest concerns the precise nature of heritage film. John Caughie sees the work of the Merchant-Ivory team as 'synonymous with heritage' and condemns the genre as 'one of the more dubious British contributions to world cinema'.[5] In the same volume, however, Richard Dyer and Ginette Vincendeau argue for a 'European heritage film', and offer a more democratic, wide-ranging definition which can include such films as *Rosa Luxemburg* and *My Left Foot*. But it is not only the debates that have diversified; latterly there has been a heterogeneity in form and content, a fissuring and a fracturing in the monolith of heritage.

The decade opened with what can be now be seen as a swansong – *Howards End* (1991) the final Merchant-Ivory adaptation of an E.M. Forster novel. Much has been written elsewhere about this film; no critics have, however, commented on the changes wrought by the casting. The plain, toothy sisters of the novel are played by Emma Thompson and Helena Bonham Carter. This allows the random, loveless, sexual encounter between Leonard Bast and Helen (Bonham Carter), that produces the illegitimate child who will inherit Howards End, to be transformed and become highly charged. The film has all the elements that characterise Merchant-Ivory films – the usual delight in English houses, gardens and landscapes, the ostentatious display of period detail and the careful tracking of the camera around the lovingly recreated interiors. This palpable pleasure in parading the visual splendour of the past undermines the social criticism of Forster's novel. Their next film, *The Remains of the Day* (1993), their last real commercial and critical success, similarly neutered, through visual excess and a focus on thwarted romance, the irony of Ishiguro's novel. Their attempt to move away from literary adaptation and make explicit an exploration of class, ethnicity and gender in *Jefferson in Paris* (1995), was a commercial disaster, bringing in only £137,000 from the British box-office.[6]

Claire Monk's investigation into the audience for heritage films seems to indicate that it is the accessibility of Merchant-Ivory films that makes them so successful at the box-office – and it is this accessibility that their detractors find so objectionable. Her research shows that the culturally privileged find the films indecently transparent.[7] This contradicts Martin Hipsky's claim that heritage audiences in America are composed of those in search of the 'cultural capital' to which they believe their educational background entitles them.[8] He also talks of the possibility of the genre becoming self-parodic, and is the only critic to comment on the use made of the films in advertising campaigns and fashion magazines. He cites the endless photospreads in glossy men's magazines of light-coloured linen suits, and certainly the films still spawn those familiar fashion shoots which depend upon a pastiche of the past – afternoon tea on the lawn , a picnic in a punt, floating dresses and starched tablecloths. Nineties fashion has been unable to escape from retro, the endless refiguring of past styles.

Adaptations of Jane Austen's novels dominated the first half of the decade. Julianne Pidduck has written a comprehensive critique of these and I shall confine my comments to the ways in which they reflect developments within heritage.[9] These adaptations do not form a cohesive canon; there are no stylistic similarities or continuities of casting.

The enormously popular television adaptation of *Pride and Prejudice* (1995) was conventional in form, if sassily scripted, but important for two reasons. Firstly, progressive depictions of gender relations were suspended to permit the portrayal of a reactionary model of masculinity – Colin Firth's smouldering, high-handed and seemingly desirable Darcy. Secondly, the links between heritage culture and the heritage industry were made explicit. Lyme Park, the house which represented Pemberley, had to organise various themed activities to satisfy the crowds who descended, including a 'Darcy trail' to show them the lake into which their idol plunged fully-clad – a bizarre conflation of fantasy, simulation and hyperreality. The costumes here were notable only in that they enabled the Bennett sisters to reveal maximum décolletage at all times of day.

Persuasion (1995) was also made by the BBC but it was also screened in cinemas across the US, where it enjoyed a commercial success comparable to that of *Sense and Sensibility* (Ang Lee, 1996).[10] The last and most sombre of the novels, it appealed to Roger Michell, the director, who claimed 'I'm trying to trash the hotel room of the BBC classic.' He was also adamant that he wanted to reject the tendency in heritage films towards 'costumes rather than clothes – I wanted these to look like clothes that had been worn. If they got rumpled, I insisted that the rumples were left.' The lighting and the colour are muted and dark, the landscapes often windswept and muddy. 'I wanted the actors to look as if they'd actually been outside ... I insisted, "No wigs".'[11]

The country houses are not filmed in sunlit splendour – and the extravagance of Bath, where the heroine, Anne (Amanda Root) is forced to accompany her vain, extravagant father and sarcastic elder sister, is seen by both Anne – and the camera – as oppressive. The cinematography and the splendid interiors are used in some of these town sequences to convey stifling opulence, undeserved privilege, and to criticise idleness, snobbery and pretension. This kind of social critique was a new departure.

Sense and Sensibility was more conventional. Emma Thompson spent four years on the screenplay and made drastic changes to the book, removing certain characters and scenes and changing others. Margaret, the youngest Dashwood sister and a negligible presence in the novel, is now a tomboy of eleven and the proud owner of a tree-house. All the scenes in which she appears are Thompson's invention, and they help to render the sisters and their economic situation more palatable to a 90s audience. Made effectively homeless by the death of their father and impoverished further by his heir, their stepbrother, they are now dependent upon the goodwill of relations until they marry. Margaret, who wants to travel to China and who advocates piracy as a career, is a sop to feminist sensibilities. Thompson was also directly responsible for a piece of self-referential casting. Hugh Grant is used in a way that plays on his role as Charles in *Four Weddings and a Funeral* (Mike Newell, 1994), and is encouraged to remind us of that amiable, charming and rather hapless man.

The Taiwanese director, Ang Lee, brought a different 'sensibility' of his own to bear on the film, commenting: 'The fact that they've come halfway across the world to ask me proves how much they don't want Merchant-Ivory', – though he added quickly – 'But, of course, they make wonderful films.'[12] Julianne Pidduck analyses in detail the visual elements of this film, and comments on the many scenes in which women are seated at, or beside, a window, though surprisingly she does not mention Vermeer. The production designer and art director had plastered their office walls with reproductions of his paintings and Ang Lee concurred in their insistence that the interior scenes be filmed using a single light source.[13] It is worth speculating as to whether he extended his interest in Dutch painters, since many of the scenes shot in Barton Cottage are curiously similar in their composition and framing to the interiors painted by Vermeer's contemporary, Pieter der Hooch.

Heritage films made during the 90s became increasingly 'painterly'. This is particularly noticeable in the use of tableaux – reminiscent at times of the way in which Peter Greenaway has used the work of different artists. Ang Lee is interested in the relationships within families rather than in the English countryside, and, lush though the landscapes may be, they are not romanticised. He insisted on removing a scene where two swans happened to sail under a bridge beside which two of the protagonists were embracing, despite the fact that the entire crew clapped at this engaging coincidence. He then went on to remove the embrace itself.[14]

Despite this attempted austerity, Thompson's screenplay ensures that the film remains firmly within the tradition of screen romance. For example, Willoughby (Greg Wise) first appears to Marianne (Kate Winslet) as he gallops out of the mist to rescue her mounted on a white horse. This could be construed as postmodern irony, were it not for Thompson's notes in her published diaries, which stress her determination to make this film unashamedly romantic.[15] Thompson's ironing out of Jane Austen's moral nuances is accompanied by broad comedy – the use of Hugh Laurie in a specially-conceived cameo, for instance – and deliberate simplification. She omits the lengthy sequence – eight pages of dialogue – where Willoughby visits Elinor while Marianne lies dangerously ill, to confess his faults and ask for forgiveness. Thompson chooses to show him as a two-dimensional character, the cad of romantic fiction: seated on his white horse, he observes Marianne's wedding from a hilltop – and then canters away, back to his rich wife and the elegant life she has provided.

There is some tension in the film as a result of the struggle between Lee's astringent, subtler vision and Thompson's commercial acumen. She seems to win out in her desire to create a film with widespread popular appeal, appealing – among others – to her own notion of the modern woman who has fantasies of a man on a white charger. The use of the wedding to end the film is also Thompson's ending – though Lee adds an anthropologist's touch. Village children walk in procession, bearing some vast, primitive floral confection, and the groom, the rich, reliable Captain Brandon (Alan Rickman) throws handfuls of gold into the air – the penultimate shot is of the coins frozen in a glittering arc against a bright blue sky.

Jude, made in the same year, set out deliberately to challenge and disrupt the heritage tradition. *Jude the Obscure*, bleakest of Hardy's novels, can hardly be prettified – and Michael Winterbottom, who had directed Roddy Doyle's *The Family* (1995) and the low-budget feature film *Butterfly Kiss* (1994), both grim and gritty, had no wish to do so. He

Christmas Day 1895. Kate Winslet as Sue Bridehead in Michael Winterbottom's *Jude* (1996)

announced that he intended not to 'fetishise the past' but to 'highlight its relevance'. His screenwriter, Hossein Amini , went further, stating that his intention was to 'destroy the heritage film from within'.[16]

The novel itself was vilified when it was published in 1895. Hardy, bewildered and distressed by its reception, never wrote another. Novel and film describe the life of a village boy who dreams of studying at 'Christminster' and teaches himself both Greek and Latin, while supporting himself by working as a stonemason. He is ensnared into marriage by Arabella, daughter of the local pig-breeder, but she quickly leaves him and he moves to Christminster – where he meets and falls in love with his cousin, Sue. He is rejected by the Dean of Admissions and is devastated; he is still more unhappy when Sue, learning of his earlier liaison, marries out of pique and is wretched. They elope together, wander the country in search of work, and, finally, a terrible tragedy overtakes their children. Sue sees this as a punishment for their sins and leaves Jude. Unlike Hardy's other protagonists, portrayed as victims of a malign fate, Jude is destroyed by the social institutions of the day – the inequities of the education system and the stigma of living together out of wedlock.

This is hardly the stuff of which heritage films are woven. The Oxbridge ambience is used quite differently here; indeed, in the film we see the embittered Jude chalking 'I have understanding as well as you' – a quotation from the Book of Job – on the college walls which shut him out. These are the very Oxbridge walls over which Charles and Sebastian clamber in *Brideshead Revisited* (Charles Sturridge and Michael Lindsay Hogg, 1981) and which allow the hero of *Maurice* (James Ivory, 1987) and his friend Clive to consort within their confines.

Winterbottom's cinematic style accentuates these anti-heritage elements. Homage is paid to Bergman, Truffaut, Renoir, Bill Douglas and Carol Reed. The characters wear clothes, not costumes – Sue in simple print frocks and Jude dressed sombrely throughout. Christopher Eccleston's gaunt face, suited to the starkness of Jude's life, replaces the soft features and floppy fringes of conventional heritage heroes. Kate Winslet, cast before she played Marianne, wears no makeup and her hair is scraped back into an unbecoming bun. The settings are carefully chosen to avoid the picturesque; the village of Marygreen is modest and muddy, the little cottage where Jude lives with his aunt is sparse, even spartan. The Oxford sequences were shot in Edinburgh and the uncompromising stone facades of that city become darker and darker.

It is not surprising that the film shocked an audience used to more lyrical adaptations; their expectations were confounded from the start. The opening sequence is shot in black and white – a vast expanse of ploughed, dark furrows stretch out towards a strip of pallid, sunless sky. A small boy trudges up and down the furrows, turning a rattle to keep the birds from feasting on the freshly-sown seed. As he walks, he passes a gibbet where the corpses of three crows are hung to deter their fellows. On impulse, moved to fear and then to pity, the boy Jude scatters the corn, calling out to the birds to eat. From somewhere in the seemingly empty landscape a brutish figure appears, with the terrifying suddenness of Magwitch in David Lean's *Great Expectations* (1946). He hits the boy hard and sends him away.

Returning home, Jude says farewell to his schoolmaster who is leaving to try and study at Christminster. Jude accompanies him out of the village and they stop on the hill so that he can show Jude where he is going. They are shot from behind, sitting on a cart, silhouetted against the skyline, in a conscious evocation of Ingmar Bergman's *The Seventh Seal* (1956). Jude looks across the valley, and rays of sunlight reach down to slant across the city in the distance – they disappear almost at once. We cut – suddenly – to the scaffolding in a church where the adult Jude is working and the film changes to colour, though that colour is muted throughout. The screen brightens in the scene where Arabella captures his attention as he sits beneath a tree reading Herodotus; she does this by throwing a pig's testicles at him, thus undercutting his pastoral idyll with the harsher realities of rural life. When he later walks in the fields with her, the sun does shine, but clouds and mist descend on the hills behind her farm as they return. They make love in the pigsty, to the sound of grunting and squealing from the occupants. There is one other significant sequence which is not infused with cold, rain, and a sense of hopeless struggle. When Sue first leaves her husband to live with Jude, we see them running along a beach and we hear their laughter. The following shot shows them bicycling towards us up a hill and she overtakes him, one of several references to *Jules et Jim* (Truffaut, 1961). Usually, though, the landscape seems hostile, and the townscapes become progressively bleaker as their lives become more difficult.

The last sequence of the film – entitled 'Christmas 1895' – shows Jude lying alone and awake in a lodging house. He walks through deserted snow-lined streets and arrives at the graveyard to find Sue already kneeling beside the headstone commemorating their children. She stands and they confront one another, the snow and the white light in sharp contrast to their black clothes. While they talk, the camera moves above and around them; after an anguished embrace Sue leaves, refusing to return to him. As he watches her walk away, he shouts after her in despair. The last image is an overhead shot of his dark figure silhouetted against the snow as the camera pulls back and the screen fades gradually to black.

The film received a mixed reception and commercially it was not successful. Winterbottom returned to contemporary material with *Welcome to Sarajevo* (1996), but two years later, Hossein Amini was given an opportunity to continue with his scheme to subvert the heritage film from within. He was employed as screenwriter on the adaptation of *The Wings of the Dove* (1998) with another director, Iain Softley, who also insisted that he did not intend to fetishise the past. Initially, the terrain seems over-familiar: the unimpeachable literary source, the London houses and country retreats of the Edwardian haute bourgeoisie, the scenes in Venetian palazzi and gondolas and the casting of Helena Bonham Carter. However, Amini and Softley have other plans and Amini radically alters the text. Robin Wood states in his monograph on *The Wings of the Dove* that 'faithful adaptation' is not only impossible but undesirable, and stresses the double impossibility of trying faithfully to film Henry James, where so much is unsaid, unspoken, unacknowledged; he writes approvingly of the changes that Amini makes, arguing that: 'If James is to be filmed at all, it is obvious that action, dialogue, décor must replace the pages of analysis of inner perception and reflection.'[17]

He does not, however, mention the temporal change – the novel, set in 1902, is updated to 1910 – which is part of the transformation of this dense, intricately-nuanced novel into a modernist text. It seems probable that Amini wished to give Kate Croy, the central protagonist, some of the characteristics of the New Woman of the period, to possess a degree of emancipation. It also seems likely that he – and the design team – were tempted by the clothes of the later period. The costumes reflect the radical and cinematically exciting changes in women's fashions effected by Paul Poiret.

Poiret , who claimed to have liberated women from the tyranny of their corsets, also rescued them from a restricted palette of colour. His interest in Orientalism was fuelled by Bakst's designs for the Ballet Russe. Consequently, fashionable women of 1910 could wear flowing, sinuous shapes in dramatic hues. Sandy Powell, the costume designer, has a highly theatrical style, frequently forcing us to look 'at' the clothes rather than 'through' them. Her costumes serve here to reinforce – or replace – James' subtle depiction of personality and interaction of character.

The credits show us that this is not to be a conventional heritage film. Deliberately modernist, they seem at first to be almost abstract – circles of light move apart, separate and come together, to the sound of a synthesiser. Finally, two circles detach themselves and move across the screen – these are to reappear much later as gondola lights in Venice.

The opening sequence is a sharp and sudden contrast to these credits – there is a swift cut to a platform on the Metropolitan Line. We see Kate sitting, seemingly waiting; she wears a vast hat with royal blue ostrich feathers, a strong visual contrast to the sepia-dominated screen. She boards the train, is offered a seat by a man whose glance she seems to welcome, and when she leaves he follows her. They enter the lift – he pulls the grilles across. As the lift ascends, the two encaged within it, the music insistent and staccato, he embraces her passionately, and she responds. There is another sharp cut to a close-up of her closed eyes – which she opens abruptly. The camera pulls back to reveal her Aunt Maud (Charlotte Rampling) beside her, making up her face, interrogating her. Maud is depicted as a harsh Bohemian siren, with a penchant for Chinese silks and turbans; she places jewels around Kate's neck before proffering her up into the world of money and power, where she may find a suitable husband.

This is Kate's dilemma and the basis of the plot. She cannot marry her lover, Merton Densher (Linus Roache), the impoverished journalist whom she embraced, without losing the patronage of her rich aunt. She meets and is befriended by a young American millionairess, Milly (Alison Elliott); when she discovers that Milly is dying of an incurable disease, she gradually hatches a rather unpleasant plan. Milly has already encountered Merton at a party and been attracted to him; Kate decides that he must court her, so that he may inherit her money. The two of them can then marry without the prospect of a life in poverty.

The thinness of the plot line is substantiated by the lavish visual spectacle – not only the use of setting, décor and costume but also the deliberate dependence on near-theatrical tableaux, stylised camerawork and the extraordinarily lush cinematography of Eduardo Serra (who worked in a very different mode when filming *Jude*). Sandy Powell's designs for Kate employ vivid colours, often linked with the décor. Kate wears a kingfisher blue dress at the soirée where Milly meets Merton; the exotic dress is echoed in the turquoise tiled, Moorish inspired décor of the house. She wears black, glittering jet, and even, on one occasion, scarlet. Milly, the unwitting victim of Kate's schemes, wears softer colours – blues, greens and russets – and lighter fabrics – chiffon, gauze, silk and lace. For her final scene with her duplicitous lover she is draped in a flowing white robe. This method of visual contrast is of course familiar; here it is taken to extremes to assist the truncated narrative.

Some scenes are reminiscent of stage sets – and the painterly tableaux are sometimes dependent on the poses and groupings to be found in Victorian narrative painting – for example, the scene where Merton kneels beside Milly to beg forgiveness as she lies, near-death, on a chaise-longue. Here again costumes and décor complement each other – the curtains, the sofa and his suit are all cream, as are the walls behind them. Milly, in her white silk robe, becomes the focus of our gaze as the camera pulls back.

James ends his novel with a conversation between the lovers – a subtle and inconclusive conflict, where the last line is Kate's cry as she leaves 'Ah, we shall never again be as we were!' In the film there is no such ambiguity and the resolution is unsatisfactory. But, significantly, Softley brings in, as the plot encourages, stylistic elements of film noir. There are

The heritage femme fatale. Helena Bonham Carter in *The Wings of the Dove* (1997)

cuts between shots of the plotting lovers gazing out of windows at the rain; and in the penultimate scene, they lie together on Merton's bed in the dim light that filters in through the blind. The woman who ensnares her lover, despite his doubts, into a plan to gain money and freedom, and is ultimately punished, is familiar to us; Softley has darkened the genre to create 'heritage *noir*.'

The juxtaposition of different generic elements and the creation of new possibilities for heritage were taken still further in *Elizabeth* (1998). The funeral of Princess Diana took place on the day the shooting of *Elizabeth* began and cast and crew saw it as an 'eerie coincidence' which could be interpreted as a reminder of a craving for ritual, pageantry and communality. But the past presented to us in this film is as uncompromising and brutal as that depicted in *Jude*. In order to become an idol, venerated by her people, Elizabeth must lose her innocence, deny her humanity and reject her sexuality.

The director, Shekhar Kapur, a veteran of Bollywood, was asked what the producers believed he would bring to the film. He suggested 'Probably lack of finesse ... something a bit melodramatic and chaotic'.[18] He wrote a 'mission statement' for the film inside his copy of the screenplay, citing 'the intrigue of *The Godfather* and the shooting style of *Trainspotting*. Michael Hirst, the screenwriter, added 'The plot is like a serpent, slithering around, and the camera became that serpent.'[19] Like Eisenstein's *Ivan the Terrible*, the production has both the scope of epic film and the stylisation of grand opera. The sequence which shows the arrest of the conspirators intercut with shots of Elizabeth praying is homage to *The Godfather*; the idea of the poisoned dress is taken from Sophocles' *Medea*.

The opening sequence shows us forcibly the brutality of the era – there is no chance that we will regard what is to follow as an exercise in nostalgia. A document is sealed and stamped – we track across shackles and chains, to the sound of screaming, and the camera observes from above the violent shaving of a woman's head, with strokes so harsh that her scalp is bloodied. From overhead, we watch as she and her fellow Protestants are dragged out through iron gates to be burnt at the stake. The camera cuts from an overhead shot of the fire to a bird's eye view of nave, chancel, and courtiers – the camera swoops down to follow the courtiers into the Gothic gloom of Mary's court. The black clothes, the gilt, the icons and the burning incense evoke the paintings of Goya.

Elizabeth herself is first seen, out of focus, dancing in the fields with her ladies-in-waiting. As the focus sharpens, she is seen to be laughing – her long hair falls over her shoulders and she wears a flowing silk dress. The very last sequence of the film shows Elizabeth's extraordinary transformation of herself into an icon. Asking 'Must I be made of stone, to feel nothing?' she looks up at a plaster statue of the Virgin Mary. There is a swift cut to a disturbing image which reminds us of the opening minutes of the film. Elizabeth's long hair is being cut brutally short by her weeping lady-in-waiting. Turning to camera, she says 'See – I have become the Virgin.' Her ladies apply white paste to her face, rouge her cheeks and – to the accompaniment of Elgar's Nimrod suite – she appears within a proscenium arch, walking down to and among her adoring courtiers, in the persona of the Virgin Queen. Her clothes have altered during the course of the film, the sensuous, revealing dresses in silks and velvets replaced by stiff, concealing garments, over-elaborate and near-theatrical.

There are countless shots through curtains, veils, grilles and other framing devices; the camera is frequently positioned so that we are looking down as if upon a stage. One such shot through gauzy drapes, seemingly tinted red, shows us Elizabeth's sly glance at the Machiavellian Walsingham as she denies any knowledge of an assassination – a contrast to her earlier involuntary looks at her lover during the coronation. The scenes at the papal court are among the most theatrical; heavy drapes frame a dark chamber, and shafts of light, cutting diagonally across, gradually reveal the seated, scarlet-clad clerics, plotting to rid England of the heretic Queen.

Even the aftermath of battle is presented in a stylised manner. A stream suddenly fills the screen and is seen in close-up to be running red with blood – the camera moves to the left to show us a body lying in the water and then pulls up and across to show countless others covering the slopes leading up to a spectacular castle. Here, as throughout, there are carefully composed tableaux – but the extraordinary camera movements make the film cinematically innovative and underscore the intrigues which Elizabeth cannot escape, the world of institutionalised cruelty to which she is committed. The film is in many ways both innovative and radical; it changes our perception of period films and how they might be made.

Shakespeare in Love could seem out of place here – but it reinforces this process in other ways. Directed by John Madden, whose first film was the more conventional heritage offering, *Mrs Brown* (1997), it may be different in mood, tone and style from *Elizabeth* but there are similarities in the uses of intertextual reference and extra-diegetic information.

There are televisual references – to *Monty Python, Blackadder* and, through casting, to *The Fast Show*. Tom Stoppard uses endless quotations from Shakespeare's entire canon, so that those possessed of cultural capital can identify them and the many other high-cultural and historical allusions. There is cinematic self-referentiality – jokes at the expense of his co-writer, Marc Norman, whose previous credits include *Cut-Throat Island* (Renny Harlin, 1995), the use of Hollywood star Ben Affleck to play Ned Alleyn, Elizabethan megastar. There are other dramatic devices and asides – including a Brechtian address to audience, 'How shall this be resolved?'

Perhaps heritage film has finally caught up with post-modern practice. As Jameson has said: 'The autorefentiality of all modern culture tends to turn upon itself and designate its own cultural production as its content.'[20] Certainly the films have been transformed, in the past ten years, from those naturalistic depictions of Edwardian manners and mores. The genre is wider and more experimental and now has the element of pastiche; *Millennial Heritage* might be a chapter heading in ten years' time.

Notes

1 Jean Baudrillard, *Essays* (Cambridge: Polity Press, 1988), p. 171.
2 The main protagonists in these debates are Andrew Higson and Claire Monk. For a summary, see John Hill, *British Cinema in the 1980s* (Oxford: Clarendon Press, 1999), pp. 73–99.
3 Richard Dyer in Ginette Vincendeau (ed.) *Encyclopaedia of European Cinema* (London: BFI/Cassell, 1995), p. 205.
4 Stella Bruzzi, *Undressing Cinema: Clothing and Identity in the Movies* (London: Routledge, 1997), pp. 36–7.
5 John Caughie, in Vincendeau (1995), p. 187.
6 Eddie Dyja (ed.), *BFI Film and Television HandBook 1997* (London: BFI, 1996), p. 37.
7 Claire Monk, 'Heritage film and the British cinema audience in the 1990s', *Journal of Popular British Cinema*, no. 2, January 1999.
8 Martin A. Hipsky, 'Anglophil(m)ia : Why does America watch Merchant-Ivory movies?' *Journal of Popular Film and Television*, vol. 22, no. 3, Fall 1994.
9 Julianne Pidduck, 'Of women, windows and walks', *Screen*, vol. 39, no. 4.
10 *Sense and Sensibility* took $4 million, *Persuasion* took $3.6 million, though *Sense and Sensibility* was also a huge success on the international market, taking a total of $134 million, Eddie Dyja (ed.), *BFI Film and Television HandBook 1997* (London: BFI, 1996), p. 38 and Eddie Dyja (ed.), *BFI Film and Television HandBook 1998* (London: BFI, 1997), p. 41.
11 Roger Michell, interviewed by Tristan Davey, *Daily Telegraph*, 7 January 1995.
12 Ang Lee, interviewed by Michael Pye, *Daily Telegraph*, 27 January 1996.
13 Ibid.
14 Press notes for *Sense and Sensibility*, 1996.
15 According to Emma Thompson, 'We all swooned. Ang laughed – "This scene is ridiculous", he said.' *Screenplay and Diaries* (London: Bloomsbury, 1997), p. 242.
16 Hossein Amini, press notes for *Jude*, 1996.
17 Robin Wood, *The Wings of the Dove* (London: BFI, 1999), p. 3.
18 Tom Charity, *Time Out*, 23 September 1998.
19 Ibid.
20 Fredric Jameson, *Postmodernism and the Cultural Logic of Late Capitalism* (London: Verso, 1991), p.146.

Chapter 13

Two Sisters, the Fogey, the Priest and his Lover

Sexual Plurality in 1990s British Cinema

Stella Bruzzi

This chapter will examine British cinema's portrayal of non-heterosexual sexualities in the latter part of the 1990s, a period which has seen a shift away from the 'new queer cinema' that emerged in response to the AIDS epidemic of the 1980s.[1] The three films to be discussed in detail here – *Priest, Sister My Sister* and *Love and Death on Long Island* – are less queer and more interested in acknowledging sexual plurality, fluidity and individuality. All three offer explorations (as opposed to definitions) of different sexualities (homosexuality, lesbianism, incest) incorporated within the structure of a journey, both metaphoric and real, undertaken by the protagonists. All three also investigate the still active and problematic division between repression and openness and play out the erstwhile conflict between remaining 'closeted' and 'coming out'. They thereby suggest that, while boundaries between the normative and the 'other' are getting progressively more relaxed, there remain obstacles preventing a full acknowledgement of alternative identities. All three films thus deploy – whether actual or metaphoric – barriers (from the confession booth to social convention) that symbolise this inherent division. The prioritisation of the 'closet'/'coming out' axis is not due to the films being old-fashioned (although they are, in different ways, consumed with the past), but due to their preoccupation that, for all the recent advancements in sexuality politics, the accommodation of the 'other' remains problematic and fraught.

Priest (1994, directed by Antonia Bird, screenplay Jimmy McGovern), which began life as a four-part BBC series, tells the story of an idealistic priest whose convictions are radically altered by his homosexuality. It is a formally conventional film, reminiscent of the British 'social problem' films of the 50s and early 60s, and not unlike Basil Dearden's *Victim* (1961) in tenor, using character interaction to debate its focal issues. The church does not merely offer a convenient backdrop; McGovern is a Catholic, and *Priest* one of the few modern films to take religion seriously.[2] In concrete terms, the film is 'about' sexuality, and parallels are made between the actions of the central gay priest, his colleague who is conducting an affair with the female housekeeper and the violent, incestuous relationship between a parishioner and his daughter. These events are then couched within a more abstract, theoretical framework that articulates the basic struggle between the repressive instinct and a contemporary call for 'coming out', exemplified by the film's extended literal and metaphoric use of the confessional. Father Greg Pilkington (Linus Roache) arrives at a Liverpool parish (wanting 'to do his wee bit for the inner city') after the last priest, struck by a crisis of faith, rips a crucifix from the church wall and rams the fence surrounding the bishop's dwellings. His fellow priest is the liberal and informal Matthew (Tom Wilkinson). From the outset, Greg's position is symbolic, his sturdy convictions (as Matthew

The confessional mode of *Priest* (1994)

comments, 'You're very certain of yourself, aren't you?') are to be put to the test, while his personal journey towards a less rigid faith enacts the rituals of the confessional.

The conflict between the repressive instinct and sexuality in *Priest* echoes Foucault's analysis of sex and the discursive strategies deployed to express sexuality. Foucault offers a radical thesis for understanding the outcome of administered censorship of the articulation of desire, suggesting that, far from banishing sex, the measures that were brought by the church and other institutions to prohibit sex and curtail the public acknowledgement of it brought into being 'an apparatus for producing an even greater quantity of discourse about sex'.[3] One location in which sex is so discursively acknowledged is the confessional. The act of confession, Foucault argues, is the locus for bringing into the open 'a thing that was hidden', thus disseminating, reinforcing and defining heterogeneous sexualities at just that moment when they are most conclusively condemned:

> It is no longer a question simply of saying what was done – the sexual act – and how it was done; but of reconstructing, in and around the act, the thoughts that recapitulated it, the obsessions that accompanied it, the images, desires, modulations, and quality of the pleasure that animated it. For the first time, no doubt, a society has taken upon itself to solicit and hear the imparting of individual pleasures.[4]

The confessional runs through *Priest* as both a metaphor and an actual location. Greg's homosexuality becomes a 'perversion', as one parishioner calls it, only when it is forced to enter the parameters of the church; beyond those confines it is granted a comparable romanticism and tenderness to other normative forms of love and affection. Despite this representation, however, the entire film is, from Greg's tortured perspective, an elaborate confessional in which his struggle between Catholicism and sex is enacted. At various stages Greg comes into direct conflict with different institutions, all of which compel him to confess his homosexuality. The climax of this collision between the public and the personal is the sequence following Greg's arrest, after he and Graham (Robert Carlyle) are discovered kissing in a car. To the policeman taking down his statement he confesses he is a priest; to the courts he pronounces himself 'guilty'; a journalist quips on the front page of the local rag, 'Not in front of the altar boys'; the church expels him from the diocese. To the police, the courts, the newspapers and the church, therefore, Greg has to state his sexuality, an action that inevitably condemns him. The confessional, however, is a paradoxical metaphor, representative of both Catholicism's hierarchical formality (symbolised by the grill dividing priest from 'guilty' parishioner) and its desire to listen and help, thus becoming the locus for the conflict between the arcane and the contemporary roles the church is allotted.

During a routine school confession, a teenager, Lisa, tells Greg she is being sexually abused by her father; Greg is subsequently visited, likewise during confession, by Lisa's unrepentant father who calls incest 'natural' and 'the one thing we'd all like to do, deep down'. Bound by the law of confidentiality, Greg cannot divulge what he has heard there unless Lisa grants him the right to, which she does not, and at this point the confessional ceases to be merely a metaphor for Greg's personal predicament, imposing instead parallels between his sexuality and the immoral, illegal sexuality of Lisa's father. Within the broader context of the film as confessional, this brutal sequence of events is handled in two ways: as a means of debating the church's inadequate, outmoded ways of dealing with social problems, and as a means of examining sexual deviancy.[5]

Greg's confession-like journey through crisis moments and denials, for instance, offers a formal mechanism for exploring his 'deviancy'. The first moment of crisis occurs as Greg returns from a wake: he enters his room, opens his closet, changes out of his priest's habit and puts on jeans and a leather jacket before cycling to a gay bar. Greg's sexuality is, intriguingly, not something he is in the process of discovering: he knows he is gay – albeit closeted – and has already familiarised himself with Liverpool's gay nightlife. Greg copes with his sexuality through compartmentalisation. The ritualised swapping of clothes is a highly charged moment; not only does it mimic (in Roache's precise, measured gestures) the dependency on ritualised action within the Catholic church, but it enforces a visual and emotional separation between Greg's two 'lives'. Returning from his sexual encounter with Graham, Greg changes back into his priest's robes (once more looking at his reflection as he does so), as if re-closeting his forbidden sexuality, thus impersonating the ritual of the confessional: he has sinned, but has absolved himself, in much the same way as he 'cleanses' his body through his sporadic trips to the gym. This elision of identity and appearance, however, is inherently fragile. Like the unco-ordinated infant Lacan invokes, for whom 'the mirror-image would seem to be the threshold of the visible world', Greg's conviction is that his selfhood is contained within what he and others see.[6] As these moments of self-assessment take place literally adjacent to the closet (in Sedgwick's words, 'the defining structure for gay oppression in this century'), Greg's vacillations between priest and gay lover enact the oscillation between wanting two separate identities.[7]

As spectators, however, we are unable to forget and re-closet the intensity of the sexual interlude that Greg has conveniently elided by changing back into his priest's clothes. Upon arriving in the gay bar, Greg, instantly the object of many a gaze he does not reciprocate, takes his drink over to another mirror, looks at himself with the same intent stare of the previous scene, takes a sip of his pint and turns round to face Graham, the one man his gaze has alighted on.[8] Although flashbacks later embellish the scene, now there is only a sharp cut to Greg and Graham in the latter's flat having sex. The sexual interludes between the two men are highly sensual, set apart from the world of the church; sex takes place, for example, against the backdrop of an open fire, the naked bodies bathed in a glowing, yellow light, and later, when the two meet on the beach, an excitable, abandoned camera circles them as they kiss – cinematic clichés for clichéd romantic moments. If Greg's church existence centres on certainty, the conviction displayed by his priest persona is predicated upon being able to successfully repress the forbidden sexuality that surfaces, as if involuntarily, in these interludes. The confessional, therefore, proves an unsuccessful purgatorial measure.

Priest consistently parallels Greg's repressed sexuality with Lisa's reluctance to talk about her abuse, most emotively at the end when the two embrace in tears during the taking of communion, but also implies that such parallels are erroneous, the products of Greg's self-flagellating guilt. After his court appearance, there is a subjective montage in which Greg's conscience juxtaposes images of himself with Graham, Lisa's family and Matthew's relationship with the housekeeper. Matthew's forgiveness and the final embrace both suggest that Greg's sexuality is not construed as a 'crime'; the failure to differentiate between his 'crime' and that of incest lies instead with the church: as Greg can only chastise the crucifix hanging in his room, begging Jesus to 'do something' with regard to Lisa, her mother is belatedly discovering her husband's abuse. The church may only have similar mechanisms for dealing with the various sexual 'crimes' illustrated in *Priest* (and the confessional is the metaphor via which its intransigence is conveyed), but 1990s society is more discriminating.

The 'problem' of equating same-sex attraction with criminality is again touched upon in *Sister My Sister* (1995, directed by Nancy Meckler, screenplay by Wendy Kesselman), a reworking of the infamous 1933 Le Mans case in which two sibling servants kill their employers.[9] *Sister My Sister*'s examination of sexuality revolves around lesbianism and the two sisters' incest, though here, unlike in *Priest*, the conflicts between the suppression and the articulation of desire are enacted as sensuous struggles on the surface or body of the film, not conducted as character interaction masquerading as social debate. Rather than being a 'social problem' film, *Sister My Sister*, alongside other films released in the mid-1990s such as *Heavenly Creatures, Fun* and *Butterfly Kiss*, is concerned with the correlation between women's transgressive sexuality and murder and recalls the recurring syndrome in modern films noirs that associates lesbianism and criminality (*Basic Instinct* or *Single White Female*, for example).[10] Whereas *Priest* contained transient moments of sensuality, *Sister My Sister* explores the impingement of closeted, illicit sexuality on the normative, heterosexual environment. As a result, the straight world is made to appear as queer as the incestuous desire unfolding in the attic. Incest is contextualised differently in Meckler's film, not so much criminal (it is consensual) but as a component of lesbianism, so that the final slaughter of Madame Danzard and her daughter Isabel by the sisters, Christine and Lea is the ultimate symbol for their brutal rejection of society's norms and its dominant moral codes.

Sister My Sister enacts the repressive hypothesis, the 'multiple implanting' of sex and particularly perversions into discourse motivated not by liberalism but by 'the endeavour to expel from reality the forms of sexuality that were not amenable to the strict economy of reproduction'.[11] The Danzard household, despite its veneer of respectability, is notably uninvolved with reproduction and heterosexuality. The house is inhabited by four women, all of whom are consciously or unconsciously attracted to one another (there is talk of Isabel's imminent engagement, but no man appears in the film at all) and little of the action

The complex sexualities of *Sister My Sister* (1995)

takes place beyond its claustrophobic walls.[12] The perversity of the environment is thereby defined by an excess of femininity. The first part of the film is a love affair, all implied through fetishism and innuendo, between Christine, the older sister (Joely Richardson), and Madame Danzard (Julie Walters), conducted in the ostensibly innocuous (and fervently feminine) domains of housework and cooking. The pervasive sexual tension is conveyed via almost imperceptible signs of delight and desire such as Madame's ritualised checking of Christine's cleaning in pristine white gloves. The arrival of Lea is an intrusion on this relationship, but before this becomes clear, there is the first dinner served by both sisters together. The sequence comprises the exchange between the four women of several charged and indecipherably erotic, tense looks as the servants dish out veal in cream sauce and perfectly spherical roast potatoes. Momentarily breaking the stifling silence, Madame reaches the heights of orgasmic rapture as she takes her first mouthful of meat, emitting, with eyes closed, muffled sounds of desire. Satiated, her tongue genteelly licks away a tiny bead of sauce that lingers on her lip.

This first, and dominant, 'other sexuality' displayed in *Sister My Sister* is non-specifically female, that is, it is not explicitly lesbian, but then neither is it heterosexual. As Teresa de Lauretis comments, although the 'first feminist emphasis on sexual difference as gender (woman's difference from man) has rightly come under attack' such an emphasis nevertheless

> did open up a critical space – a conceptual, representational, and erotic space – in which women could address themselves to women. And in the very act of assuming and speaking from the position of subject, a woman could concurrently recognise women as subjects *and* as objects of female desire.[13]

If one interprets *Sister My Sister* through feminist orthodoxy and how it has recently changed with regard to the position of lesbianism in particular, then one can observe a schism occurring in the text between the 'female continuum' Madame Danzard ostensibly desires (between femininity and lesbianism) and the separatism manifested as incest later implemented by the two sisters.[14] As it is in a more orthodox sense in *Priest*, the focal conflict in *Sister My Sister* is between 'respectable' old morals constructed around repression and the more contemporary call to 'come out'. Old sexuality is represented by Madame, who is, it could be argued, simply frustrated, and yet her life is substantially more pleasurable than this dull analysis implies. (In fact, 'frustration' is exhibited more by Isabel, who dislikes all the things that satisfy her mother and rather ravenously consumes chocolates to compensate). Madame would remain perfectly content in this twilight world of fetishism and oblique erotic communication; it is only when overt sexuality begins to surface, that she begins to experience resentment and unease.

The first incestuous kiss between Christine and Lea occurs as the two are reconciled following an argument. Christine has finished making Lea an embroidered petticoat, which Lea duly puts on (back-lit and slightly soft focus from the light streaming in through the bedroom window) as Christine sits expectantly with her eyes closed. Upon opening her eyes, she admires her sister's beauty and they kiss. The kiss encompasses two patterns of desire: incest and lesbianism, the former allied to Christine, the latter to Lea.[15] Like Father Greg's compartmentalisation, the impulse in much feminist theory has been to differentiate between various sexualities and genders, to distinguish between male and female, between straight and gay or lesbian, or between the generic category 'women' and lesbians.[16] Part of what sets recent films such as *Sister My Sister* apart from their predecessors is that previously-affirmed boundaries are now irrevocably blurred, with the acknowledgement of plural sexualities and, within this, perversions. While Christine's desire for Lea is object-specific, replacing her previous attachment to a Sister at the convent and her ritualised 'courtship' with Madame Danzard, the commencement of an incestuous relationship draws out not only Lea's lesbianism but her attraction to sex generally. This first incestuous kiss, for example, immediately precedes a scene in which Isabel offers Lea a chocolate, an exchange that marks the beginning of their flirtation; soon after, during the sisters' visit to the portrait photographer, Lea likewise responds to the flirtatious comments of the photographer. Lea's sexuality is thus not object or orientation-specific as is Christine's, and neither is she bound by a single definition of herself.

Lea's sexuality is performative. When commenting about drag, Judith Butler sheds doubt upon the notion of gender fixity and the concomitant static distinction between the 'imitation' and the 'original', proposing instead that 'In imitating gender, drag implicitly reveals the imitative structure of gender itself – as well as its contingency.' Gender parody is thus a parodic performance of 'the very notion of an original', not of the original itself.[17] Sexual plurality as explored in *Sister My Sister* and as exemplified by its multiple layers and patterns of arousal, similarly posits that no-one is unerringly affiliated to one sexuality, that, as with gender, sexual orientation is fluid and uncircumscribed. Lea embodies this, as her physical attachment to Christine provokes an explosion within her of a more generalised desire, and correspondingly triggers in the film as a whole an increasingly intense sensuality. As the narrative moves to its violent conclusion, the action is punctuated, for example, by increasingly close-up images of the kitchen tap dripping. This tap has no consistent meaning, except maybe to represent the growing realisation that the incest cannot remain hidden, but it does possess a consistent point of identification: Lea.

With the emergence of an illicit, overt and complex sexuality, the dual murder of Madame Danzard and Isabel could be interpreted as a radical response against such an intrusion. Both Madame Danzard and Christine (the two figures who set in motion the sexual continuum played out in the film and who, in turn, precipitate the final confrontation) have something to lose if pluralism triumphs: Christine will never have an exclusive hold over Lea, and Madame will be compelled to admit the unconscious perversity of her own desires. The latter is affronted by the sisters' incest (despite its compatibility with her own sexuality) because – quite apart from being illegal – it breaks the 'house rules' of implicit as opposed to explicit erotic expression. The two pleasures – subliminal and overt – are, for Madame and Christine, incompatible, although Lea is naively capable of straddling the two domains. It is thereby apposite that the residual anger between the two elder characters finally 'comes out', as Madame shouts at a dishevelled Christine, 'God forgive me for what I have harboured here ... you smell of it' and Christine initiates the murders by gouging out Danzard's eyes. The repressed on both sides finally rises in extreme response to a flexible definition of sexuality that suits neither.

Because of the manner in which *Sister My Sister* involves the spectator, primarily through the mechanisms of fetishism, the film's bloody outcome in part represents the death of the initial, delicious, more innocent, sexuality. The discovery of an alternative sexual consciousness that can accommodate very different sexualities is thus perceived as ultimately destructive. Conversely, in *Love and Death on Long Island* (written and directed by Richard Kwietniowski, 1998, from a novel by Gilbert Adair) Giles De'Ath's comparably obsessive (though hardly illegal) journey towards sexual freedom is affirmative. While *Love and Death* is similarly nostalgic for the erotic possibilities offered by the repressive mentality (the references to *Brief Encounter*, Chatterton, Verlaine and Rimbaud), it embraces positively the more contemporary insistence upon 'coming out'. What sets the film apart from the others previously discussed, is that Giles' literal and metaphoric voyage of self-discovery is not motivated by circumstance but by personal predilection. Giles (described in the *Radio Times* listings for a radio interview as an 'erstwhile fogey, now cult' author) is a widowed writer who, symbolically, is not yet in tune with the modern technological and communications age: he uses a pen not a word-processor, he does not possess a television, and when he ventures to 'the pictures' it is with the intention of seeing an adaptation of Forster's *The Eternal Moment*. Giles conforms to the 'Queer Wits' stereotype, the amusing homosexual character favoured by straights, 'provided of course that the queer in question shuns any overtly sexual behaviour'.[18] Significantly, Giles' acerbic wit diminishes as the narrative progresses, marking the transition from repressed to open sexuality, the transitional moment being his visit to the cinema. Realising that what is showing is not Forster but the teen flick *Hotpants College 2*, Giles gets up to leave, but finds himself mesmerised by the appearance on the screen of Ronnie Bostock. This accident is the catalyst for Giles' journey towards both homosexuality and modernity; he goes in search of Ronnie on Long Island, acquires a video, television and answerphone, and orders home-delivery pizzas.

Initially, *Love and Death* revolves around Giles' total immersion in his Ronnie fantasy: the adolescent search for images of Bostock in teen magazines then lovingly transferred to a scrap book of 'Bostokiana'; the incessant re-viewing of the B-movie star's notably unimpressive oeuvre (*Hotpants College 1*, *Skid Marks* and *Tex Mex*). Giles' fantasies are, at this stage, secret, something to be indulged in the seclusion of his fogey's study and his daydreams (for example, imagining competing on *Mastermind* on the subject of Ronnie). Within the security of the closet, this existence is safe and amusing. Giles' journey becomes fraught with danger, however, when he ventures forth beyond the narrow confines of his study and his imagination to pursue the real rather than the imaginary Ronnie Bostock to his home in Long Island. Whereas Giles (like anyone in the grips of a similar obsession) believes in the potential correspondence between idol and reality, the film stresses the divergence between the grandeur of Giles' emotions and the insubstantiality of his chosen object of desire. As Giles arrives in Long Island and goes in search of his idol's home, the two domains are brought alarmingly close, finally merging when Giles engineers a meeting with Ronnie's partner Audrey and receives an invite to meet Ronnie upon his return from Los Angeles.

To help legitimise and bridge the gulf between emotional investment and its actual object of affection, Giles invents a fixated godchild, Abigail, as the source of his copious information about Ronnie's career, an alter ego who, in turn, gives him license to impose his own aggrandising and flattering parallels between, for instance, Ronnie's films and Shakespeare. During Giles' intellectual ruminations, Ronnie (played by Jason Priestley of *Beverly Hills 90210*) looks on bemused, a simpler mind attempting to grasp the lofty ideas of the sage.[19] While the schism between ideal and reality remains intact for the spectator, Giles wants to live his fantasy, to press for a fusion of the two. The culmination of this desire comes as Giles tells Ronnie his ideas for a screenplay he pretends he's been commissioned to write that centres on a deaf-mute of Ronnie's age obsessed by television images who surrenders himself to the 'desire to fall in love'. As a symbolic hybrid text, this derivative and melodramatic scenario functions as a metaphor for Giles' regeneration: it collapses Ronnie's image with Giles' desires and previous actions; it posits a future working relationship between the two; it expresses Giles' underpinning desire to surrender himself not just to fantasy, but to physical love.

Giles' journey thereby begins to transgress the understood boundary between the imaginative and the physical, between the safety of the closet and the relative danger of being 'out'. Cocooned until Audrey's belated recognition of his motives, Giles' ultimate expression of wanting to amalgamate the two realms is his 'confession' to Ronnie on the eve of his departure back to England. Against the backdrop of the diner 'Chez D'Erv' (a modern day equivalent of the station café in *Brief Encounter*), Giles tells all, and in so doing divulges to the very object of his new desire his fantasy existence. He insists Ronnie is too young to marry Audrey, that he is 'prepared to devote myself to your career' and become Verlaine to Ronnie's Rimbaud (for which Ronnie understands Rambo), finally saying, quite simply, 'I love you'. In response to this outpouring, Ronnie adopts his bland, familiar look of confusion and vacuous pity, leaving Giles after gently placing his hand on his shoulder, echoing, no doubt unconsciously, Trevor Howard's parting gesture in *Brief Encounter*. Giles is left to muse, 'dear God, what have I done?'.

Love and Death on Long Island concludes with Giles leaving, but only after he has sent Ronnie a fax telling him 'our story' – the narrative (fantasies and all) of the film. Giles comprehends this action as the ultimate expression of his desires, his 'outing', but it also signifies the continued potency of fantasy (by its very nature a function of the closet). Throughout *Love and Death*, Ronnie has been, in the tradition of melodrama, the image onto which Giles has projected his desires – desires that Ronnie consistently fails to live up to, except in Giles' imagination. Likewise the fax concludes with Giles trying one last time to make Ronnie conform to what he wants him to be:

> Well, Ronnie, there it is, the end of our story – and also the beginning of a new story for me, but perhaps you'd worked that out for yourself. But what of you my darling? For no one on earth knows you better than I do.

What Giles 'knows' is the Ronnie of his imagination, a figure who has indeed precipitated his 'new story' but who, beyond incorporating Giles' suggestion of Walt Whitman's lines 'Now, voyager, sail thou forth to seek and find' into his graveside eulogy in *Hotpants College 3*, is no more part of that reality than he was before they met. As he quotes Whitman, Ronnie's image is blotted out by the beam from the cinema projector, a corny metaphor, perhaps, for the notion that Ronnie never can embody the depth of Giles' love and identification with him. It is not unimportant that the film's final image is a close-up of the first handshake between Ronnie and Giles on the beach: the moment when fantasy and embodiment meet, but also the moment when the divergence between the two is cemented.

Love and Death on Long Island, in charting Giles' progress towards self-fulfilment, signals the death of the prior need for a *Brief Encounter*-esque suppression of emotion. In this, like both *Priest* and *Sister My Sister*, it functions as a parable of enlightenment and individualism. All three films represent a current trend in British cinema's treatment of 'other sexualities' as exemplary of plurality and a freedom not circumscribed by received notions of sexual identity. Jonathan Dollimore posits that one of the progressive differences of our time is that people have 'begun positively to identify the difference of the other'. These three films go one step further than earlier new queer cinema in that they represent the diversity of that other, so it is not merely heterosexuality's binary opposite, but is celebrated as the site where fixed identity and definition are dispensed with.[20]

Notes

1 See Honey Glass, 'Queer', *Sight and Sound*, October 1997; Ruby B Rich, 'New queer cinema', *Sight and Sound*, September 1992 and Sarah Street, *British National Cinema* (London and New York: Routledge, 1997) for definitions of queer cinema.

2 Cf. Donald Lyons, 'Priests', *Film Comment*, May/June 1995, for a discussion of cinema's representation of priests. Most of the time – as in Hitchcock's *I Confess* (1953) – the church's rituals are mechanisms for facilitating plot and narrative problems; in *Priest*, the actual convictions of the Roman Catholic church are the focal point, whether or not they are questioned and found wanting.

3 Michel Foucault, *The History of Sexuality: Volume One* (Harmondsworth: Penguin, 1976), pp. 4–5.

4 Ibid., p. 63.

5 Unlike *I Confess* in which the law of confidentiality is used as a convenient device in a murder plot, the similar situation in *Priest* brings up the debates surrounding the church's role within the community.

6 Jacques Lacan, 'The mirror stage as formative function of the I', in *Ecrits: A Selection* (London: Tavistock, 1977), p. 3.

7 Eve Kosofsky Sedgwick, 'Epistemology of the Closet' in Henry Abelove, Michèle Aina Barale and David M. Halperin (eds), *The Lesbian and Gay Studies Reader* (London and New York: Routledge, 1993), p. 48.

8 It also seems significant, in relation to the film's play on mirrors and reflections, that Linus Roache and Robert Carlyle are physically quite similar.

9 *Sister My Sister* uses the same story as Genet's play *The Maids*, although the latter focuses more on class issues and sado-masochism.

10 For some further discussions of this tendency see Lynda Hart, *Fatal Women: Lesbian Sexuality and the Mark of Aggression* (Princeton: Princeton University Press, 1994) and

Yvonne Tasker, *Working Girls: Gender and Sexuality in Popular Cinema* (London and New York: Routledge, 1998).

11 Foucault, *The History of Sexuality*, pp. 37 and 36.

12 The male photographer Christine and Lea go to is heard but not seen.

13 Teresa de Lauretis, 'Sexual Indifference/Lesbian Representation', in Henry Abelove, Michèle Aina Barale and David M. Halperin (eds), *The Lesbian and Gay Studies Reader* (London and New York: Routledge, 1993) pp. 141–2.

14 Cf. Eve Kosofsky Sedgwick, *Between Men: English Literature and Male Homosocial Desire* (New York: Columbia University Press, 1985).

15 This is the ostensible reason for Lea's subsequent 'recovery' and re-integration into society following her spell in prison and for Christine's total, irreversible collapse.

16 The dominant impulse has, until recently, been towards differentiating along gender lines, to bracket women's experience together and to pit that experience against men (cf. Simone de Beauvoir, *The Second Sex*, London: Picador, 1988). This has been replaced in many ways by theorists such as Monique Wittig who, in 'One is not born a woman' (reproduced in *The Lesbian and Gay Studies Reader*) argues for the uniqueness of the lesbian experience because it circumvents men entirely. Judith Butler's *Gender Trouble: Feminism and the Subversion of Identity* (London and New York: Routledge, 1990), problematises the very notion of gender and a rigid gendered identity.

17 Judith Butler, *Gender Trouble*, pp. 137 and 138.

18 Andy Medhurst, 'Licensed to cheek', *Sight and Sound*, October 1997, p. 35.

19 Ronnie's idea of an 'artsy' movie, for example, is Alan Parker's *Birdy* (1984).

20 Jonathan Dollimore, *Sexual Dissidence: Augustine to Wilde, Freud to Foucault* (Oxford: Oxford University Press, 1991), p. 330.

Chapter 14
Unseen British Cinema

Geoffrey Macnab

> With a few exceptions, if a British film deserves distribution, it will get it ... a lot of
> films that do get a release don't warrant it – as the figures show.
>
> (Nick Thomas)[1]

In May 1998, the film trade magazine *Screen Finance* revealed that 'nearly 60 per cent of the films involving a UK producer that went into production in 1996, have yet to be screened at a UK cinema'.[2] At first glance, this is an astonishing statistic. These were feature films, most involving a huge outlay. Without a theatrical release in their own domestic market, they stood little chance of recouping the money lavished on them. Admittedly, 1996 was a boom year for British film-makers. There were more than eighty films completed in the UK involving British producers, roughly double the figure of 1983, the year the Eady Fund was abolished.[3] Arts Council Lottery funding, which became available to the industry in the autumn of 1995, had stimulated production as had the optimism engendered by the increase in cinema attendance and by the success of *Four Weddings and a Funeral* (Mike Newell, 1994), *Trainspotting* (Danny Boyle, 1996) and *The Full Monty* (Peter Cattaneo, 1997), which were made on modest budgets and broke box-office records. Funding for film-makers suddenly seemed more readily available than ever before. As one industry source puts it, there was suddenly 'more money around than viable projects'.[4]

Many of the new films were begun without a guarantee of distribution. In Britain's small, fragmented and production-led industry, this was only to be expected. Rather than wait around trying to pre-sell their projects to sales agents and distributors, film-makers preferred to raise production finance as best they could and worry about clinching the deals which would get their films shown later. They were speculators, operating on the Micawber-like principle that something would turn up. Their philosophy may have seemed reckless and naive but, given the nature of the marketplace, it was understandable. As *A Bigger Picture*, the 1998 government-commissioned report into the industry noted, production remained a cottage industry. 'Typically, companies are established to develop, finance and produce a single film, and then start again from scratch on their next project.'[5]

In Hollywood, the seven major studios are vertically integrated. They can guarantee continuity of both production and distribution. In the post-war heyday of the Rank Organisation and ABPC, the British industry was similarly structured. Both companies had their production and distribution arms as well as their own cinemas. They gradually realised, though, that production was the most expensive and risky side of the business.

Showing other people's movies, especially those made in Hollywood, made much more sense financially.

With no big studios to support them, British producers are left to work on the hoof and their films are often under-capitalised. This puts them in a Catch 22 situation. Without the guarantee of distribution, they have little chance of raising big budgets or of attracting stars to their projects, but without stars and budget already attached they cannot attract the distributors. As *A Bigger Picture* noted, 'the average budget for the wholly British films produced in 1997 was less than £3.5 million compared with over £18 million for the overseas films made in the UK'.[6] British producers rarely have much money to invest in research and development and are sometimes obliged to rush films into production sooner than they should do.

Exhibitors habitually claim that they will show anything that makes them money. 'Emotive statements are made without any objectivity behind them', protests Richard Segal, Managing-Director of Odeon Cinemas, when asked why so few British films are considered worth an airing. 'We choose films on commercial merit – country of origin is not a criterion we look at.' He insists that ninety-nine per cent of the films that are brought to Odeon's attention by distributors will be given some form of cinema release. 'Typically we'll always give the distributor the ability to demonstrate a film's commerciality.'[7] Nevertheless, if confronted with a choice between showing an American film about baseball (a sport with virtually no following in the UK) and a low-budget British movie, it is safe to say most multiplex exhibitors would opt for the former. *Land And Freedom* (1995), Ken Loach's award-winning film about the Spanish Civil War, wasn't shown in the multiplexes; *Major League* (David S. Ward, 1989) was. Admittedly, Loach's previous film, *Ladybird Ladybird* (1994), had been given a national release by UIP, but (ironically) many argue that it should not have been. An uncompromising story about a battered wife at loggerheads with social workers who deem her an unfit mother, it was precisely the kind of film that needed careful handling and it was scarcely surprising that it failed to find an audience.

At the end of 1997, there were around 2,400 screens in the UK, a rise of more than 200 on the previous year, and new cinemas are still being built. In theory, this ought to make it easier to release British films. In practice, the reverse is often true. As one consultant noted, 'the increasing number of multiplex screens has made it more difficult to release smaller films because it has led to a trend towards wider releases supported by television advertising. As a result, smaller films and smaller distributors are being squeezed out of the market.'[8]

The British films that did make an impact tended to be those handled by aggressive US distributors. BBC Scotland's *Mrs Brown* (John Madden, 1997) was distributed by Miramax as was *The English Patient* (Anthony Minghella, 1996) and *Little Voice* (Mark Herman, 1998). *The Full Monty* was distributed (as well as fully financed) by Fox Searchlight. However, there are some signs that modestly budgeted films handled by British distributors can also reach an audience, if marketed imaginatively enough. Entertainment Film Distributors enjoyed an unlikely success with its low-budget rugby film, *Up 'n' Under* (John Godber, 1997), the first feature the company had fully financed. It boasted no big stars, the subject matter was esoteric (rugby is not the most popular sport in Britain) and the director, playwright John Godber, had never made a film before. The film opened to lukewarm reviews at around the same time and in the same cinemas as James Cameron's *Titanic*. Nevertheless, thanks to an aggressive promotional campaign, it became a popular second choice at the multiplexes and made well over £3 million in the British market alone. Enter-

This Year's Love (1999) and *Up 'n' Under* (1997) – British films for British audiences

tainment subsequently repeated the success with the romantic comedy, *This Year's Love* (1999), another low-budget film which made $5.3 million in its first four weeks. The success of these two pictures, neither of which was likely to appeal much anywhere outside the UK, proved that it was still possible to make British films for British audiences and turn a profit.

'UK distributors suffer from the lowest rentals of the world, averaging twenty-five to thirty-five per cent of box-office, and some of the highest marketing costs', observed *Variety* in late 1998.[9] This increased their reluctance to pick up British films, most of which require painstaking publicity campaigns if they are to reach an audience. The less popular a film, the higher the percentage of the box-office returns the exhibitors demands. 'With less successful films, we keep more of the take because of the severe fixed costs which we now face, particularly with multiplexes', explains Richard Segal.[10] In other words, when a film flops, the distributors suffer most. They pay the print costs and the press and advertising bills. Given the level of risk, they don't have much incentive to handle British product, which is almost by definition deemed 'difficult'. Unless they are involved in the financing of a film (as was the case with Entertainment and its two box-office hits) they are likely to shy away from British pictures on purely business grounds.

US independent film-makers operate under roughly similar conditions to their British counterparts. As Segal points out, many US films that we don't hear about, made outside the studio system, don't receive distribution either. The key difference is that US distributors are on the lookout for product which they can exploit in the art house market and have the resources to launch films in an altogether more lavish way than British distributors. October spent more than $4 million on publicising its British pick-up, *Hilary and Jackie* in the US, in advance of the 1999 Oscars, while Miramax is alleged to have spent $6 million promoting its 1995 Oscar-winning foreign language success, *Il Postino* and has spent even more on its campaign for Robert Benigni's holocaust comedy, *Life is Beautiful* (1998), helping earn Benigni a Best Actor award and the film to win the Oscar for Best Foreign Language Film in 1999.

Screen Finance's statistics suggest that dozens of feature films made in Britain throughout the 1990s have simply been left to gather dust. Many others have been given only limited releases, perhaps showcased for a week or two in London's West End or booked in for short runs at regional art house theatres. What are these films like? They encompass a wide variety of genres and turn out to be as heterogeneous a mix as the films that actually did receive distribution. Some were shot for a pittance. Others boast impressive budgets. Some were state-funded. Some were made with private capital.

What follows is a survey, exploring the production histories and uncertain fates of a handful of these films. The intention is to give an idea of the range of Britain's unseen cinema and to hint at the different reasons why the films failed to make it into British theatres, and what the consequences of that failure were.

1 THE CO-PRODUCTION: *BULLET TO BEIJING*
(George Mihalka, Canada/UK/Russia, 1995)

Bullet to Beijing is a belated sequel to the three Harry Palmer spy thrillers (*The Ipcress File, Funeral in Berlin, Billion Dollar Brain*) made in Britain in the late 1960s. Michael Caine again stars as Palmer, brought out of retirement by the British government to prevent North Korea getting hold of a deadly virus called 'The Red Death'. As Harry's new boss, Alexei (Michael Gambon), tells him, 'I'm not being overly dramatic, Mr. Palmer, when I say the fate of the world is in your hands.' Although *Screen Finance* lists the film as British, *Bullet to Beijing* is an international co-production, originally made for an American cable TV channel. A theatrical release would have been an added bonus. As Michael Caine explains, 'with that kind of film, which was made for $7 million, you've got to spend $5 million opening it. Unless it's superlative (which quite frankly this wasn't) that isn't going to happen. If the picture had really worked, they would have put it out. But you can't put something like that out against the *Die Hards* and bloody *Star Wars* and all those big pictures.'[11] In the event, *Bullet to Beijing* finally surfaced in Britain on video in spring 1997. Some critics warmed to its old-fashioned qualities. 'Compared with such precision-tooled Hollywood thrill machines as *The Fugitive* and *Speed,* the low budget, meandering small talk and pedestrian pacing are oddly refreshing,' wrote Tom Tunney in *Sight and Sound.*[12] A second Harry Palmer film, *Midnight in St Petersburg,* made straight after the first with many of the same cast and crew, also went straight to video.

Twenty years ago, a film like *Bullet to Beijing* would not have been made without a guarantee of a theatrical release. It is a testament to how the market has changed that such a film can bypass the cinemas and still recoup its costs. In one of his last interviews before his death in 1998, veteran TV and film producer Lew Grade pointed out that in the 1990s, if a producer makes a film for a 'decent budget', by which he meant not less than £8 million, 'there's very little money you can lose because of all the different venues that are available to you – with cable, video and satellite to fall back on, you can't lose a lot. When I started, all there was was cinema and television.'[13]

As if to underline Grade's point, British satellite broadcaster BSkyB has set up its own production arm, Sky Pictures, which aims to make around a dozen medium-budget British films a year which, at least in the first instance, will bypass the British cinemas altogether. Titles include *Best,* a biopic of football legend George Best starring Linus Roache, and *Milk,* a comedy starring Dawn French. They will premiere on Sky and only then will it be decided if they are to be given a theatrical release.

2 THE LOW-BUDGET INDEPENDENT: *BOB'S WEEKEND*
(Jevon O'Neill, 1996)

Described by the *Observer's* film critic Philip French as 'an immensely enjoyable surreal comedy', Jevon O'Neill's debut feature *Bob's Weekend* was warmly received at the 1996 London Film Festival.[14] Nevertheless, more than two years later, the film is still languishing on the shelf. Set in Blackpool, downbeat, hard to categorise, it epitomises the kind of low-budget British movie that distributors and sales agents are loath to handle. As O'Neill acknowledges, the film is not easy to pitch. It is neither a romantic comedy in the vein of *Four Weddings* nor a warm-hearted tale about Sheffield steel workers. The *Wonderful Life*-style story follows Bob (Bruce Jones), a woebegone middle-aged man who has just lost his job and learned that his wife is having an affair. He heads for Blackpool, planning to end his life, but after a series of bizarre encounters with local oddballs, discovers a new zest for life. 'Jones', wrote French, 'is extremely touching as a natural optimist undergoing a dark night of the soul that leads him back into the light, and his performance gives a unity to a movie of varying moods.'[15] The film also stars Brian Glover and Ricky Tomlinson, actors who (like Jones) have worked with Ken Loach and are well-known on TV.

O'Neill shot *Bob's Weekend* for a budget of £365,000. 'We spent £120,000 in cash and the rest was in deferments.'[16] Much of the money came from O'Neill's own savings. He used his earnings from his career as a successful director of commercials and pop promos to subsidise the film. None of his investors (who included family and friends and contributed anything from £200 to £25,000), cast or crew have yet been paid. They seemingly have faith in O'Neill, even if the distributors do not. 'It has done what it needed to do for me in terms of a calling card. Everyone is aware of it and it has allowed me to get into the position to make my next film, but it would be nice now to get people to see it and to receive the financial returns.'

O'Neill is currently in negotiations to shoot a much more ambitious film, a £5 million comedy based on the popular children's TV series, *Mr Benn*. He has already signed up John Hannah (*Four Weddings, Sliding Doors*) to play the lead role. Ben Kingsley is also pencilled in to appear. Thanks to *Bob's Weekend*, the industry takes O'Neill more seriously. He is no longer regarded as a first-time director and, he claims, *Bob's Weekend* is more attractive to distributors now than it was when it was made because its star, Bruce Jones, has gone on to become a leading actor in *Coronation Street*, Britain's most popular TV soap opera.

O'Neill points to a central paradox about the way British distributors operate. 'They are in a risk business but they don't want to take risks. I don't understand being in a market where audiences respond to what is different but are always given more of the same.' His point is borne out by the fact that the three biggest British successes of the 1990s – *Four Weddings and a Funeral, Trainspotting* and *The Full Monty* – were all considered risky projects by financial backers and have since spawned a host of lesser imitators.

O'Neill still has hopes that *Bob's Weekend* might be rediscovered. For that to happen, he suggests, he needs a distributor to acquire all UK rights 'and give it a cinema release to boost the TV price and the video price'. In the meantime, he is proud to have made the film without public funding or indeed help from any outside sources.

3 THE DOCUMENTARY: DONALD CAMMELL: *THE ULTIMATE PERFORMANCE*

(Kevin Macdonald and Chris Rodley, 1998)

British cinema prides itself on its documentary tradition. From John Grierson and his followers in the 30s, to Humphrey Jennings and Harry Watt during the war, to the Free Cinema group in the late 50s, documentary-makers have had a major influence on British film culture. In the 1990s, the tradition survives but now British documentaries, whether shorts or feature-length films, are almost exclusively confined to television. Kevin Macdonald, co-director of *Donald Cammell: The Ultimate Performance*, points out that in the US, feature documentaries are regularly given theatrical distribution and are treated little differently from foreign-language art house films. In Eastern Europe, there are studios exclusively geared to producing documentary films.

Discussions about the difficulties British films face in securing theatrical distribution are rarely extended to include documentary. Nevertheless, there are certain documentaries which clearly work better on the big screen than on TV. The 1997 IMAX-3D film *Everest* (already the biggest grossing documentary in British film history) is a case in point. Its chief selling points are scale and spectacle. When Macdonald and co-director Chris Rodley conceived *The Ultimate Performance*, their documentary portrait of artist and film-maker, Donald Cammell, they did so with the express intention of showing the film in cinemas. They felt that the project had a cult appeal which would attract cinemagoers: Mick Jagger and Marianne Faithfull appear; there is music from the Rolling Stones, and locations include London, Paris and the Mexican desert. But despite their attempts to make the film cinematic, Macdonald and Rodley discovered that television exercises such a stranglehold on documentary culture that it was well-nigh impossible to get their film a theatrical release.

'The problem with documentaries is that they are very difficult to fund and that the only real sources of finance are the TV stations', explains Macdonald.[17] The majority of British documentaries are made for television, often as a part of a series (*Modern Times* and *Dispatches*, for example) and commissioning editors want their films to be showcased on their channels. The BBC is sometimes reluctant to allow even feature films a 'theatrical window'. Stephen Frears' *The Snapper* (1993) was shown in cinemas almost everywhere else in Europe, but in the UK was premiered on television. Given the popularity of Roddy Doyle (from whose novel the book had been adapted) and Frears' own track record, the film would have stood a fair chance of finding an audience in British cinemas if it had been given the chance.

The Ultimate Performance's co-funding by the BBC and by Scottish Screen's Lottery fund turned out to be a schizophrenic arrangement: whereas Scottish Screen demands that all its projects should have a theatrical release, the BBC wanted the documentary to be shown on television first. In the end, a botched compromise was reached. *Donald Cammell: The Ultimate Performance* was shown for a few days at the Glasgow Film Theatre and booked in for a one-week run at the ICA cinema in London. Then, less than a fortnight later, it turned up on television. The documentary was reviewed on the film pages of some national newspapers but there was no budget for advertising and, with such a short-run, no time for word-of-mouth to build. 'With documentary much more than with features,' says Macdonald, 'you are reliant on recognition of the subject matter. People will go and see the documentary because they're interested in that subject. With features, they'll go because they like the sound of it, the story or the stars.'[18] Once *The Ultimate Performance* had been shown on the BBC, its UK theatrical life was effectively over although, ironically, it went on to win prizes at various film festivals, where it was treated as a cinema rather than a television film.

4 THE STAR-DRIVEN COSTUME DRAMA. *THE SERPENT'S KISS*
(Philippe Rousselot, 1997)

The Serpent's Kiss is the story of a young seventeenth-century Dutch architect hired to build a new estate for an English landowner and his wife. As he pursues his commission, he is drawn into a web of sexual and political intrigue. The fate of this lavish costume drama, made for more than £8 million by a French director with established producers (including Robert Jones, who had just had a massive international hit with *The Usual Suspects*) and three well-known British stars (Ewan McGregor, Greta Scacchi and Richard E. Grant) suggests that it is not only low-budget British films which fail to secure theatrical distribution.

In theory, a star-driven period melodrama with top-notch production values should have been an attractive proposition for distributors. The success of such films as Shekhar Kapur's *Elizabeth* (1998), John Madden's *Mrs Brown* and *Shakespeare In Love* (1998) suggests that there is still an appetite for British costume dramas. *The Serpent's Kiss* was also given the ideal launch pad when it was chosen as one of only two British films in competition at the 1997 Cannes Festival. This meant that it was seen by international buyers and critics. The response was largely favourable, even if the reviews pointed out that the film covered similar territory to Peter Greenaway's *The Draughtsman's Contract* (1982). The film opened in France in May 1997, within days of its Cannes premiere. Since then it has only surfaced in one other market, Iceland, where it went straight to video.

It is unclear why *The Serpent's Kiss* has not yet appeared in British cinemas. Possibly, the sales agents scared off buyers by asking too high a price, but *The Serpent's Kiss* risks falling between two stools. It is neither a big-budget studio film nor the kind of low-budget independent film that small-time British distributors would feel comfortable in handling.

The long-term prognosis for the film is not entirely gloomy. In late 1998, Mark Peploe's

Mark Peploe's *Victory* (1998) was released three years after completion

Victory was finally released in British cinemas (albeit with only five prints), three years after it was completed. This was another period drama, an adaptation of a Joseph Conrad novel with a middle-ranking Hollywood star (Willem Dafoe) and a well-known European actress (Irène Jacob). The Feature Film Company, its eventual distributors, described *Victory* as 'an unlucky film' because its British, French, German and American backers all seemed to have different ideas about how the film should be handled. The FFC acquired *Victory* relatively cheaply and despite its lacklustre box-office performance, they are confident that it will reach an audience on video and on satellite TV.

In early 1999, J&M, the UK-based sales agents of *The Serpent's Kiss*, was still hopeful about securing British distribution for the film, possibly with the Disney-owned Buena Vista International. Producers and sales agents prefer holding out for a major American distributor such as UIP (which released *Sliding Doors*, the most commercially successful British film of 1998) or Buena Vista, rather than see their film handled by smaller, independent British distributors. And *The Serpent's Kiss* still had one other major asset which kept it an attractive box-office proposition: its star, Ewan McGregor, appeared on British screens as Obi Wan Kenobi in George Lucas' *Star Wars* sequel, *The Phantom Menace*, one of the most eagerly awaited films of 1999.

Conclusion

At the time of writing, there is no real sign that the distribution logjam is easing. Although fewer films are being made than in the boom year, 1996, production is still relatively buoyant. In May 1997, the Arts Council of England awarded funding worth £92 million to three new consortia, all of which promised to function like mini-studios over the six years of their franchise. The three were DNA ('Duncan and Andrew') formed by Duncan Kenworthy and Andrew Macdonald; The Film Consortium, which pooled together some of the best-known names in the industry in Scala (Steve Woolley, Nik Powell), Skreba-Greenpoint (Simon

Relph, Ann Scott) and Parallax (Ken Loach, Sally Hibbin); and Pathé Pictures. Given that Pathé is a French company, this was the most controversial of the franchise winners. But as veteran producer David Puttnam observed, the significance of the Lottery franchises lay not simply in who won or lost them but in the opportunity for the industry to indulge in some long-overdue self-analysis. Producers, distributors and exhibitors were expected now to bury their differences. 'This extraordinarily fractious industry was, for the first time in the twenty-five years I've been in it, obliged to analyse its strengths and weaknesses and to work out how it would structure itself in the event that it was allowed to behave like a proper industry.'[19]

Much hinges on the performance of the three Lottery franchisees. They have promised to produce more than seventy films over the six years of their franchise term. It remains a moot point, though, as to what sort of distribution those films will receive. For all the franchisees' bold talk about functioning like mini-studios, only one – Pathé – has its own distribution arm and in early 1999, most British films' chances of receiving theatrical distribution remain as uncertain as ever. The Film Consortium has secured a distribution deal with the Hollywood-owned UIP but it remains to be seen whether this will be to its long-term advantage. Most of the production companies associated with The Film Consortium, for instance Parallax (*Land and Freedom, My Name is Joe*) and Skreba (*The Slab Boys, The Land Girls*), make precisely the kind of challenging, independent fare which needs specialist handling. For all its muscle, UIP, more accustomed to releasing studio blockbusters, does not necessarily look an ideal partner.

The government's Film Policy Review Group, which was set up to address structural problems in the industry, advocated the creation of an All Industry Fund to compensate for market failures arising from the structure of the industry. Voluntary contributions were to be raised from exhibitors, distributors, video companies and broadcasters all of whom stood to gain from better developed and better marketed British films. It was hoped that this fund would raise around £15 million a year, and that a substantial part of it would go toward distribution. But the broadcasters and Hollywood studios refused to contribute and the All-Industry Fund was quietly shelved in November 1998.

'Critically what the industry needs to do is to create more distribution companies who will aggressively distribute British films', argues PolyGram's Stewart Till, who co-chaired the Film Policy Review Group. 'I still think that British films aren't marketed as aggressively as they should be.'[20] Throughout the the 90s, PolyGram Filmed Entertainment was the one British film company (albeit Dutch-owned) with the same muscle as the Hollywood majors. Like the studios, it was vertically integrated, with its own production, distribution and sales arms. PFE marketed and distributed its films with an energy and imagination rarely seen before in the British film industry. On the back of ingenious promotional campaigns, *Four Weddings and a Funeral, Shallow Grave, Trainspotting* and *Bean* all became substantial hits. PFE proved beyond any doubt that British films, regardless of budget or genre, could consistently perform at the box-office if they were handled with flair. The company's record in 1998 was exceptional: *Lock Stock And Two Smoking Barrels* (Guy Ritchie), *The Borrowers* (Peter Hewitt), *Spice World – The Movie* (Bob Spiers) and *Elizabeth* were among the top half-dozen British films of the year. Nevertheless, in the summer of 1998, it was sold off by Philips, its parent company, along with the rest of the PolyGram group, to Canadian leisure conglomerate Seagram which already owned the Hollywood studio, Universal.

At one stage, it looked as if Seagram planned to close down PFE, something Stewart Till warned would be cataclysmic for the British film industry. In the event, the company was absorbed by Universal but maintains its European operations under the new name, Universal Pictures International. However, 1998 had already seen the disappearance of two other long-established British distribution companies: First Entertainment and Rank (which had been taken over by TV conglomerate, Carlton) and although UIP announced in early 1999 that it would be setting up a division to distribute low-budget, art house fare, sceptics saw this as a public relations exercise to counter threatened EC anti-monopoly legislation.

The overall figures remain as stark as ever. According to *Variety*, US films accounted for seventy-six per cent of the total UK box-office in 1998. The British films themselves were responsible for around twelve per cent and many new British features didn't receive a theatrical release. The tribulations of PFE, the teething difficulties faced by the Lottery franchisees and the collapse of the All Industry Fund hardly suggest that the industry was setting itself on a new, firmer footing. Nevertheless, by the spring of 1999, there was at least some reason for optimism as cinemas continued to be built at a prodigious rate and new independent distributors set up shop in the UK. These ranged from heavyweights like Icon Film Distributors (co-owned by Mel Gibson) and Roseland (set up by Merchant-Ivory) to less well-known outfits like Redbus and Downtown. Whether or not they succeed in the long run, they are already picking up the kind of low-budget British films which a year or two ago would probably never have been seen in cinemas.

Notes

1 Nick Thomas, editor, *Flicks*, in interview with the author, November 1998.
2 *Screen Finance*, 14 May, 1998, p. 1.
3 The Eady Fund was a levy on British box-office receipts established in the late 1940s. The money raised went back into British film production.
4 David Thompson, BBC Films, in interview with the author, July 1997.
5 *A Bigger Picture – Film Policy Review*, DCMS, March 1998.
6 Ibid.
7 Richard Segal, in interview with the author, January 1999.
8 Karsten-Peter Grummitt, quoted in *Screen Finance*, 14 May, 1998, p. 9.
9 *Variety*, 14-20 December, 1998, p. 64.
10 Richard Segal, as above.
11 Michael Caine, in interview with the author, October 1997.
12 *Sight and Sound*, May 1997, p. 59.
13 Lew Grade, in interview with the author, April 1998.
14 Philip French, *The 40th London Film Festival programme*, November 1996.
15 Ibid.
16 Jevon O'Neill, in interview with the author, January 1999.
17 Kevin Macdonald, in interview with the author, January 1999.
18 Ibid.
19 David Puttnam, in interview with the author, April 1997.
20 Stewart Till, in interview with the author, January 1999.

Chapter 15

Travelling Light

New Art Cinema in the 90s

Claire Smith

One

> The contemporary film-maker should aspire to the condition of internal exile: alert, cynical, open.
>
> (Iain Sinclair)[1]

A number of films have emerged in the 90s which do not fall easily into categories of art or experimental cinema, documentary or fiction. The film-makers share a marginal gaze which when cast on the British landscape transforms banal, insignificant locations into sites of awesome beauty: eerily familiar, startlingly alien. They share a documentary impulse combined with a keen sense of irony, a taste for coincidence, visual puns, tenuous connections and they employ structures of fiction to varying degrees in their work.

The discourse at the heart of the work is by no means confined to the screen, indeed in the light of the current interest in spatial theory, it is difficult to conceive of an individual idiosyncratic vision, an epithet which suggests the work lies beyond or disconnected from social, cultural, historical processes. This is important because spaces such as docklands, shopping centres, industrial parks have been particularly significant to academics for some time as sites of contestable meaning. These films arise out of and contribute to the wider tradition and focus of such studies.[2] Their contribution has been to re-present these sites on cinema screens rather than in academic journals and in so doing add to the discourse.

There are echoes here of that earlier group of British documentary makers of the 30s. Internal exiles as displaced intellectuals, returning from observing foreign cultures to face a changing society and an uncertain position within it, journeying into an unknown Britain, documenting the problems, reporting their findings, remaining steadfastly out of the frame. Unlike their predecessors, the new film-makers cannot envisage a practical transformation of the unspecified problem which lurks in most of their evocations of the country. The landscape they film is imbued with irony, through the act of filming they offer an alternative, outsider's perspective on a recognisably British landscape.

The films are stylistically very different. It is hard to equate the anarchic mad dash of Andrew Kotting's camera in *Gallivant* (1997) with the insistent stare of Patrick Keiller's in *London* (1995) and *Robinson in Space* (1997). It is the gravitation towards insignificant sites, empty, lost spaces which draws them together along with the fact that they managed to secure funding and distribution, (without wanting to over-emphasise the extent of that distribution), and that they emerged as a group via mediation which forged connections between them and rescued them from the critical void which usually surrounds experimental work.

In order for something to be absent from the discourse it has to be presumed to exist in the first place. If we are aware of experimental film practice as anything more than an act of blind faith, it is because people *emerge* from it. The films which emerge speak of the interface between the artistic concerns of the film-maker and the cultural remit of the funders; the consolidation of innovation with the need to envisage a target audience. They also speak of contemporary criticism which provides a framework for the appreciation, or neglect, of new work.

Two

Officially films like those, and maybe this one on paper, shouldn't exist. You know, no-one should be interested in them, no-one should bother to make them and no-one should bother to see them. Of course the exact opposite is true.

(John Maybury)[3]

Common to all these directors is the strong sense of bewilderment that they managed to get their films made at all. They made feature films which stood little chance of making it through the process. At the time of writing there are three main access points to national funding for independent film production: BFI Production, British Screen and the Arts Councils, all of which have benefited from Lottery funding since its introduction in 1995. Feature film production is expensive and risky and the cultural remit of the funding bodies has to be balanced by commercial considerations. This means that the BFI Production Fund favours the work of directors who have already exhibited 'a proven cinematic style' and while the Arts Councils encourage proposals of 'vision and imagination' they must also show the ability 'to communicate to the target audience.' [4]

For a film to be able to prove its viability it must be 'sold' on paper. The script has to contain elements to convince the funders that it will translate to an audience, and this emphasis is often at odds with much innovative film practice which can offer no guarantees. Work which does make it through this process is sometimes seen as having so watered down its experimental impulse as to have sold out. Another danger is that the relative success of these chosen features can cast the experimental sector in the role of training ground, a 'nursery slope' for new big talent, future bankable names.[5] James Mackay (responsible for producing much of Derek Jarman's work) bemoans the difficulty in convincing funding bodies to back an innovative proposal: 'I believe that this kind of fussing around in developing ideas does nobody any good and seems to favour a cinema that is developed from books rather than a cinema which comes from a film language.'[6] Iain Sinclair in his prose travelogue *Lights Out for the Territory* makes much the same point. 'So many films die as proposals, as more and more of the murky material that has to be discovered and dealt with – as the payoff for undergoing all this stress – is dredged out, talked through, de-energised.'[7]

These are not ideal conditions for innovation. An experimental film practice which challenges cinematic process in every aspect, seeks not only aesthetic alternatives but also alternative methods of production, distribution and exhibition. To this end it is most often produced through, and organised around, co-operatives and independent festivals in opposition to the mainstream industry and funding institutions. Of course nothing is that easy to contain, distinctions can always be challenged and the waters muddied as territories overlap. Just as film-makers can move across practices bringing with them a migrant perspective which unsettles and defamiliarises their adopted territory, so too can the organisation of funding bodies shift, altering their remit, enabling them to take greater risks to fund more experimental proposals or, alternatively, tying their hands.

The tradition of an institutionally acceptable art cinema in this country, which offers an alternative to mainstream film-making, disrupting classical narrative conventions whilst proffering an aesthetic closely aligned to European cultural mores, is often entwined with an experimental impulse which investigates and challenges the medium. It could be argued that this merging of identity owes as much to the policy of the funding bodies as it does to the concerns of the film-maker. In this sense Michael O'Pray suggests that the involvement of television in British film production in the 80s led to the production of hybrid art/experimental features, particularly in Jarman and Greenaway's co-productions with the BBC and Channel Four's with the BFI, to the extent that it became difficult to conceive of a separation between the two forms.[8]

This hybridity, the result of a fusion of institutional requirements with the concerns of the directors who emerged out of an experimental arena, finds expression in John Maybury's feature *Love is the Devil* (1998). In contrast to the wandering camera of Andrew Kotting *et al.*, *Love is the Devil* is a film of claustrophobic interiors, submerged in a confined and incestuous 60s Soho Bohemia. Focusing on the relationship between Francis Bacon and his lover George Dyer, their story is told through a fairly conventional narrative, but visually, seductive colour conspires with digital effects and fish eye lenses to produce the beguiling distortions so evocative of Bacon's paintings.

There is also a parallel between Maybury's move to feature/art cinema from experimental/visual art tradition and that of Derek Jarman. Both came from a fine art background; Maybury met Jarman at the London Film-makers Co-op (LFMC) and worked on both *Jubilee* (1978) and *The Last Of England* (1987). Maybury has directed pop promos as well as experimental films and the ease with which he moves between these practices suggests that *Love is the Devil* may not signal the beginning of a career in the industry but an experimental foray into another aspect of moving image production.

Love is the Devil received £360,000 of Lottery funding from the Arts Council of England, was a critical success and introduced Maybury to a wider audience. However it was not his first feature. In an interview for *Vertigo*, he outlines a very different experience for the funding of *Remembrance Of Things Fast* (1993), a challenging, hour-length experimental film which investigates a relationship through an energetic collage of high-tech images.

> I got twenty-five grand from the Arts Council and they were expecting me to make a ten minute piece maybe. Because of my previous work in promos I was able to go to post production facilities and say 'I can give you ten grand but I need a hundred hours' when ten grand would normally buy me five to ten hours.[9]

Love is the Devil (1998) – art and experiment

His knowledge of the system enabled him to make a feature which would usually be impossible. He admits that often this isn't enough: 'On *Love is the Devil* the elements were right at the right time. The combination of forces meant that it could become something more. This is an organic thing that couldn't happen that way in any other situation.'[10] His comments issue a challenge to the contemporary film-maker: it is possible to get around the limitations of funding if you know what you are doing. However the visibility and success of a project relies on a combination of forces over which no one individual or institution has control. A fortuitous collision, a matter of being in the right place at the right time perhaps?

Three

> We all become nomads, migrating across a system which is too vast to be called our own, but in which we are fully involved, translating and transforming bits and elements into local instances of sense. It is this remaking, this transmutation, that makes such texts and languages – the city, cinema, music, culture and the contemporary world habitable: as though they were a space borrowed for a moment by a transient, an immigrant, a nomad.
>
> (Iain Chambers)[11]

In 1992, Patrick Keiller, a few critically well-received shorts tucked under his belt, secured backing from the BFI Production Board for a feature-length project. He had only a fraction of the script in place, the rest was to be assembled after filming: a real gamble tempered by the fact that it would be a kind of documentary, produced on a low budget (£180,000).

London was released in 1994 to critical acclaim, heralded as 'The brightest sign of life in British cinema since early Greenaway.'[12]

In *Lights Out for the Territory*, Iain Sinclair forged connections between Keiller and a counter cultural cinema which foregrounds the immediacy of the act of filming the landscape, a psychogeographic imagination which links him with such film-makers as Michael Reeves and Chris Petit.[13] On the production of Reeves' *Witchfinder General* (1968), Sinclair points out:

> The methodology of this kind of production had much in common with such diverse future titles as Patrick Keiller's *London* and Chris Petit's *Radio On* (1979). In no case was the generating idea written out, enough was held back for the immediate occasion of the shoot: the excitement of the present tense was preserved.[14]

An approach which allows the weather and landscape to fuel the image rather than subverting them to narrative impetus produces tension between the subject and camera, feeding the transformation which enables somewhere to be seen in terms of somewhere else. In this way Reeves' horror film, starring Vincent Price as the eponymous witchfinder, is also 'a Suffolk western, a British cowboy picture', while Petit in his road movie *Radio On* sweeps such a European eye over the British locations that he 'should immediately have been asked to return his passport'.[15]

At the heart of all journeys lies a reason for travelling, a quest. In Petit and Sinclair's film *The Falconer* (1998) this is to pin down the 60s experimental film-maker Peter Whitehead. The journey, littered with red herrings, unfolds through layers of mock documentary interviews and secret rendezvous captured by surveillance cameras, but ultimately leads nowhere. The audience is required to adopt a meditative approach to the film, as if on a journey themselves, viewing the images with the detachment of a passenger gazing out of a train window. As Sinclair says of *Radio On*, 'You are encouraged to let go, let the attention waver, drift with the music'.[16] Keiller's two features require a similar approach. The arrangement of certain shot sequences, in semi-self-contained groups which cast a new light on and question the meaning of each shot, are themselves inseparable from the overall flow of the films, rendering it impossible to make total sense of what passes before our eyes. In fact we are overloaded with information to the point where we find ourselves sinking in this excess of dates, quotes and images. The steady pacing is relentless. As information washes over us it becomes impossible to assimilate every detail. Instead we must give ourselves over to a structure of feeling through which we may make occasional connections. The effect is engrossing in spite of the fact there can be no climax, no obvious pay-back except the elusive promise of a chance to re-imagine or solve the problems of London and England respectively, the ever-present promise of the journey's end; a promise which is only half delivered, tempered in the narrative flow by Robinson's perceived failure.

London chronicles an attempt to transform the city through the eyes of fictional flâneur, Robinson, aided by his travelling companion, the narrator, while simultaneously providing a contemporary document of a city in the midst of recession. The narrator has recently returned from abroad and although Robinson has not left the country for several years he was, we are informed, an enthusiastic flâneur on foreign territory. They are both equipped with an exile's perspective which is adamantly applied to the city. We are made aware of Robinson's anxieties, his despondency, his attraction to earlier literary flâneurs – Montaigne, Rimbaud, Baudelaire. He is an outsider, trailing the flip side of London's heritage, wandering invisibly through a crowd he will never be a part of. He stares from a distance, resolutely detached, moving only in the gaps between a procession of static shots.

His attempts to re-visualise the landscape are dependent on his ability to achieve a perspective rooted in nostalgia and memory, the detachment of a traveller who is able to skim erotic/exotic pleasure off an alien landscape. As the narrator informs us, '"Romanticism" wrote Baudelaire "is a mode of feeling" – for Robinson it is the ability to get outside oneself as if he were in a Romance.' He de-familiarises London, projecting his desires, forgotten histories and strange associations over the city. His problem is that the sites are stubborn. His attempts to transform can verge on the quixotic as incongruities in the shots themselves or the juxtaposition of images and narration filters perspective and fractures the authorial voice. Yet at the same time the specific process of cinematic representation works beyond Robinson's flâneurist sensibilities to transform the everyday into a revelation of the intersection between political, cultural, historical and geographical processes. If in Robinson, Keiller instils the desire to transform through a recognition of alternative readings, focusing on the dialectical nature of sites and the atmosphere of conspiracy which exists in the everyday, it is through the cinematic process that the transformation is fully realised.

In *Robinson In Space*, the manufacturing industry, once the staple of Britain's economy, is now manifest as a spectre in heritage sites and popular memory or revived under foreign ownership. Robinson sets off on his journey around England with a determined nostalgia for modern times past, only to discover along the way an economy which is buoyed by the invisible manufacture of intermediate products and of which the chemical industry is one of the leading players.

The travelogue/documentary organised around Robinson's quest to solve 'the problem of England' and filtered through his friend's narration is a confusing journey which distorts our bearings. There are no supplementary maps to plot our course or totalising views of a city viewed from a comforting distance. Keiller's film does not seek to define actual space but presents a series of postcards, ripped out of context, imposing and solid. Too close to imagine their position in relation to the overall landscape or too distant for us to be able to make sense of what we see, confused as roads and bypasses obscure the view.

Even as the camera disrupts and disorientates our perspective of the country we are constantly, often ironically, made aware of the existence of borders. We leave and enter territories whether these be geographical locations, political constituencies or communications networks. Motorways, ports and railways give way to satellite communications, internet connections and secret spy installations. At the same time the ghosts of previous journeys, historical and fictional, leave traces so that at any one moment, in any frame, we could be in many places at the same time. This layering of boundaries over the same physical site complicates any attempt to conceive of a single reading of the landscape. It is transformed as a result of the acknowledgement of overtly arbitrary definitions as well as the transformation of subject through the cinematic process.

Keiller's appropriation of lost space focuses attention on the absence of visible community for which Robinson yearns. As in *London*, the quest stems both from the urge to document and the desire to transform the landscape and it is in the contingency between these representations that the curious power of the film resides. He forces us to stare with unwarranted concentration at industrial parks and supermarkets, framing the images in classical proportions, holding them for a few seconds too long. The journey is an elegy to solitude, we feel detached and isolated from the subject on screen. Yet viewing the films in the cinema is an oddly communal experience, there is a deal of pleasure to be had in this recognition of England from an 'internal exile's' perspective, filtered through a cultural heritage which hovers over the static images of dilapidated estates and Travel Lodge Inns. The tension between the individual's capacity to negotiate space and the urge to be part of a visible community conspires to produce an unnerving but ever-present suggestion that life is elsewhere or rather that community is only possible, indeed defined, through a recognition of isolation, detachment and solitude. This is a view from the margins, an outsider's epistle, projected against a backdrop of shifting structures, continuing anxieties and momentary euphorias.

The Lux Centre, the new home for the LFMC and London Electronic Arts funded by Lottery money opened in September 1997 with a screening of Andrew Kotting's *Gallivant*. Kotting is a long-term member of the LFMC with roots in experimental shorts as well as performance art and the film was the first BFI film to receive Lottery funding. In *Gallivant* his attraction to the margins is taken to the geographical extreme as he journeys clockwise around the British coastline. While Keiller absents himself and his characters from the frame, Kotting hurls himself, his daughter (Eden), his grandmother (Gladys), his crew and as many chanced-upon eccentrics in front of the camera as he can. Keiller journeys with a quiet, steadfast political motivation, Kotting's quest is personal. He does not shy away from the fact that time is running out for his central characters. Both Eden and Gladys have limited life expectancy and we are made aware that this could be their last chance to get to know each other as well as their country. The seaside locations and shots of great-grandmother and daughter on the beach in matching red coats add to the home movie appeal of the film, but it is decidedly more than this.

Where Keiller envisages the city through a palimpsest of fictional narration, literary and historical heritage, contemporary events and images, Kotting has Gladys and Eden to interpret the coastline of Britain and commune with the found cast. Three generations getting

Gallivant (1997) – the attraction of margins

to know each other, their history, their language (Eden communicates in sign language), getting to know the country, tied securely to the present tense. Allusions to decay and death, a sense of time running out, shabby seaside resorts, dissatisfied locals, and time lapse photography suggesting the erosion of the land by relentless waves, accentuate the passage of time but do not swamp the film. This is no melancholy piece. Kotting is a hyperactive host, his antics (whether viewed as surreal performance or, as Gladys puts it, buggering-about) complement his fast and loose approach to film-making, jump cuts, black and white inserts, constant recourse to signs and symbols, weather maps and hand signals. At all times personal motives are foregrounded as is the process and paraphernalia of film-making. The constraints of low-budget film-making set the parameters of these films as limitations are turned into stylistic strengths. For both Kotting and Keiller, sets and locations are the found landscapes they encounter on travels with cameras which at once defamiliarise and transform.

Four

> This new British cinema (born of the polytechnic and art schools) – promoting
> psychogeography, the journey, the quest, a close examination of random particulars . . .
> a vitalising alternative to the once lively, now largely inert, documentary programme
> fillers of mainstream TV.
>
> (Iain Sinclair)[17]

The wave of optimism which accompanied the opening of the Lux and the premiere of the first film made with Lottery money did not last. A year later, at a conference on 'The State of Independence', the mood had darkened considerably. The cinema was packed with filmmakers, producers, representatives of funding bodies and critics eager to discuss the implications of the findings of the government's Film Policy Review Group, *A Bigger Picture*. The need for a voice in the debate, for visibility, for acknowledgement of the importance of cultural film-making, are stressed. Plans for a rationalisation of independent film funding do little to ease the anxiety. The Film Council which would provide one national access point for funding, incorporating BFI Production, British Screen, Arts Council films and the promised Alpha fund (which could divert Lottery money into cultural film-making) is regarded with suspicion by many in the independent sector as yet another example of the centralising tendencies of a government with an overtly populist agenda.

There was also conflict; not everyone can agree on what constitutes independent cinema. A voice in the crowd suggested that the only true independent source of funding for filmmakers is the dole, an institution which is itself under threat from recent government initiatives. Although the report was widely held to be an admirable attempt to come to terms with the needs of the film industry, there was little doubt that the role of innovation and experiment was not under the review group's remit.

So what does a view from the margins have to offer? The motif of absence is one which is as central to an understanding of the discourse surrounding cultural film-making as it is to an understanding of Keiller's films. This is Britain after all, a place where modernism did not so much refuse to take root as dematerialise, to hover out there somewhere in that space reserved for underground culture, manifesting itself every now and then in experimental practice which, through no fault of its own, secures distribution and becomes visible for a moment, or surfaces in hybrid form.

Between the third and fourth 'chapters' of *Robinson in Space*, the travellers, weary and sick from a poor diet of supermarket food and insipid coffee, arrive at a West Bromwich chemical manufacturers, Robinson Brothers Ltd. The camera focuses its fixed stare on a factory yard: blue barrels containing who knows what pile up at the back, a lone figure sidles away in the middle distance. The space is empty; an absence of people, an absence of visible product, a melancholy image which is disrupted by the narration informing us of the warm and generous hospitality they received courtesy of the Robinson Brothers (Robinson claimed they 'were kindly looked after for two weeks while we convalesced'.) The narrator quotes Doreen Massey: 'amid the Ridley Scott images of world cities ... Baudrillard visions of hyperspace .... Most people actually still live in places like Harlesden or West Brom.' But the absence of people in the image unsettles the text. The sequence is disrupted, the fourth journey begins, at a bus stop, in the rain.... 'waiting in a bus shelter with your shopping for a bus that never comes'. At which point a bus arrives for Robinson, but he has already disappeared 'to a sexual encounter with a stranger he encountered on the internet'.

There is nothing to hold on to, no way of getting your bearings as arbitrary connections, signs, fictional encounters compete with the reality, the everyday nature of the sites to question and defamiliarise them. The Hyundai works, on its international industrial estate is parodied by the familiar red brick of innocuous West Brom which is in turn parodied by its international connections. The sites which occupy the new film-makers seem to conspire with the recognition of absence at the heart of British culture, the absence of labour and product, of innovation and a visible community. Wastelands, industrial estates,

Robinson in Space – the primacy of landscape over script

out-of-town supermarkets are non-places, complicit evocations of the atmosphere of exile which pervades the work. Yet as old structures dissolve so new sites of contact emerge. As Robinson's mobile phone and portable computer provide him with the means to transcend barriers (for a limited time at least), so the film-makers manage to create their images of Britain against the odds, layering perspectives, encouraging alternative, nomadic visions.

The connection between Keiller, Kotting and Petit is the primacy of the landscape over script, the possibility of fortuitous connections between the act of filming and the subject, a sense of getting one over on the institutions and a DIY approach. They travel lightly over the surface of the landscape, seemingly self-sufficient.

The last decade has seen the development of digital technologies and the attendant avail-ability of cheaper equipment. Now if you want to make a film to high production standards it is possible to do so on a limited budget. Chris Petit in an article for *Vertigo* suggests that soon we will all have it within our power to produce a film:

> There is now no excuse not to make a movie. In the past you could always blame someone else ('they turned down my script'). Now there is only yourself to blame ... Which is precisely what is both good and bad about the way things are now ... The good and bad of it is, you're on your own.[18]

The emergence of these films proves that it is possible to work around the structures, to produce innovative work on a low budget. In celebrating the individual's capacity for trans-formation, for existing in the gaps and carving out an alternative experimental vision, it would be a mistake to underestimate the importance of the structures which allow for such interpretation. A critical approach which allows for the possibility of chance connections and fortuitous opportunity but never for one moment ignores the parameters which limit the way in which we are able to perceive these visions, lies at the heart of this cinema. Keith Griffiths begins his essay, 'Anxious visions' with a quote by Paul Klee: 'Art does not portray what is visible, but renders visible.'[19] In revealing a forgotten/unknown Britain, effecting transformations of the everyday, using strategies to render ambiguous, these film-makers do just that.

However in writing about those films which emerge into the discourse it is necessary to ask what it is that renders art visible. The visibility of this largely experimental work can be seen as a serendipitous intersection between the desires of the facilitators, restricted and often thwarted by the commercial imperatives of funding institutions, the formal and theoretical concerns of the film-makers themselves, and the mediation of these films in the contemporary discourse which surrounds them. It is this revelation/forging of connections of the individual to their contemporaries as well as to a hidden British film history pro-moting an exile's perspective, that forms the identity of the new cinema.

Notes

1 Iain Sinclair, 'Big granny and little Eden', *Sight and Sound*, September 1997, p. 21.
2 Of particular relevance to Keiller's films are: Michel de Certeau, *The Practice of Everyday Life* (Berkeley, CA: University of California Press, 1988), the work of Henri Lefebvre, including *Critique of Everyday Life* (London: Verso, 1991); Doreen Massey, *Space, Place and Gender* (Cambridge: Polity Press: 1994); Marc Auge, *Non-Places: Introduction to an Anthropology of Supermodernity* (London: Verso, 1995).

3 John Maybury, interview with Ben Gibson, 'Love is the Devil', *Vertigo*, no. 8, Summer 1998, p. 31.

4 Susan Forrester, *The Arts Funding Guide: 97/98* (London: Directory of Social Change, 1996), pp. 122–32.

5 *A Bigger Picture – The Report of the Film Policy Review Group* (London: DCMS, 1998), p. 19.

6 James Mackay, 'Low Budget British Production: A Producer's Account', in Duncan Petrie (ed.), *New Questions of British Cinema* (London: BFI, 1992), p. 56.

7 Iain Sinclair, *Lights out for the Territory: 9 Excursions in the Secret History of London* (London: Granta, 1997), pp. 293–4.

8 Michael O'Pray, 'The British Avant-Garde and Art Cinema from the 70s to the 90s', in Andrew Higson (ed.), *Dissolving Views* (London: Cassell, 1996), p. 189.

9 Maybury, 'Love is the Devil', p. 35.

10 Ibid., p. 31.

11 Iain Chambers, 'Cities Without Maps' in J. Bird (ed.), *Mapping The Futures* (London: Routledge, 1993) p. 193.

12 Tony Rayns, 'Berlin notes', *Sight and Sound*, April 1994, p. 4.

13 Iain Sinclair, *Lights Out*, p. 298. See also his *Sight and Sound* review, 'London, necropolis of fretful ghosts' (June 1994).

14 Sinclair, *Lights Out*, pp. 293–4.

15 Ibid., pp. 293 and 314.

16 Ibid., p. 313.

17 Sinclair, 'Big granny', p. 21.

18 Chris Petit, 'The freefall death of the cultural critic and other related matters, or, the art of nonchalance', *Vertigo*, no. 8, Summer 1998, p. 9.

19 Keith Griffiths, 'Anxious visions', *Vertigo*, Winter 94/95, p. 47.

Chapter 16
Men in the 90s

Claire Monk

To begin by quoting Thomas Elsaesser out of context, the 1990s could aptly be summarised as 'hard times, interesting times' for men and masculinity as represented in the British cinema of the decade.[1] Hard times, that is, for many of the male protagonists of 1990s British films; interesting times in terms of the emergence of men and masculinity as key themes of 1990s British cinema, and the diversity (and at best richness) of representations this engendered.

To an almost unprecedented extent, 1990s British cinema seemed preoccupied with men and masculinity in crisis. These crises spanned the post-industrial economic desperation of the male no-longer-working class represented by the stripping ex-steelworkers of *The Full Monty* (Peter Cattaneo, 1997), the penniless Catholic father in Ken Loach's *Raining Stones* (1993), the tormented ex-miner turned party-hire clown in *Brassed Off* (Mark Herman, 1997); the damage by dysfunctional or absent fathering suffered by half brothers Jack and Tommy in Peter Chelsom's dark comedy *Funny Bones* (1995), by Ray in Gary Oldman's brutal drama *Nil by Mouth* (1997) and by the vulnerable Nottingham youths of Shane Meadows' *TwentyFourSeven* (1998); the scatter-gun existential rage of the itinerant rapist/seer Johnny in Mike Leigh's *Naked* (1993); and Charles's emotional inarticulacy in *Four Weddings and a Funeral* (Mike Newell, 1994).

The decade also produced a range of more fluid and provocative images of masculinity in films which engaged with the changeability (and in some cases loudly celebrated the polymorphousness) of gender and sexual relations rather than mourning the passing of patriarchal certainties. While the commercial and artistic successes of the later 1990s seemed dominated by post-industrial male trauma, it should be recalled that *The Crying Game* (Neil Jordan, 1992), an IRA thriller organised around gender confusion and ambiguously tender male bonding between captor and captive, remains one of 1990s British cinema's biggest international hits. Further examples range from the last works of Derek Jarman to the flawed attempt to depict a multiracial, polysexual youth culture in Isaac Julien's ill-received *Young Soul Rebels* (1991) to US director Todd Haynes' personal vision of the artifice and sexual ambivalence of British 70s glam-rock masculinity in *Velvet Goldmine* (1998). Also significant are the North London 'new men' of the romance *Truly, Madly, Deeply* (Anthony Minghella, 1991), Ewan McGregor as bisexual object of desire in *The Pillow Book* (Peter Greenaway, 1996) and the transsexual romance of Richard Spence's groundbreaking but barely released *Different for Girls* (1996).

It is significant, though, that (with a few high-profile exceptions) such post-patriarchal masculinities received a limited circulation, confined to art cinema distribution or marginalised on the mainstream exhibition circuit. It is true that one face of Britain in the 1990s was the acceptance of an increasingly wide spectrum of sexual identities and practices – in particular, it appeared that male gayness had gained mainstream acceptance as a lifestyle (or cluster of lifestyles).[2] But this decade of sexual liberalism was also a decade in which homophobia still lingered and in which the apparent ascendancy of women in the post-industrial workplace heralded a resurgence of masculinism and misogyny.

I would argue that this post-feminist male panic, and the resultant mix of masculinist reaction and masculine self-scrutiny, have been the defining influences shaping the dominant images of men produced in the British films of the decade. My core argument will be that 1990s British cinema's intensified attention to men should not be read as denoting a progressive, liberalising or egalitarianising shift in the gender and sexual politics of British cinema or society. What was new about this preoccupation with men was its self-consciousness, its confessional and therapeutic impulses (its admission of male neediness and pain) and its attentiveness to men and masculinity as subjects-in-themselves. However, the emergence of this impulse within the mainstream of British cinema at a moment when the fallout of post-industrialism and Thatcherism collided with the gains of feminism, produced a strand of male-focused films whose gender politics were more masculinist than feminist.

While 1990s British cinema's preoccupation with men was clearly the product of a perceived crisis in male economic power and gender privilege, the images of men and masculinity it spawned were often complex, hybrid and contradictory. Their ambiguities cannot be adequately analysed without reference to the wider mesh of socio-economic changes from which this preoccupation with men emerged. Of particular relevance to my arguments in this chapter are the rise of a 'new lad' media and consumer culture and the 1990s tendency for commercially-aspirant British films to deploy equivalent narrative, casting and marketing strategies to those associated with post-classical Hollywood.[3] The meanings generated by such films tended to be pluralistic, fragmentary and often contradictory rather than ideologically cohesive.

In this context, the ambiguous or contradictory images of men in many 1990s British films can be read as a strategy of commercial and political pragmatism intended to multiply and maximise audience appeal rather than as mere incoherence. Men were addressed as a social problem, a political interest group and a consumer market often simultaneously within the same film; and the commercial and political need to address both male and female grievances meant that the line between critique and celebration of the masculinities being portrayed was often blurred.

Furthermore, the 1990s trend towards the increasing centralisation of British box-office success among one or two films per year meant that the representations of masculinity in a small number of major international British hits – The Crying Game, Four Weddings and a Funeral, The Full Monty – received an exponentially wider circulation than those in relative box-office failures. This trend made box-office revenues an increasingly questionable indicator of a film's socio-cultural resonance or cinematic interest, and in such a commercial climate it became increasingly unlikely that images of masculinity which might challenge rather than flatter the perspective and prejudices of the mainstream cinema audience (those aged 18–25, and implicitly heterosexual and male) would receive the support from distributors and exhibitors necessary to ensure a wide release. Gentler and weaker male characters tended to be found in niche hits from genres (such as romance and period drama) associated with an older and/or female audience. More provocative or less complacent images of masculinity – such as those in Different for Girls, John Maybury's Love is the Devil (1998) and Jez Butterworth's Mojo (1997) – tended to be confined to art cinemas or denied adequate UK exhibition.

The representations of men and masculinities projected in British films of the 1990s are most accurately understood in terms of a range of contradictory tensions within 1990s British society between, on the one hand, growing sexual liberalism, greater female participation and achievement in the world of work and increasing fluidity of gender roles, and on the other, a reactionary upsurge of masculinism and misogyny. Nineties British cinema could be summarised as a cinema which both engaged in critically deconstructing and interrogating the masculinities it portrayed, and participated in an increasingly sophisticated media and consumer culture which was aggressively multiplying its attempted appeals to men on the basis of lifestyle. The sections below discuss some of the most significant of these trends in male representation.

New Men

The main media-led fashion in masculinity of the late 1980s/early 1990s, the 'new man' – characterised in a frenzy of media discussion as supportive, in touch with his emotions, keen to share equally in the predominantly female burdens of childcare and housework and open to spending money on his appearance – had only a marginal impact on the images of men favoured by 1990s British films compared to the more enduring, influential and populist 'new lad' trend which followed it. The reasons for this may lie in the fact that the 'new man' was a media construction who owed more to advertisers' desires to create a new consumer market sector than to an actual or incipient increase in equality in the gendered division of unpaid labour.[4]

While the appeal of the new man to women – the promise of a combination of sensitivity, sex appeal and support in household tasks – was obvious, his popular appeal as a role model to the majority of men was far from clear. Once the growth of the new lad media market (instigated by the launch of *loaded* magazine in 1994) had demonstrated that it was amply possible to sell designer fashion and beauty products to men by appealing to their sexism rather than by exploiting the imagery of proto-feminist reconstruction, the new man's days as a consumer lifestyle model (in reality, his primary function) were numbered.

In keeping with the new man's primary appeal to women, and especially those of child-rearing and/or first-time homemaking age, the appearances of new men tended to be limited to films and genres – such as contemporary romances and costume dramas – with a known appeal to female filmgoers.[5] The one out-and-out new man hit of the decade was *Truly, Madly, Deeply*, a weepy but emotionally-mature exploration of bereavement, mourning and new love in which both the dead partner and counsellor from beyond the grave (Alan Rickman), and the eventual new love (Michael Maloney), of the grieving heroine (Juliet Stevenson) are models of reconstructed, post-feminist sensitivity. Two indices of the Maloney character's quirky, non-traditional masculinity are that he works with Down's Syndrome children and that he performs spontaneous magic tricks in public. However, the credibility of these characterisations rested heavily on the film's middle-class North London therapy-belt setting and the quality of its performances. The new man's rare appearances in films with contemporary settings tended to be concentrated in such relatively affluent and metropolitan milieux: another performance by Rickman, as an enigmatic hippy millionaire reacting in peculiarly laid-back fashion to his wife's torrid affair with her brother in Stephen Poliakoff's *Close My Eyes* (1991), and Richard E. Grant's widower left holding the baby in the romantic comedy *Jack & Sarah* (Tim Sullivan, 1995), are two further examples.

A far wider range of representations with affinities to the new man ideal can be found in the shy, weak, flustered and often overtly proto-feminist male heroes and lovers of 1990s post-heritage period dramas. This affirms the importance of these films as an arena in which debates around gender and sexuality were often worked through more radically than in mainstream films with contemporary settings, but also confirms the new man's status as a fantasy object, and suggests that his qualities were less likely to be received cynically by audiences when presented outside the context of the present. In *Sense and Sensibility* (Ang Lee, 1995), for example, the shy Edward (Hugh Grant) – object of the sensible Elinor (Emma Thompson)'s unspoken affections – is not only more satellite than protagonist in a drama in which active female characters are central, but is presented as a victim of the same patriarchal inheritance system which oppresses the film's women. While the death of their father deprives sisters Elinor and Marianne (and their mother) of their home because their brother has inherited everything, Edward's status as inheriting son gives his family leverage to control his life by forbidding him to marry Elinor or enter the clergy. However, such examples serve to confirm the new man as a figure who was most feasible within the parameters and concerns of middle-class cinema.

Hard Times

If the new man – a figure who implicitly signified an easygoing, voluntary sacrifice of male power and privilege – did not find wide favour in 1990s British films, this was largely because the dominant mood colouring the British films of the decade was that men were already, non-voluntarily, disempowered. The structural changes of the post-industrial era had, by the 1990s, virtually obliterated two employment strata overwhelmingly dominated by men – unskilled workers and middle-management – from the workforce. By contrast, the 1990s saw women making increasingly confident inroads into the expanding white-collar and service industries, placing them among the most significant recruits to an expanded middle class.[6] Even though this feminisation of the workforce was substantially founded on the flexibility of women in tolerating work which was part-time, insecure and ill-paid, the impression grew of a society in which women were in the ascendancy in the workplace and beyond. By contrast, masculinity – especially jobless, skill-less masculinity – was increasingly defined as a problem. Educational underachievement by boys relative to the gains being made by girls; evidence that increasing numbers of young men were continuing to live in their parental home well into their twenties; and a recorded increase in mental illness and suicides among young men, all added to the diagnosis that young masculinity especially was in trouble. New reproductive technologies added to the male terror of obsolescence: a terror which is, in effect, the central narrative problem explored in *The Full Monty*. In the words of the film's hero Gaz (Robert Carlyle): 'A few years more, and men won't exist. . . . We're obsolete. Dinosaurs. Yesterday's news'.

As the 1990s progressed, it became increasingly evident that a central project of much British mainstream cinema was to work through such concerns, and the wider sense of a male crisis. Some of the most commercially successful of these films – *Brassed Off* and particularly *The Full Monty* – transformed the problems of male unemployment and social exclusion and related psychic crises into incongruously feelgood comedy, and it seems significant that it was these films which felt most able to offer male audiences a symbolic, if inevitably problematic, solution. But the predicament of the jobless working-class/underclass male was also a central subtext in more pessimistic films such as *Naked, Nil by Mouth,*

Antonia Bird's *Face* (1997), Scott Michell's *The Innocent Sleep* (1996), and a range of youth-orientated dramas in which crime and/or drugs were central – *Shopping* (Paul Anderson, 1994), *Trainspotting* (Danny Boyle, 1996), *Twin Town* (Kevin Allen, 1997) and Shane Meadows's *Smalltime* (1996) and *TwentyFourSeven* (1997).[7]

There are clear distinctions in the stance on male crisis adopted by the films in these various strands. With the exception of Meadows's work, the youth-orientated films presented young male joblessness and social exclusion as taken-for-granted states with no history, no proposed solution and no expectation of change. With detached irony, they framed the male underclass not as a 'social problem' but as a subcultural 'lifestyle' with certain attractions for a young, post-political male audience. Rather than attempting to arouse anger or social outrage, *Trainspotting* and especially *Twin Town* encouraged a knowing, empathetic complicity between audiences and the films' young male inhabitants. These films address the anxieties of young male viewers by portraying the young male underclass in terms of an appealing subculture of dissent from the demands of adulthood, women and work.

Importantly, this stance meant that the youth-underclass dramas, although targeted to appeal to young men, were not structured around an attempt to capitalise on male resentment of female advancement. While both *Twin Town* and *Trainspotting* present paid work and serious study as female activities, suggesting a society in which traditional gender roles had been inverted, they show little outrage at the supposed excesses of female empowerment or the loss of the male 'right to work'. Indeed, girls and women were marginal figures in both films, suggesting that the female pursuit of work and qualifications was itself marginal to the young male's sphere of interest. In *Twin Town*, female work (represented by the dubious job as a massage-parlour 'receptionist' undertaken by the car-nicking male protagonist's sister) is portrayed as unworthy of emulation or respect.[8] In *Trainspotting*, Diane (Kelly Macdonald), the ultra-assured young woman who picks up Renton (Ewan McGregor) at a disco but is revealed next morning to be still at school (and in uniform), is infinitely more empowered than any of the male characters; but the film copes with this by confining her to a single narrative episode and presenting her assurance as an excess and therefore a joke.

By contrast, the comedies of male post-industrial unemployment, *The Full Monty* and, to a more extreme degree, *Brassed Off*, were explicitly, and bitterly, preoccupied with male disempowerment. Moreover, despite their nominal subject matter – the loss of working-class male labour power – both films consistently and pointedly expressed the problems of the post-industrial male in a 'feminised' society as problems of gender, rather than economic, relations.[9]

Masculinity and class: from *Four Weddings and a Funeral* to *The Full Monty*

The crises of masculinity with which the films discussed in this chapter are concerned are class-specific and there is an interesting trajectory from the southern, bourgeois social-ritual-centred comedy of *Four Weddings and a Funeral* in 1994 to the northern, working-class unemployment comedy of *The Full Monty*, which displaced it as British cinema's biggest all-time hit in 1997–8. Each film is, in its way, narratively organised around the exploration of contemporary British gender relations and around the articulation and resolution of a problem of masculinity: Charles's inability to express emotions or commit himself to a relationship in *Four Weddings*; the unemployed males' desperation for work, loss of self-esteem and consequent relationship difficulties in *The Full Monty*.

The obvious differences between the two films suggest that in the mid-1990s a quantum shift took place in British cinema's preferred (and most exported) projection of the contemporary nation in terms of class and gender. However, in the context of the parallel shifts in political leadership from John Major to Tony Blair, and in the preferred official articulation of national identity from warm beer and cricket to Cool Britannia (with its vision of a middle-class nation built on 'creative' entrepreneurialism) it is vital that the *Four Weddings–Full Monty* shift should not be read at face value as symbolising a simple transference of national identity from southern bourgeois professionals to northern unemployed labour. Rather, I would suggest that in *The Full Monty* (and also in *Brassed Off*) working-class masculinity functions as the sign for a wider, cross-class range of male experience. The appeal of these films to a wide, especially male, audience can be explained in terms of their appropriation of working-class masculinity and its problems as an emblem for a wider range of male insecurities and fears in need of reassurance.

It is noticeable, for example, that in both *Brassed Off* and *The Full Monty*, the working class whose passing is being mourned is defined as a community of *men*. Both films are preoccupied not with the effects of post-industrial male unemployment on the community at large, but with its impact on men. The crises played out in their narratives arouse audience emotions not around a lost era of stable employment and the old industries in themselves but around the lost homosocial communities these industries represented and the silent yet powerful masculine emotional bonds associated with them. *The Full Monty*'s steelworks is long closed; it is Gaz's discovery that the working-men's club (traditionally, and notoriously, an institution from which women without men are banned) is being used as a male stripping venue for female-only audiences that provides the film's initial narrative trigger. From the opening scenes of *Brassed Off*, we are repeatedly told that the colliery closure the film's miners are fighting is probably a *fait accompli*. It is the possibility that the colliery

Brassed Off (1996) – Gloria (Tara Fitzgerald) in a community of men

brass band (and, analogously, the masculine emotional community rooted in the work-place) will also die that is presented as the ultimate tragedy.

It is this arousing of powerful emotion around the idea of men as a community under threat that explains the widespread and powerful appeal of these films for male audiences. Both films play out a drama in which the male social and emotional bonds once associated with the workplace and the working-men's club are threatened, mourned, struggled for – and finally restored. Thus the solution they offer to the anxieties of a wider 1990s male audi-ence is one of emotional acknowledgement, catharsis and reassurance.

However, this solution raises the problem of misogyny. In *Brassed Off*, the threatened community to be remembered and preserved is expressly one which excluded women (who were not allowed to play in the colliery band any more than they were permitted to enter the working-men's club). Flugelhorn player Gloria (Tara Fitzgerald) is permitted to join the band – despite her 'class enemy' status as a successful woman and representative of management – because she is the film's love interest and has patriarchal links with the pit: her dead grandfather was the coal-face partner or 'marrer' of bandleader Danny (Pete Postlethwaite). But even Gloria is kept in her place throughout the film by means of sexist humour (she is repeatedly referred to as 'Gloria Stits') and put-downs; and the claim by the miners that the report she is preparing on the pit's viability is merely cosmetic and will be ignored by her bosses proves to be true. *Brassed Off*'s other female characters – lacking youth or beauty and therefore redundant in terms of the film's value system – are portrayed without exception as grotesques or heartless bitches.

New Misogyny, New Laddism

What was startling about *Brassed Off* was that its misogyny was both systematic and gratu-itous (in the sense of being extraneous to the film's needs). However, its puerile humour, resentment of women and loathing of the older female body – traits which the film's writer-director Mark Herman reprised in his next hit, *Little Voice* (1998) – were consistent with a resurgence of misogyny in the wider culture. Misogyny had, of course, never gone away, but in the 1990s gained a new respectability in some quarters, provided it was cloaked in post-modern irony or humour, or justified in terms of a backlash against the gains of fem-inism. The trend for sexist humour and the acceptable sexual commodification of women (typically defended as willing self-commodification for profit and a post-feminist exercis-ing of female sexual power) were particularly associated with 'new laddism', itself a male backlash against the media- and female-imposed ideal of the new man.

Although new laddism found its official media organ with the launch of the men's monthly magazine *loaded* in 1994, the new lad's endurance suggested that (in contrast with the new man) his media inventors had astutely tapped into a male mood (and a new lifestyle market, older and more affluent than the word lad implied) already latent in the culture. The new lad ethos was neatly encapsulated in *loaded*'s cover line: 'for men who should know better'. At best, the new lad stood for a humorous, hedonistic and above all regres-sive escape from the demands of maturity – and women. In film terms, *Trainspotting, Twin Town* and especially the jokey East End crime thriller *Lock Stock and Two Smoking Barrels* (Guy Ritchie, 1998) all owed much of their success to lad appeal. The only two noticeable female characters in *Lock Stock* ... are a card-dealer and a comatose stoned girl, who is treated as a piece of furniture: other characters literally sit on her.[10] Aspects of the editor-ial content of *loaded* and the other men's monthlies which remodelled themselves in its image, and research into the attitudes of their readers, suggests that the new lad was reactionary not only in his attitude to women. A 1998 readership survey conducted by the men's magazine *Maxim* revealed that more than sixty per cent of its selected sample of 16–30-year-old males wanted the death penalty to be restored, while forty per cent wanted to see the police armed.[11] In spring 1999, *loaded*'s founding editor James Brown was sacked from his new post as editor of rival men's monthly *GQ* after running a feature which named Rommel as one of the '200 most stylish men of the 20th century'.[12]

The Ambiguity of Critique

The analyses of problematic masculinity offered by two of the most ambitious and important British films of the decade, *Naked* and *Nil by Mouth* require a more complex response. Both of these films reveal the difficulties inherent in attempting the analytical representation of pathological masculinity and male brutality on screen. The refusal of *Naked*'s writer/director Mike Leigh to take a stance on the behaviour of his tormented protagonist, Johnny (David Thewlis) – a serial interrogator and abuser of women – asserting that he'd 'rather let [the film] speak for itself' made *Naked*'s coruscating pessimism all the more disturbing, but also laid it open to charges of misogyny.[13]

My initial objection to *Naked* rested on the uniform passivity or masochism of virtually every woman Johnny encountered (the initial rape victim excepted): I felt that the totality of this absence of resistance defied credibility. Re-evaluating *Naked* retrospectively, I feel that it tapped into some depth of despair which I failed to recognise at the time; but this does not absolve the film from criticism. *Naked*'s attempt to show, but not comment on, misogyny and sexual violence is hugely problematic. Our distance as viewers from Johnny's position is never clearly delineated, producing a complicity with, rather than distance from, his perspective on the film's women – a perspective which is nastily interrogatory even when he is not dishing out violence or humiliation. Andy Medhurst argues that:

Nil by Mouth (1997) – the pathology of masculinity. Ray Winstone as 'Ray'

> Johnny... is indulged by the film to a rather frightening degree – he might be a rapist but
> at least he's not posh.... And where are the women? Fucked, hiding and bleeding,
> basically, peripheral or allegorical in this remorselessly male landscape.[14]

The fear that *Naked* may have drawn the bulk of its audience from those who enjoyed this,
is not allayed by the available audience data, which suggests that seventy-nine per cent of
Naked's UK cinema audience was male.[15]

By contrast, actor Gary Oldman's *Nil by Mouth* – a more formally innovative film than
Leigh's, indeed, one of the most cinematically extraordinary British films of the decade –
scrupulously resists the pitfalls of voyeurism in its depiction of a South East London
working-class marriage pushed to the brink by husband Ray (Ray Winstone)'s alcoholic
rages and horrific violence towards his wife Val (Kathy Burke). This care is undoubtedly
connected with Oldman's deep personal investment in the project: Ray is a portrait of his
father, himself an alcoholic; the film was shot in locations familiar to Oldman from his
childhood; and his sister, 'Laila Morse' (an anagram of *mia sorella*) performs in the film as
Val's stoically supportive mother Janet.

What is especially significant vis-à-vis *Nil by Mouth*'s stance on the dysfunctional masculinity it portrays, is the constant tension between intimate involvement and critical
distance achieved by the film's director of photography Ron Fortunato. The headline on
Sight and Sound's feature about the film – 'Being there' – precisely summarises the relation
to events this produces for the viewer.[16] The camera places us among the characters, yet its
constant, rapid mobility and the *vérité* framing militate against the identification expected
of a conventional close-up. Our sense of separation from the characters is intensified by the
fact that our view of them is almost always mediated by other objects. We are placed in the
position of being squashed up against the characters, of having them invade our space, yet
of constantly having to work to make sense of what is going on.

When we first encounter Ray – ordering a large round of drinks at a bar – the camera
seems to have caught him by accident. It is only on a second viewing that the significance
of the round Ray is ordering becomes clear. He orders a round for himself and his male
mates before recalling that he is, nominally, out for the night with Val, her mother and her
friends and is supposed to be buying them drinks. Having delivered the round to Val's
party, he returns to his mates as rapidly as possible. Thus, from the outset, *Nil by Mouth*
establishes a sense of homosocial space. Even at home, Ray's social mingling is entirely with
other men: if the women come in, the men go upstairs, or out. This homosociality is
marked as pathological by means of the contrast between Ray's all-male social circle and
Val's mixed-sex group of friends. Indeed, it is Ray's jealous rage when Val refuses to let him
stop her from playing pool with a male friend that precipitates the beating from Ray in
which Val loses the child she is carrying.

The masculinity of Ray and his friends is also marked as problematic by the style and
rhythms of dialogue. *Nil by Mouth* has received much praise for the authenticity of its
working-class language; but the male discourse expressed in the film has more specific qualities. That the film opens with a monologue from Ray that we cannot readily make sense
of is significant. Ray and his mates never stop talking, yet most of their discourse communicates next to nothing. Their bar-room chat is more patter than communication. Their
lingo is ripely male, yet full of childish diminutives ('bluey' = blue movie; 'hardy' = hard-
on). At least two meanings to the film's title are explicitly suggested within the film (the
medical ban on eating and drinking imposed on Ray's father in the advanced stages of

alcoholism, and Ray's starvation of affection by his father), but the foregrounding of incessant male speech suggests a third one: if we don't catch everything these men are saying, maybe that's because they're saying nothing – nil by mouth. By contrast, the film's women speak less, but their utterances have a utilitarian function in contrast with the men's endless anecdotes about orgies and 'bent birds'.

Nil by Mouth's circular dialogue and cyclical narrative accrue to suggest a gendered cycle of damage: the reproduction of damaged and damaging relationships between father and son and between man and woman. Thus the film functions at the structural level as an eloquent, yet sympathetic, critique of traditional 'hard' masculinity and its impositions on women. Yet even a film as lucidly analytical as *Nil by Mouth* is ambiguous, and capable of multiple, perhaps less progressive, readings, in its portrayal of Ray. For understandable reasons, the camera lingers on Ray, not Val, during his vicious attack on her; and also at other times, as if trying to seek out the reasons for his war with himself, and others, as a man. But the film's concentration on Ray (who does, after all, represent Oldman's own father), coupled with the power of Ray Winstone's performance, lends its critique of masculinity considerable ambivalence. Despite its seemingly critical stance on Ray and his mates, the film spends far more time with them than with Val – suggesting an enduring fascination, more widely evident in 1990s British films, with the unreconstructed world of men.

Notes

1 Elsaesser's phrase originated as a comment on the impact of Thatcherism on 1980s British cinema. Thomas Elsaesser, 'Images for Sale: The "New" British Cinema', in Lester Friedman (ed.), *British Cinema and Thatcherism* (London: UCL Press, 1993), p. 52.

2 The discursive shift to characterising gayness as a *lifestyle* – i.e. as a group identity defined by shared *consumption practices* – did, of course, also imply a depoliticisation (and commodification) of gay identity, a shift much criticised by some gay commentators.

3 See Thomas Austin: 'Gendered Displeasures: *Basic Instinct* and Female Viewers', *Journal of Popular British Cinema*, no. 2, 1999, p. 6. For a fuller analysis of these strategies in relation to post-classical Hollywood, see Thomas Schatz, 'The New Hollywood', in Jim Collins, Hilary Radner and Ava Preacher Collins (eds), *Film Theory Goes to the Movies* (New York and London: Routledge, 1993), pp. 8–36.

4 Several surveys undertaken during the decade confirmed that by 1998, British women were still spending far more hours on housework per week than their male partners even though they were also working full-time.

5 See, for example, the data from *Caviar 12* (London: BMRB International Limited, 1995) analysed by Claire Monk in 'Heritage films and the British cinema audience in the 1990s', *Journal of Popular British Cinema*, no. 2, January 1999, Table 2.2, p. 30.

6 In 1975, members of the professional, managerial and clerical occupational grades ABC1 comprised 36.2 per cent of the UK population; by 1997–9, the percentage was 48.4 per cent (figures rounded up to one decimal place). Source: NRS survey, cited in 'Definitions Fuel Debate', *Guardian*, 15 January 1999, p. 3.

7 For a more detailed discussion of *Smalltime*, see Claire Monk, 'From underworld to underclass: crime and British cinema in the 1990s' in Steve Chibnall and Robert Murphy (eds), *British Crime Cinema* (London: Routledge, 1999), pp. 172–88.

8 *Shopping* differed substantially from this model in that its youth criminal subculture was bi-gendered, with its main female character, Jo (Sadie Frost), portrayed as a strong and

autonomous figure of greater maturity than the male protagonist Billy (Jude Law). However, like the other films discussed, it offered reassurance to young males by defining the world of legitimate work as marginal.

9 My argument here, and those concerning *The Full Monty* and *Brassed Off* below, are expanded upon in Claire Monk, 'Underbelly UK: the 1990s Underclass Film, Masculinity and the Ideologies of "New" Britain', in Justin Ashby and Andrew Higson (eds) *British Cinema: Past and Present* (London: Routledge, forthcoming).

10 I would like to thank Claire Meeghan, one of the students in my 1998 British Cinema seminar group at Middlesex University, for this observation.

11 'New lads back death penalty', *Evening Standard*, 28 October 1998, p. 19.

12 'Browned off', *Guardian*, 22 February 1999, 'Media Guardian', pp. 4–5; '200 most stylish men of the 20th century', *GQ*, March 1999, pp. 47–56.

13 These charges were made by only a small number of critics, including myself, but caused much irritation to Leigh. See Claire Monk: 'Naked' (review), *Sight and Sound*, November 1993, p. 48. I would like to take this opportunity to explain that part of my review was omitted from the published version, causing important nuances of my argument to be lost.

14 Andy Medhurst, 'Mike Leigh: Beyond embarrassment', *Sight and Sound*, November 1993, p. 10.

15 Source: *Caviar 12* (1995) vol. 1, Table 23/5.

16 Nick James, 'Being there', *Sight and Sound*, October 1997, pp. 6–9.

Chapter 17

Not Having It All: Women and Film in the 1990s

Charlotte Brunsdon

'Media women work too hard to have children', the *Independent* headlined a half-page report by Maggie Brown on the interim findings of the British Film Institute's 'Television Industry Tracking Study' in 1994.[1] This study used detailed questionnaires and diaries from a sample of 520 television workers in creative grades to track their origins, conditions and aspirations in a period of great change in the industry. The shift to casualised and short-contract labour is revealed to have particular consequences for women and maternity. Two-thirds of the men in the study have children, compared to thirty per cent of the women. The difference is not explicable, the researchers argue, by age, origin or education. As one female independent producer put it, 'The same pay for twice as much work, anti-social hours, no maternity pay or nurseries – it is becoming again a young man's industry'.[2]

A woman freelance researcher without children commented: 'There isn't any room in the television industry at the moment to want both [children and career]. There is no maternity leave. When you are working freelance, you are working month to month. Suppose I am working 8 to 10 at night. How does that fit in?'[3] The difficulty of having 'both', as this woman poignantly puts it, is clearly a significant issue for women working in tele-vision at the end of what could be seen as feminism's century, and data on the continuing casualisation of the notoriously unstable film industry does not suggest that the position of women there is any better.[4] Nevertheless, some women are managing to have something, and I want to look in this essay at some of the films and television programmes made by and about women in the 1990s.

I want to investigate the representation of female experience in British film of the 1990s, and particularly what I would suggest is a noticeable concern across a varied body of work, the question of how to 'do' femininity. I will suggest that it is useful to think about film and television together – not so much in terms of their increasing industrial interdependency – but in terms of visual style and the circulation of images and representations. In partic-ular, I want to use the notion of 'having it all' to represent both a continuing aspiration and a recognised fantasy of post-feminist femininities.

The most significant films directed and written by women in the early 1990s are Sally Potter's *Orlando* (1992) and Gurinder Chadha's *Bhaji on the Beach* (1993), films which draw on, and transform, quite different traditions in British cinema.[5] *Orlando*, the second feature of a director who has been working since the 1970s with a continuing concern for issues of gender, reveals a modernist inheritance in its highly formal structure, its explicit interpretation of Virginia Woolf and its lingering on the surface and texture of the image. This avant-garde inheritance, strongly evident in Potter's earlier films, *Thriller* (1979) and *The Gold Diggers* (1983), is, in *Orlando*, used to figure English heritage (the Elizabethan Age, the country house, the empire, Victoria) in a way which renders it strange. Thus Potter uses her own concerns to interrogate what was, by 1992, perhaps the most significant cycle of 1980s British films, the heritage film.[6] She re-stages English heritage as a drama of gendered performance and inheritance, in which Orlando, crossing sexes, loses his property but greets the future having produced a daughter and a novel.

In contrast, *Bhaji on the Beach*, which was written by Meera Syal, directed by Gurinder Chadha and produced by Nadine Marsh-Edwards for the British Film Institute, addresses itself — like Horace Ové's *Playing Away* (1986) — to another strand of British cinema heritage, Ealing Studios.[7] As with Ealing's comedies, *Bhaji* sets up its story with a carefully-differentiated group and a circumscribed time frame, here a trip to Blackpool for a group of Indian and British Asian women in the mini-bus of the Saheli Women's Centre, Birmingham. The 'Ealing-ness' of the trip to Blackpool, in which different individuals will come to slightly different understandings of their situation, is transformed, as the juxtaposition of the title suggests, by the evocation of the traditions of popular Indian cinema in the imagination of Asha (Lalita Ahmed), and also, simply, by the very Asian-ness of the three generations of the day-trippers to the traditional English working-class resort.[8] Chadha and Syal, however, are concerned to show the multiplicity of Asian female identities, ranging from the traditional older 'aunties' such as Pushpa (Zhora Segal), the sophisticated Indian visitor, Reka, who declares Blackpool to be 'just like Bombay', to the younger British women with their different choices of marriage, medical training and community activism. Chadha and Syal are concerned with questions of feminine destiny and identity, but they show these being lived out in the complex post-colonial hybridity of contemporary Britain, embodied, in one of the film's finest moments, through the Punjabi rendering of the Cliff Richard 1960s hit, 'Summer Holiday' as the day trippers set off.

Orlando and *Bhaji* focus significantly on female experience. Other female-directed feature films such as *Priest* (Antonia Bird, 1994) and *Beautiful Thing* (Hettie MacDonald, 1995) find women directing stories principally concerned with male homosexuality, while Ngozi Onwurah's *Welcome II the Terrordrome* (1994) addresses a failed version of the culturally hybrid Britain we find in *Beautiful Thing* and *Bhaji* through the form of a deeply pessimistic futuristic fantasy.[9] Here though, I wish to pick up on a thread of desperate-ness in the staging of female experience, discussing two striking films of the later 1990s, *Stella Does Tricks* (Coky Giedroyc, 1996) and *Under the Skin* (Carine Adler, 1996) with some reference to *The Girl with Brains in her Feet* (1997) which was directed by Roberto Bangura from a script by Jo Hodges. Each of these films has a very sombre core, addressing an impossibility or intolerability in their heroine's lives. They each, with different degrees of success, address and contest the dominant traditions of British film-making and the look of the provincial. But it is not just in relation to British cinema history, with its angry young men, that these desperate young women are significant. My own sense is that, in the 1990s, an address to a female audience and the representation of dilemmas of feminine destiny has become significantly more 'prime-timed' and that films such as these should not be seen separately from the (mainly regional) ensemble female dramas that we find in prime time television. Series such as *Making Out* (wr. Debbie Horsfield, 1987), *Band of Gold* (wr. Kay Mellor, 1995 and 1996) and in 1998, *Real Women* (wr. Susan Oudot) and *Playing the Field* (wr. Kay Mellor), offer often prestigious female casts with individual characters each dramatising one of the perceived choices of femininity. These, in turn, can also not be completely separated from costume dramas such as the 1995 BBC *Pride and Prejudice* that Bridget Jones liked so much, or the 1998 *Far From the Madding Crowd* so explicitly scheduled and marketed against the World Cup.[10] In the later 1990s, the drama of, in Rachel Brownstein's words, 'becoming a heroine', is figured across a range of texts and media, many of which occupy more culturally central positions than has been traditionally the case with feminine-gendered fiction.

We need to approach these fictions as the product of several different histories. Firstly, there is the recognition of women as a differentiated audience for film and television. Since the later 1970s advertisers and schedulers have been increasingly interested in high income, high-spending career women, the women who might be thought to have it all.[11] Secondly, with the proliferation of domestic television sets and the incursion of the masculine-identified satellite channels (sport and films) into the network audience, there has been a femininisation of the prime-time network television schedules.[12] Finally, there is the coincidence of the industrial compulsions on the culture industries to innovate with the long march through the institutions of female writers, directors and producers. That is, the demand for new product can be partly met by the difference of the imagination and concerns of both an older generation, such as Kay Mellor or Sally Potter, who have finally secured some kind of recognition, and a younger generation, brought up with the concerns of 1970s feminism to some extent taken for granted.[13] The high proportion of women under thirty participating in the BFI study underscores this point. Here, the role of television in national cultural life in Britain is particularly significant, and can usefully be contrasted with the situation in France. In Britain, where the employment of women in the audiovisual industries has increased significantly in the last fifteen years, few directors are recognised as auteurs – however, there is a spread of women working as writers, documentary film-makers, animation makers and producers across film and television (for example, Molly Dineen, Candy Guard, Lucy Gannon, Debbie Horsfield, Beeban Kidron, Nadine Marsh-Edwards, Lynda La Plante, Verity Lambert, Kay Mellor, Winsome Pinnock, Jane Root, Jennifer Saunders, Janet Street-Porter, Meera Syal, Jeanette Winterson) in a way which contrasts strongly with the national recognition of the isolated figures of Diane Kurys, Agnes Varda and Coline Serreau as auteurs in France.

The increasing interpenetration of film and television in Britain is recognised as a key feature of the British audiovisual landscape, but there are different interpretations of the significance and consequences of this interpenetration once we move beyond clichés such as 'British cinema is alive and well and living on television'. It is possible to distinguish between what we might call 'the view from television' and the 'view from cinema'. It is the former that is less often voiced, but is most vividly expressed in John Caughie's essay, 'The logic of convergence', in which he discusses the 'peculiarly British hybrid' of an emergent art cinema which is 'balanced precariously between a European sensibility and the North American market' and which is economically dependent on television.[14] While scrupulous to welcome individual works within this emergent cross-media mode, Caughie raises a series of questions about what he sees as the logic of the elision of what is 'local, awkward and complex within the nation' (what is representative) in favour of a representation of the nation, 'capturing the images around which the complexity of the nation can identify itself as a unity, representing itself to the outside and securing its continuity on the global market'.[15]

This distinction is suggestive in relation to the fictions I am discussing, because I think it may be more difficult to conceive of, and market, these clearly feminine stories as 'representation' of the nation – except perhaps when the heroine is Elizabeth I. Writers such as Debbie Horsfield and Kay Mellor, whose work is always strongly regionally located, offer a very vivid account of what is 'local, awkward and complex within the nation', as, in a different way, do A.L. Kennedy and Coky Giedroyc with *Stella* and Roberto Bangura and Jo

Hodges with *The Girl with Brains in her Feet* and I would suggest that the interpenetration of film and television is still, for these dramas of female subjectivity, mainly enabling. Precisely because there are real equivocations in the fit between being a woman and representing Britishness, these fictions are, of necessity, representative, rather than representation, in Caughie's sense. It is *The Full Monty* and *Trainspotting*, both self-consciously boys' stories which have had to sustain the burden of representation, not these feminine fictions.

Desperate Girls

The production circumstances of *Stella Does Tricks* and *Under the Skin* are similar: both were produced by the British Film Institute with budgets under £700,000; both were partly developed outside London (Glasgow and Liverpool) through regional incentive money; both were photographed by Barry Ackroyd (who has also worked with Ken Loach) and both are début features by female directors. Each film has a very intense focus on its heroine, rarely including shots, let alone scenes, in which she is not present, and each, for a culture thought to be embarrassed by the sexual, has a substantial sexual content. *The Girl with Brains in her Feet* , made independently by Lexington Films for just under £1 million also has a provincial setting (1970s Leicester), and was a first feature for both writer and director. These are stories of desperate girls, and I want to sketch out some elements we might wish to consider when approaching them.

Stella Does Tricks is the more familiar as a British film. Ackroyd's cinematography here is more 'Loach-like': low-key, naturalistic, inconspicuous. The locations of London and Glasgow are offered in a relatively conventional visual vocabulary. London is tightly framed in medium and medium long street shots – always showing more than the figures on which the frame is focused, but never stretching to give a sense of space or distance. It is a city of seedy hotels and cafés, flats and a dusty inner city street park. The camera rarely rises above eye-level and we only see the sky briefly in the park. The only place of beauty, apart from the corrupted respite offered by the park (where Stella has to masturbate her pimp, Mr Peters, while they pretend to eat ice cream), is the flower stall at which Stella works after her escape from prostitution. Again, this is tightly framed, and we never see an establishing shot, but the stall is introduced through a close-up pan of a row of flowers which is picked up later in an extreme close-up on a bunch of purple lilac. The stall is the source of the plants which Stella brings home to transform the bed-sit she shares with Eddie. Glasgow, in appropriate contrast for a city visited in the film mainly in memory and fantasy, is more spacious and is revealed more often in twilight long shots, particularly around the pigeon-loft, Stella's father's pride and joy. Glasgow, in these longer, spacey shots which include a park and a cemetery, is still a place where things might have been going to be all right.

Stella Does Tricks is a film about a young Glaswegian woman working as a prostitute in London under the aegis of Mr Peters (James Bolam), whose favourite she is for the first part of the film. Stella (Kelly Macdonald), as Mr Peters puts it, has the ability to 'go away in [her] head', and the London scenes are intercut with Glasgow scenes of uncertain status which include the motherless Stella as a child, her father (Ewan Stewart), an unsuccessful stand-up comedian who drinks too much and her stern Auntie Aileen. While some of the Glasgow scenes are clearly memory, others, such as a conversation between her father and Aileen in which he asserts that all she needs is love as they look out on the child Stella dancing in the rain in the street below are omniscient flashback, while yet others could be

Beyond naturalist
representation.
Stella Does Tricks (1997)

fantasy. Stella decides to leave Mr Peters when he makes her take crack after an evening in
which he was unable to trace her (she was avenging the beating of another girl) and takes
refuge with Eddie, a heroin addict. Together, they travel to Glasgow, where Stella revenges
herself on both her respectable aunt and her abusive father. When they return to London,
Stella gets a job in a flower stall and starts decorating the flat, still with dreams of going
away, but Eddie doesn't clean up.

The film has a doubled structure, first introduced in the ambivalences of the title. Stella
does at least two types of trick. In the American slang, she works as a prostitute ('does
tricks'); but she also, in bursts of exhilarating energy, performs spectacular feats, such as
swimming underwater or releasing a flood of condom balloons into her Auntie Aileen's
respectable suburban garden. The film shows both types of tricks, the squalid encounters
with middle-aged men filmed in a way which refuses any eroticism and renders the clients
both pathetic and exploitative, and the increasingly angry tricks Stella performs in
vengeance for both past and present wrongs. She gives a client a fearsomely hot British
sweet, a Fisherman's Friend, instead of hashish, for anal stimulation. She smashes car head-
lights, breaks car aerials and mirrors on her way home. And in what becomes cumulatively,
a vengeance of fire, she sets light to a car, her father's pigeon loft and his crotch. Stella does
tricks indeed, but her best one, the one she can't quite pull off, is the escape from prostitution and the reinvention of herself, and, in her fantasy, Eddie, as normal.

The doubled structure, the London/Glasgow opposition, attempts to give Stella interi-
ority and motivation. We see how it is and how it was. The motherless child, the weak,

affectionate father – and gradually come to see that there is a further doubling, in Stella's painful love for Mr Peters and her memories of her abusive father. Stella, we see, has been formed in abusive relations to fathers, and yet she is, as she tells Mr Peters 'more than you think I am'. She is shown to be, above all else, a performer, a teller of stories: 'Sisters, sisters, picture this, I can picture any fucking thing, that's my thing, I have the technology.' Stella's technology, her imagination, is her most significant attribute, and through giving Stella the ability to fantasise the film seems to figure her as enunciator, and attempts to break with the tradition of naturalist representation of the prostitute as victim.

In contrast, the heroine of *The Girl with Brains in her Feet*, is much less able to articulate her desires and must go along with the shaping actions of those around her. Set in Leicester in the 1970s, this is the story of growing up for thirteen-year-old Jacqueline (Joanna Ward), who is a talented runner, good at lessons and able to draw and paint. As her middle-class art teacher says to her, 'Jacqueline, you have the ability to be lots of things. It's all going to be up to you.' But Jack, more interested in the arcane secrets of sex in 1970s Britain, isn't quite sure what she wants and doesn't understand that some choices exclude others. With its emphatic 1970s soundtrack, the film contributes an interesting inflection to British cinema's representation of the past. Instead of frocks and country houses, Jack's story, adolescence in a white working-class area, life with her white mother and no contact with her black father, offers a rather less elegant tale of an everyday 1970s life – paper rounds, the school bus, hanging round the chippy and trying out tampons, sex and cigarettes. At the same time, the slightly retro feel of the film marks it apart from the British naturalism which has been the main tradition for the representation of working-class life – this is, stylistically, a film of a certain kind of life made by those who have left it.[16]

The retrospective setting has one particularly interesting element in that the film-makers choose to deal with the everyday racism of 1970s England by including racist comment, such as the sympathetic games teacher's admonitions to Jack, before a contest with another school, that the competitors might have 'a darky up their sleeves', without emphasis or

Growing up in the 1970s – *The Girl with Brains in her Feet* (1997)

textual contestation. The film relies on a contemporary audience to notice the casual racism, and shows the way that Jack takes for granted this type of comment. Her mother, wishing that 'a nice coloured family would move into the area' and trying to put Jack's hair in 'those West-Indian plaits', is the only liberal in matters of ethnicity. Jack's sexual naiveté is her undoing, and still inarticulate, it turns out not only that she can't do what she wants, but that she has in fact done just what her mother did before her and unintentionally become pregnant. The only race she wins is to find out what 'it' is like.

Under the Skin offers the most elaborated engagement with the interior life of its young heroine. Carine Adler's film is about the response of a young woman, Iris (Samantha Morton), to the death of her mother (Rita Tushingham) shortly after she has been diagnosed with cancer. The film evokes the intensity of Iris's grief through the intensity of its concentration on Iris, with only two scenes excluding her image, and even here she is the subject of conversation. Iris has an intermittent voice-over narration in the film, although often what she describes is in counterpoint to the image, most notably in her detailed descriptions of her casual sexual encounters laid over firstly, the cremation of her mother and secondly, a choir singing ecclesiastical music. Like Stella, Iris both is and isn't in control of her narrative, shown most powerfully through her repeated denial, as she says to her boyfriend Gary, shortly after her mother's death, 'You think this is something to do with Mum don't you, well it isn't, it isn't.'

This is a film which tries to show emotion, rather than to tell us about it, and the manner it chooses is very risky for Iris's mode of expression is increasingly humiliating sexual encounters. Thus much of the visual and verbal imagery of a film which is concerned with exploring the uncontrollable modes of grief and the explosive eruption of sibling rivalries after the death of a parent is the imagery of masturbation and desperate sex. Rather than allow Iris's voice-over to describe her loss, the film instead offers us the spectacle of Iris's self-degradation as her journey through her grief, showing us not sex as pleasure, but sex as a grief-torn attempt at both connection and obliteration, sex as the expression of pain and anger.

Expressionism and the interior life of a heroine – *Under the Skin* (1997)

The intensity of the film is enhanced by its simple structure and limited location and cast. Iris moves from the stability of living with Gary and working in a shop, visiting her mother and seeing her pregnant married sister regularly, to an empty flat which she furnishes with the flowers from her mother's funeral, and where she trawls through the suitcase of her mother's clothes and accessories, dressing in her underwear, her chemotherapy wig and her sunglasses. For a location-shot Liverpool film, this does not look quite as one would expect. Instead of the emphasis on location and natural light characteristic of much British naturalist cinema (like *Stella*), this film is much more expressionist. The lighting, particularly on Iris, is sharper and darker, the use of colour vivid and luminous.[17] That other, less ostentatious cinematography is present, particularly in scenes where Iris is with her sister Rose, or in her mother's or sister's house and nearby streets. But it is rendered, rather than simply real, as so often in British cinema, rather more fragile and likely to be disrupted. For example, shortly after the mother's death, the two sisters walk along the road together – undramatic lighting and framing confirming the normality of their suburban environment. Rose starts to cry, saying how much she misses their mother, whinily claiming precedence and Iris responds sharply 'Don't start'. Rose continues to assert her special connection with their mother, 'I spoke to her every day' and suddenly there is a cut as abrupt as Iris's 'Don't start' and the *mise-en-scène* explodes as Iris stalks past a corrugated iron fence, running her hand along the noisy, unstable metal, setting up banging echoes as the frame judders and the image seems also to lose balance in her headlong rush of fury, grief, denial and jealousy.

Later in the film, when Iris, through a friend, has found a job in the Lost Property Office, she recounts what she has lost in one month: 'Two pairs of shoes, a bag, a boyfriend, a mother'. What the stylistic variation of the film suggests is that she is in danger of losing her very grounding – and this can be read as an interrogation of the kinds of stories that British cinema has traditionally told. For, unusually in British cinema, this is a story about emotion not being repressed, even if it is denied. Iris's grief interrupts the naturalism with which the north of England is usually represented, the mobile body-led camera, the saturated colour and the use of slow motion offering a different representational repertoire.

Each of the feature films has unique qualities, but their very production – the imagination of their stories, the production personnel, and the prediction by funding bodies that there would be an audience – is dependent on wider cultural shifts which also underpin the 'prime-timing' of feminine experience on network television through drama serials and other programmes aimed at female audiences.

The female ensemble dramas are quality productions which represent the escape of strong female characters from their traditional television place on day time and soap opera into prime time. The identifying trope of this type of drama, made internationally famous from another point of view in *The Full Monty*, is that of 'women watching male strippers', condensing as it does the scandals of female sexual desire, public bawdiness and all-female groups, whilst I would suggest that its dramatic questions are always bound up with the status of marriage for the contemporary woman.[18] The commencement of two of these series within a couple of weeks of each other on BBC television in spring 1998 suggests some generic recognition at the level of production, particularly as each, presumably unintentionally, opened the first episode round a waiting wedding dress. Each distributed different feminine destinies across the different cast members. Thus for example, *Real Women* (Susan Oudot, BBC, tx 26/2/98–12/3/98) centres on five characters who were friends at school. One is a housewife with children, a mum. One is married and trying unsuccessfully to conceive. One, a career woman, has just had an abortion. One is a lesbian, but has not told her friends. The fifth is just about to give up being a bad girl to get married. The series, which ran over three weeks, is structured round these women's lives in the period shortly before this wedding, and opens with the bride's sight of the waiting wedding dress. Their different destinies and attitudes are explored, and the terrain of the series is female, not male experience. This involves discussion of what happens to a woman's body when she becomes pregnant and has children, the conflict between career and maternity, the disappointments of marriage, and the self-hatred of lesbianism. Similarly, broadcast in the following week, *Playing the Field* also opened with the waking bride's sight of her waiting wedding dress. Other characters in this series include an adulterous, childless, married businesswoman, a young woman who thinks her mother is her sister, a married woman with children who is jealous of her husband, a lesbian woman, a grandmother with a large family and a young woman who has been abandoned by her parents. Here too, 'having it all' is both recognised – the individual women do live femininity differently, there is a plurality to femininity – and recognised as impossible precisely through this dispersal of destinies. The series as a whole 'has it all', but it can retain its claim on realism by granting this to no single character.

All these fictions are, in quite fundamental ways, women's fictions. They focus on female characters and they engage with the emotion and desire of these characters. *Under the Skin*, the most audacious text, is perhaps more clearly careless of male viewers – like Iris, the film doesn't care what people think, while *Playing the Field*, with its central trope of the women's football team, is attempting a quite complicated audience address, invoking class loyalties and traditionally male pastimes to invite in a male audience. The texts are unimaginable without second wave feminism, but they are also post-feminist in a number of ways. In both *Stella* and *Under the Skin*, the heroine both is, and isn't, sexually autonomous. The range of sexual experience is considerable – as Stella observes to Eddie when he suggests they celebrate 'straight' by screwing in the coach lavatory, 'I've done it fucking everywhere'. She does choose to have sex with Eddie but that is the only sexual choice she makes. Iris chooses to pursue her desires for anonymous sexual encounters, but is clearly driven by other emotions. These desperate girls feel answerable to no-one, although in fact their ambitions are very conventional, Iris wanting to 'give the singing a go', Stella bringing home plants and slowly wallpapering the flat. These are 1990s girls, and I think finally cannot be understood in isolation from other circulating discourses of femininity. They are in some ways each like parodies of the successful achieving superwoman feminism is now associated with.

When we look at these desperate girls in conjunction with the ensemble dramas, there arises an interesting issue of the relation between medium and meaning. Without wanting to suggest that either medium is essentially like this, it is clearly the case that the drama serial format, with weekly episodes over a limited run, has been, in Britain, most productive for the ensemble narratives, while the feature format seems to have been most clearly associated with the exploration of an individual subjectivity. The necessity for the end of episode hook that will attract a viewer the following week makes for a greater range of tone in the serial drama, all of which offer humour as well as sadness, while the feature films have a more singular and focused intensity. This in turn leads to the curious phenomenon in which life seems harder for the celluloid heroines, desperate in different ways, while the ensemble dramas, busy dramatising the different feminine destinies that have now received some recognition, offer at least a kind of camaraderie of a 'a woman's lot' in their repeated insistence that no-one can 'have it all'. If these desperate girls in some ways stand against the manicured achievement of the superwoman, the drama of 'how to be a woman' is simultaneously also being played out in drama series in which each character – and not all are white – inhabits a particular female identity – mother, working woman, single girl, lesbian, pregnant woman, adulteress, etc. Here, as with *Bhaji on the Beach*, I think the range of possibilities, the different ways of doing femininity – and still being recognised as a woman – has been extended. Series such as *Real Women* and *Playing the Field* choose to engage with changing ideas of appropriate femininity, reiterating the impossibility of 'having it all'. For Stella, Jack and Iris the question is whether they can have anything at all.

Part of the analysis of *Stella Does Tricks* and *Under the Skin* has appeared in 'Des filles désespérées' in *Iris* no. 26, 1996, pp. 149–62. Thanks to Karen Alexander and Kate Ogborn of the BFI and Michael Daniels of Alliance Releasing.

Notes

1 Maggie Brown, 'Media women work too hard to have children', *Independent*, 5 December 1994, p. 7; Brown is reporting on a presentation to launch the *BFI Television Industry Tracking Study. The First Year: An Interim Report* (London: BFI, 1995). The diaries quoted in her article have remained confidential to the BFI and are not part of the first interim report. Slightly more use of quotation is used in the second report: *BFI Television Industry Tracking Study: Second Interim Report* (London: BFI, 1997).

2 Maggie Brown, ibid., interview.

3 Maggie Brown, ibid., quoting from a diary in the BFI Tracking Study.

4 *Cultural Trends 30* records that the British film industry in the 1990s is dominated by 'small companies with fewer than 10 employees and high numbers of part-time and self-employed workers'. This survey of published statistics on the audiovisual industries does not distinguish between film and television. Sara Selwood (ed.), *Cultural Trends 30*, (London: Policy Studies Institute, 1999) pp. 9–10.

5 *Orlando* was a UK/USSR/Fr/It/Neth co-production, obviously raising the thorny issue of the definition of a British film.

6 On *Orlando*, see Julianne Pidduck, 'Travels with Sally Potter's *Orlando*: gender, narrative, movement', *Screen*, vol. 38 no. 2, 1997 pp. 172–89. The founding polemical account of heritage cinema is Andrew Higson's 'Re-presenting the National Past' in Lester Friedman (ed.), *British Cinema and Thatcherism* (London: UCL Press, 1993).

7 *Playing Away* is centred around a cricket match in a traditional Suffolk village with a visiting team from Brixton.

8 On *Bhaji*, see, for example, Sarita Malik, 'Beyond a Cinema of Duty' in Andrew Higson (ed.), *Dissolving Views* (London: Cassell, 1996) and Gargi Bhattacharya and John Gabriel, 'Gurinder Chadha and the *Apna* generation: Black British film in the 1990s', *Third Text*, 27, 1994, pp. 55–64.

9 The Spanish/French/British co-production, *El Efecto Mariposa (The Butterfly Effect)* (Fernando Colomo, 1995), which is set in London and also ventures into the future, provides an interesting European contrast to the 'hybrid utopia' British films. Paul Gilroy's hostile review of *Welcome II the Terrordrome* ('Unwelcome', *Sight and Sound*, vol. 5.2, 1995, pp. 18–19), gives an indication of what is at stake in these utopian/dystopian visions of the future of the cultural hybridity of Britain.

10 As was Kay Mellor's first venture into feature films, *Girls' Night* (d. Nick Hurran, 1997). On its repeat screening, the *Radio Times* reported that 'Anyone wrapped up in France 98 would have missed this feel-good weepie from director Nick Hurran, which was released in late June in a bid to lure World Cup widows into the cinema'; 'Film of the Week', *Radio Times*, 10–16 April 1999, p. 43.

11 This is particularly clear in the USA, where demographics are more explicitly invoked in the production process. For example, *Ally McBeal*, first shown in Britain in 1998, was commissioned by Fox from David E. Kelley with a brief to appeal to 'women of 18–34 and provide an alternative to the predominantly male audience of *Monday Night Football* on the rival network ABC'. See Janine Gibson, 'Will this girls' night in make the boys switch off?', *Independent Media Section*, 25 May 1998, p. 4.

12 In this context, the flood of 'make-over' and cookery shows in the 8.00–9.00 slot on network tv is relevant.

13 Of course, there is not just an 'older' and 'younger' generation – at present, the most significant female players in British film and television may well be the 'in-between' generation, which includes, for example, Jane Root, appointed Controller of BBC 2 in 1998.

14 John Caughie, 'The logic of convergence', in John Hill and Martin McLoone (eds), *Big Picture, Small Screen* (Luton: John Libbey Media, University of Luton Press, 1996), p. 217.

15 Caughie, ibid., p. 223.

16 'All those involved with the film were keen to avoid the semi-documentary style championed by directors Ken Loach and Mike Leigh', thus Robert Bangura (director) described his stylistic inheritance. 'I love Ken Loach, but the films I am inspired by are *A Taste of Honey, Alfie, The Loneliness of the Long Distance Runner*. They treated their working class subjects in way which was quite lyrical and often quite romantic.' (Press Pack, Alliance Releasing, 1997. p. 9). Whether *The Girl* . . . embodies these aims is a different matter.

17 Kate Ogborn, the film's producer, named the look of *Chungking Express* (Wong Kar Wai, 1994) as a key influence on the production team (interview with author, 4 September 1998).

18 This is of course, also present in *Bhaji*, which offers, in compressed form, many of the characteristics of the ensemble drama.

Chapter 18

Failure and Utopianism: Representations of the Working Class in British Cinema of the 1990s

John Hill

'The number of British films that have ever made a genuine try at a story in a popular milieu, with working-class characters all through, can be counted on the fingers of one hand', observed Lindsay Anderson in 1957.[1] The 'new wave' films of the late 1950s and early 1960s which followed sought to change this situation by placing working-class characters at the centre of their narratives but they did so at a time of economic and social change. Hence, films such as *Room at the Top* (Jack Clayton, 1959), *Saturday Night and Sunday Morning* (Karel Reisz, 1960) and *A Kind of Loving* (John Schlesinger, 1962) all demonstrated a certain anxiety about the demise of the traditional working class (associated with work, community and an attachment to place) in the face of growing consumerism, Americanisation and suburbanisation.[2] A similar concern for the decline of the traditional working class is also apparent in the working-class films of the 1980s and 1990s. However, unlike the earlier group of films, there is now little sense of the corrupting effects of affluence or embourgeoisement. Rather it is the damage wrought by de-industrialisation, mass unemployment and poverty typical of the Thatcher years (1979–90) – when employment in manufacturing fell by two million – that is foregrounded. This theme is explicit in the opening sequence of *The Full Monty* (Peter Cattaneo, 1997) which begins with footage of a promotional film from the early 1970s for 'Sheffield – City on the move', celebrating the city as the 'the beating heart of Britain's industrial north'. The film then cuts to twenty-five years later when the shots of men at work contained in the promotional film are replaced by shots of a disused factory in which former steelworkers, Gaz (Robert Carlyle) and Dave (Mark Addy), accompanied by Gaz's son Nathan (William Snape), scavenge for scrap metal.

However, it is not only the loss of traditional industries, and their consequences for the social and political traditions of the working class, that these films map. For the decline in manufacturing, and growth of long-term male unemployment, are also seen as precipitating a weakening of the ideologies of masculinity which have traditionally underpinned both work and trade union action. Thus, in focusing on unemployment and industrial decay in the north of England, the 1980s and 1990s films often suggest the crisis in masculinity associated with the collapse of those social roles such as wage-earner and head of the family that have traditionally sustained a sense of male identity. In the 1980s, films like *Educating Rita* (Lewis Gilbert, 1983), *Letter to Brezhnev* (Chris Bernard, 1985), *Rita, Sue and Bob Too* (Alan Clarke, 1986) and *Business as Usual* (Lezli-An Barrett, 1987) suggested this by the way they characteristically subverted the conventions of earlier 'new wave' dramas by focusing on the concerns of working-class women rather than virile (and employed) young men.[3] If, in so doing, the 1980s films adapted elements from the 'woman's film' (and combined an interest in both class and gender issues), then the 1990s films are more characteristically 'men's films' in which there is a much greater concentration on the dramatic conflicts faced by working-class men. This is evident in Ken Loach's series of working-class dramas – *Riff-Raff* (1991), *Raining Stones* (1993), *Ladybird Ladybird* (1994), and *My Name is Joe* (1998) – as well as a group of comedy dramas – *Brassed Off* (Mark Herman, 1996), *Up 'n' Under* (John Godber,1997) and *The Full Monty* (1997) – that appeared during the same period.

Ken Loach[4]

Loach, who began his television and film career in the 1960s, provides something of a bridge between the 'new wave' working-class films of the early 1960s and the films of the 1990s and, in a number of respects, his films show a remarkable degree of consistency in their concerns. Thus, just as Loach's work in the 1960s – such as his groundbreaking television plays *Up the Junction* (1965) and *Cathy Come Home* (1966) – reminded audiences that not everyone was enjoying the benefits of post-war affluence, so his films in the 1990s have emphasised the plight of those who have had to pay a heavy price for the economic upheavals of the 1980s. There are, however, significant differences as well.

Thus, while the 90s films draw attention to the widening of economic divisions characteristic of the Thatcher years, they also reveal how de-industrialisation, mass unemployment and anti-trade union legislation have not only significantly altered the social character of the British working class but have undermined the prospects for self-confident forms of working-class action as well. Loach's work has always been pessimistic about the prospects of radical political change in Britain. His television dramas *The Big Flame* (1969), dealing with a workers' take-over of the Liverpool docks, and the episode in *Days of Hope* (1975) dealing with the General Strike of 1926, both end on a note of betrayal and failure. However, in the late 1960s and early 1970s, it was at least still possible to imagine how organised, collective action might mount a serious challenge to the power of capital (and also to conduct an impassioned debate about reformist versus revolutionary political strategies). In the later films, this sense of political possibility is missing. Thus, in *Riff-Raff*, Loach's comeback film of the early 1990s, the fear of unemployment and absence of trade union rights have successfully put the film's assortment of casual labourers at the mercy of unscrupulous, cost-cutting employers. While the film ends with an arson attack on the building site by two of the men, this is less a considered political act than a desperate hitting out at a system that they lack the power to change. As in *Raining Stones*, where Bob (Bruce Jones) is driven to a violent attack on an uncaring loan shark, it is individual acts of anger, rather than organised political activity, which now constitute the main form of resistance to the status quo.

These individual alienated acts of defiance characteristic of the films set in Britain are contrasted with the emblematic moments of revolutionary action provided by the Spanish Civil War of the 1930s in *Land and Freedom* (1995) and the Nicaraguan revolution of the 1980s in *Carla's Song* (1996). The characters who leave Britain to join these political struggles abroad, however, either experience a degree of disillusionment (*Land and Freedom*) or fail to become fully involved (*Carla's Song*). It is Hispanic 'others' – the beautiful Nicaraguan dancer Carla (Oyanka Cabezas) in *Carla's Song*, the committed Spanish revolutionary Blanca (Rosana Pastor) in *Land and Freedom*, along with the Paraguayan folk singer and political refugee, Jorge (Vladimir Vega), in *Ladybird Ladybird* – who are seen to embody the purity of political purpose that the British working class lack. Characters in the

contemporary British dramas may, as in *Riff-Raff*, demonstrate considerable resourceful-
ness and fortitude in the face of economic adversity but such behaviour is shown as a
defensive response to imposed circumstance rather than – as in *Land and Freedom* and
Carla's Song – an active taking control of, or remaking of, the characters' lives.

However, while Loach's films may chart the erosion of working-class traditions, they do
not sentimentalise the plight of the characters. Working-class characters are neither intrin-
sically good nor bad in Loach's films but moulded by the economic and social conditions
in which they are located. As such, Loach's films rarely ask us to identify with characters so
much as to observe, and understand, their predicaments. This is evident, for example, in
Raining Stones where Bob's obsessive determination to find the money for his daughter's
communion dress is shown as foolhardy (given that he is repeatedly warned that the expenditure on a new dress is unnecessary and will lead to debt) yet also understandable in so far
as it symbolises such an obvious attempt to hold on to the last remnants of his sense of self-
worth. It is also evident in *My Name is Joe* in the way in which our perceptions of, and
sympathies towards, Joe are radically transformed half-way through the film when his violent past is revealed in a disturbing flashback that echoes Ray Winstone's alcohol-fuelled
violence in *Ladybird Ladybird*.

It is this strategy of observation, rather than involvement, that is also the hallmark of
Loach's cinematic style. Loach's films commonly make use of real locations that demonstrate the often grim actualities in which people live (the Langley estate in Manchester in
Raining Stones, Ruchill in Glasgow in *My Name is Joe*). The films also employ a mix of professional and non-professional actors and Loach seeks to downplay the sense of an actor's
performance through improvisation and even surprise (whereby an actor is sometimes kept
in the dark about developments in the script). What in particular distinguishes Loach's style
is his employment, to varying degrees, of techniques, such as the avoidance of dramatic
lighting and compositional effects or the use of unbroken takes, that have an affinity with
traditional documentary film-making. In this way, the films maintain a degree of distance
from the characters they observe and inhibit some of the emotional involvement that techniques used to strengthen the spectator's identification with characters would encourage.
Thus, in the emotional confrontation between Stevie (Robert Carlyle) and Susie (Emer
McCourt) near the end of *Riff-Raff*, the camera holds back from the action and the close-
ups and reverse angles that would normally accompany such a dramatic climax are avoided.

Indeed, much of the power to unsettle in Loach's films may be seen to derive from the
apparent impassivity of his cinematic style in relation to the disturbing or moving nature
of events in front of the camera. Thus, while Loach's films make use of a distanced obser-
vational style that draws on documentary conventions, many of them also rely on the
dramatic machinery associated with melodrama: impossible choices and misjudgements,
chance and coincidence, a foreshortened sense of cause and effect. Thus, for all of its claims
to documentary realism, *Ladybird Ladybird* may also be read as a maternal melodrama that
achieves many of its emotional effects through the employment of melodramatic themes
(the enforced separations of mother and children) and plot devices (the dramatic coincidence of fire breaking out at the refuge when Maggie's children have been left alone; the
surprise of the social workers seizing a new-born baby). What separates Loach's work from
conventional melodrama, however, is not only the way that it discourages too strong an
emotional identification with characters but its insistence upon the economic and social
underpinnings of their actions. In this way, the impossible dilemmas and unbearable
choices that characters face are seen to derive less from personal traits (or moral short-

comings) than economic circumstances, such as poverty, unemployment and homeless-
ness, which are beyond their control. Thus, despite the film's unflattering portrait of
Maggie's anger and aggression (and its blocking of straightforward emotional identification with her), *Ladybird Ladybird* nonetheless refuses to indict her as a bad mother and
pinpoints how the obstacles to her achievement of happiness result from her lack of social
and economic power.

This combination of social observation and melodrama is also apparent in *My Name is
Joe*. Like *Raining Stones*, the film is set in the bleak new world of the housing estate in which
unemployment, debt, drug-taking and crime have become commonplace. Typical of this
world are the young couple, Liam (David McKay) and Sabine (AnneMarie Kennedy) and
their baby Brendan. Liam has been in prison for drug dealing but is seeking to go straight
and keep clean. Sabine, however, is both on junk and on the game and has plunged the
family into massive debt. Their situation comes, in turn, to weigh heavily on the film's main
character, Joe Kavanagh (Peter Mullan), an unemployed ex-alcoholic seeking to put his life
back together again.

A chance for happiness is offered to Joe when he encounters Sarah (Louise Goodall), a
health worker involved with Liam and Sabine. Although a number of critics appeared to
think that romance was a new ingredient in a Loach film, romantic (and even passionate)
encounters occur in most of his 90s films – Stevie and Susan in *Riff-Raff*, Maggie (Crissy
Rock) and Jorge in *Ladybird Ladybird*, David (Ian Hart) and Blanca in *Land and Freedom*,
George (Robert Carlyle) and Carla in *Carla's Song*. Romance in these films is shown to offer
redemptive possibilities, providing characters with the opportunity to change or to discover
new aspects of themselves, but Loach avoids celebrating love as a form of humanist triumph over social obstacles by dramatising how its success or failure also depends upon
economic and political factors. Thus, in *Carla's Song*, George leaves Carla at the end of the
film when he realises that he is unable to reconcile his love for her with the violent realities
of war. Similarly, the romantic relationship between Joe and Sarah exists in a specific social

My Name is Joe (1998) – social observation and melodrama

context (Joe is initially unsure, for example, about whether he can even afford to go out on a date) and is ultimately ripped asunder by the weight of economic and social circumstances (and the dilemmas which they generate).

As in traditional melodrama, Joe is faced with competing demands and loyalties. Discovering the extent of Liam and Sabine's plight, he tackles McGowan (David Hayman), the local drug-dealer, with whom he went to school. In doing so, he is confronted with a perverse, sociologically-grounded variant of the melodramatic choice between duty and love: for if he helps Liam, a member of his surrogate family (the football team which he manages), by agreeing to transport drugs for McGowan, he risks his own happiness with Sarah by plunging back into the world from which she has offered him escape. He opts, from the best of motives, to assist Liam but from then on his relationship with Sarah is in jeopardy, as is revealed in the highly-charged scene where Sarah discovers that he has lied to her (and used the proceeds from his activities to buy her a ring). Joe attempts to reverse his decision but succeeds only in making matters worse, with events culminating in one of the gloomiest endings in any Loach film when Joe returns to the drink and Liam hangs himself. In this way, the fatalistic logic of melodrama (and its exaggerated sense of dramatic consequence) is harnessed to the socially-deterministic impulses of naturalism.[5] For, typically of Loach's work, Joe's decision is seen not simply as a matter of personal morality but one that has been forced upon him by his socio-economic situation. As he attempts to explain to Sarah, 'we don't all live in this nice tidy wee world of yours ... some of us cannie go tae the polis ... some of us cannie gae to the bank for a loan ... some of us cannie just move hoose and fuck aff out of here ... some of us don't have a choice'.

Sarah's failure to grasp (or fully sympathise with) Joe's predicament also highlights the barriers of class that still divide them. It is in the character of Loach's documentary realism (and its emphasis upon observation) that it should emphasise the role of those middle-class authority figures who impose most heavily on the day-to-day lives of the working classes (rather than the less visible members of the economically dominant class). Hence, it is the failure of the professional middle classes – such as teachers and social workers – to understand, or provide relevant support, to the working class that characteristically arouses criticism in Loach's films. Thus, in *Ladybird Ladybird*, the social workers constitute a malign presence, cruelly interfering in the lives of others and adding to their misery rather than helping them. In *My Name is Joe* there is rather more sympathy for the 'helping professions' and a greater recognition of the burdens that are imposed upon them. The scenes at the health centre show basically good people struggling against the odds to care for the unwell and the needy ('I've put a lot of work into this family' declares Sarah as she attempts to dissuade a doctor from dropping Sabine and her family from the register). The point the film makes, in this regard, is not so much that the social services are incapable of providing help but that the need for them is exacerbated by unemployment and poverty, precisely the two areas where interference is most required but not provided. Nevertheless, for all of her caring and nurturing qualities, there is still an implicit indictment of Sarah's lower middle-class outlook in failing to make the imaginative leap into Joe's world, and it is her rejection of him that precipitates the film's final downward spiral of events. Sarah does make an appearance at Liam's funeral at the film's end but, by this time, it is unlikely (and would be out of keeping with the film's materialist logic) that their relationship can be repaired.

While not denying the power of Loach's vision of misery and frustration, there is something remorseless about the way in which the narrative imposes its determinist grip. In comparison to much of Loach's earlier work, the plot is tighter in its construction and the inexorable drive from bad to worse is more pronounced. A sense of pessimism dominates almost completely. Moreover, unlike previous films, there is no character who might offer a more politicised perspective on events. While such characters can run the risk of undermining the surface realism to which the films aspire, it is nonetheless common for Loach's films, especially those written by Jim Allen, to incorporate a degree of political argument. Thus, in *Riff-Raff*, Larry (Ricky Tomlinson) good-naturedly lectures his fellow workers on the iniquities of the Tories and the men's lack of political consciousness. In *Raining Stones*, Jimmy (Mike Fallon) is a community activist who argues with his son-in-law Bob about the need to change the system and reprimands a local Labour councillor for his ineffectiveness. In *My Name is Joe*, however, such a voice is absent and it makes the film's tale of defeat all the more definite.

The Full Monty

There is, in this respect, a sharp contrast with more popular films such as *Brassed Off*, *The Full Monty* and *Up 'n' Under*. Like Loach's films, they share a concern with the decline of the traditional working class and the problems of de-industrialisation and unemployment, but unlike Loach's films they move towards more optimistic conclusions. In all three cases, the films revolve around a recovery of pride and self-dignity in the face of economic adversity and social decay. Moreover, in contrast to the working-class films of the 1950s and 1960s, the stress is on collective action rather than individual escape. Thus, in the case of *Brassed Off*, the brass band (which according to band leader Danny, played by Pete Postlethwaite, 'symbolises pride' 'more than owt else' in the village) is able to go on to secure victory in the national championships despite the vote to close the pit (and the loss of morale that this involves). In *Up 'n' Under*, a rugby league team from the industrially-decaying north (where jobs are under threat and cash is scarce) regains its pride and team spirit ('supporting each other ... sweating and working and putting it together') by winning against a well-drilled, semi-professional side. In *The Full Monty* it is also community spirit upon which the film places most value. Thus, while the men in the film are confronted with unemployment, it is less work, or money, that they are seen to need (Gaz turns down his ex wife's offer of a job and Dave runs out on his) than the support and self-respect that participation in the group, and the strip-show, provides.

In contrast to the relative pessimism of Loach's films, these films offer a certain utopianism about the possibilities of collective action. Richard Dyer has suggested how the representations of working-class life found in the television soap opera *Coronation Street* manifest a utopian impulse by virtue of the emphasis which is placed on community and mutual concern.[6] These comedies share with television soap operas a representation of working-class life in terms of a geographically-bounded community in which (even in a city the size of Sheffield) everyone appears to know everyone else. They also make use of many actors familiar from television and place an emphasis upon ensemble playing. In doing so, they celebrate the recovery, in a post-industrial context, of the collective spirit that such communities have traditionally stood for, even if the shared experience of work which they originally grew out of has disappeared. In this respect, the idea of working-class community is mobilised less in the service of class politics than as a metaphor for the state of the nation. Writing of the British working class in the 1950s, Geoff Eley suggests how it came 'to embody a powerful representation of the national essence ... an allegory of

national wholeness . . . after the wounding and divisions of the war and depression'.[7] In the
1990s, the representations of the working class found in films such as *Brassed Off* and *The
Full Monty* continue to carry this allegorical dimension and, in doing so, to give voice to a
certain yearning for 'national wholeness' in the face of economic and social divisions and
the rise of self-interested individualism that characterised the Tory years. In this respect,
the films also offer a certain populist alliance in which middle-class characters are incorporated into the community represented by the working-class characters. In all three films,
upwardly mobile characters, such as the gnome-loving Gerald (Tom Wilkinson) and Gaz's
suburbanised ex-wife Mandy (Emily Woof) in *The Full Monty*, the management consultant Gloria (Tara Fitzgerald) in *Brassed Off* and the professional trainer and gym owner
Hazel (Samantha Janus) in *Up 'n' Under*, all end up as part of the group at the end of the
films. However, in returning to the traditional working-class community for a model of
wholeness, there are also implications for how the national community is then imagined,
particularly in relation to gender.

As has already been noted, the declining economic and political power of the traditional
working class is commonly linked in these films to a certain erosion of traditional forms of
working-class masculinity and male dignity. Thus, in Loach's films, such as *Raining Stones*,
it is the men's inability to support their families financially that is responsible for much of
what happens. In *The Full Monty*, this connection between unemployment and the erosion
of masculinity becomes central. Thus, the film constantly highlights the ways in which
social and economic changes have encouraged an apparent reversal of gender roles (and
also generational roles in so far as the unemployed men revert to a kind of adolescence,
wandering the streets and playing in the park, while Gaz's son Nathan assumes an air of
adult indulgence and helps to finance the men's activities). Not only do the women generally have jobs while the men do not but women have also increasingly appropriated
traditionally male spaces. Thus, in a key sequence, the working-men's club is taken over by
a group of women, gathered together to watch men strip, while Gaz illicitly observes a
woman, in a symbolic appropriation of phallic power, urinate standing up. The trauma (or
symbolic castration) to which this gives rise is reflected in the subsequent melancholy chat
at the job club when Gaz asserts that men have become, like dinosaurs and skateboards,
'not needed no more' and 'obsolete'.

To this extent, the regaining of self-respect that *The Full Monty* involves becomes associated not just with the recovery of community but of the forms of masculinity associated
with the traditional working class. There is, however, a degree of ambivalence in how this
is achieved. For, in order to retrieve their dignity, the men become strippers, assuming a
role that has historically been allotted to women. In so doing, they are confronted with
broadly feminist concerns surrounding appearance and the display of the body. In another
key scene, where the men are making use of Gerald's wife's sunbed and exercise bike and
are looking at a copy of the woman's magazine, *Cosmopolitan*, they are forced to consider
how they will be looked at in much the same way as men have traditionally looked at
women. As a result, members of the group develop an anxiety about their appearance: Dave
frets about his weight and wraps himself in cling film while Horse (Paul Barber) acquires
a penis enlarger.

However, the adoption of the role of strippers by the men does not lead to the same
eroticisation of the male body as would be the case with women and, as many critics were
quick to complain, the final scene avoids the full frontal display that the film's title
promises. The effect of this is to rescue the characters from the degree of indignity which

such shots would have entailed and reinforce the sense of triumph for the men which the strip show involves. As Richard Dyer has argued, the actual display of the male penis 'can never live up to the mystique of the phallus' and the film's discretion in this regard makes the men's recovery of their masculinity symbolically more potent.[8] Indeed, given that representations of the male working class have so often involved – as Colls and Dodd suggest – a 'celebration' of the male body (either at work or in sporting activity), then the film's ideological achievement (and this is also the case with *Up 'n' Under*) is to permit the reconstruction of masculinity around men's bodies that are either fat or out of condition.[9] As Dave tells the audience, 'we may not be young, we may not be pretty, we may not be right good but ... we're here'.

As such, the film may be seen to hold out the possibility of overcoming the crisis of masculinity, less by a re-learning of male roles than by the re-establishment of the bonds amongst men, particularly those associated with traditional male, working-class culture. It is for this reason that Claire Monk complains that *The Full Monty*, along with *Brassed Off*, seeks to resolve the problems of class disadvantage in terms of gender relations and the 'healing powers' of the all-male group.[10] Thus, through their involvement in the group, Dave is able to regain his sexual potency while Gaz wins the respect of his son (and consolidates his role as a 'proper' father).

There are of course, qualifications. In the case of *Brassed Off* and *Up 'n' Under*, the success of the men is also dependent upon the involvement of women and the films confront the initial reluctance of the men to change. 'Traditionally this is a male-only excursion', Danny tells two wives when they attempt to board the band's bus.) However, the women who do become members of the group – Gloria in *Brassed Off* and Hazel in *Up 'n' Under* – partly do so on the basis of their links with men (Gloria is the granddaughter of the 'best bandsman' Danny ever played with, while Hazel was married to a rugby international) and by adapting to its masculine norms (by becoming 'one of the lads' as Hazel herself puts it). The inequity involved here is clearly revealed by the ending of *Up 'n' Under*. It initially looks as though Hazel, the strong woman who has trained the men, will secure victory for the team with her final kick of the game. However, she hits the bar and it is Arthur (Gary Olsen), the ageing rugby obsessive, who saves the day for the team and, by implication, male pride.

The position of women in *The Full Monty* is rather more complex. At one level, the film follows in the tradition of earlier working-class realism by associating a number of its women characters, such as Gerald's wife, Linda (Deirdre Costello) and Gaz's ex-wife, Mandy, with either consumerism or a desire for social improvement that threatens, or compounds the problems of, the men. Thus, one of the least likeable characters in the film, at least until her 'reproletarianisation' at the film's end when she becomes a part of the cheering crowd, is undoubtedly Mandy whom the film repeatedly identifies with suburbanisation and social climbing (as well as a new, rather priggish middle-class partner). While some of the women (such as Dave's wife, Jean, played by Lesley Sharp) are treated more sympathetically, women remain peripheral to the film's main action. This does not seem to have affected the film's appeal to female spectators, however. One of the striking characteristics of the cinema audience for the film (particularly in the UK) was the high proportion of women (who often attended in groups). So, while at a diegetic level, the film may be read as being about the re-empowering of men, it was nonetheless enjoyed by female audiences because of the degree of role reversal as well as the incongruity and just plain silliness involved in the men's actions. As such, the conditions under which the film was viewed could hardly be said to have sustained a simple ideology of masculine solidarity.

Moreover, the group that is forged in *The Full Monty* cannot be regarded as fully traditional. It is significant, for example, that two of the men – Lomper (Steve Huison) and Guy (Hugo Speer) – are revealed as gay. The character of Lomper provides a perfect example of how the film seeks to provide collective solutions to personal problems. Lomper is a social misfit, set upon suicide, before he is rescued by Dave and successfully integrated into the group. However, his route to health also involves his coming out and the development of a relationship with Guy. While this may have a certain air of contrivance about it, it also begins to re-imagine the traditionally heterosexual world of the northern working-class community in a more inclusive manner than is found in either *Brassed Off* or, indeed, the films of Ken Loach from which gay characters are entirely absent.[11] As Dave wittily observes, reworking a traditional northern aphorism, 'there's nowt as queer as folk'. The inclusion of the black character Horse in the group also establishes a degree of difference from the male working-class community as traditionally imagined. Although there were complaints that the film had, in conception, been more multicultural in character, it is still significant that the black character, and his relatives, are simply accepted as a part of the drama without it becoming an issue or problem. Once again, this is in contrast to the universe of *Brassed Off* and the films of Loach from which, with a few exceptions, black characters are absent.[12]

Conclusion

Since the 1950s, there has been a steady decline in the proportion of manual workers in the British workforce. Moreover, an increasing proportion of manual workers (close to fifty per cent) are either women or black people.[13] In this respect, the traditional idea of a predominantly white, male working class has become problematic and it is this changing situation that British films of the 1990s have struggled to come to terms with. Thus, in seeking to re-instate the importance of class politics (as in the films of Ken Loach) or in celebrating a model of community based on the traditional working class (as in the populist comedies), there has been a tendency to marginalise, or under-estimate, the experience of women and black and Asian workers. What the films have done successfully is provide – despite the persistence of politicians in arguing for the classlessness of British society – a reminder of the continuing economic divisions within Britain as well as giving voice to the desire for a different kind of society in which community and social attachment are accorded greater importance. What they have done less well is dramatise a model of community that can fully embrace social and cultural diversity and which looks forward rather than back.

Notes

1 Lindsay Anderson, 'Get out and push!' in Tom Maschler (ed.), *Declaration* (London: MacGibbon & Kee, 1957), p. 158.

2 See John Hill, *Sex, Class and Realism: British Cinema 1956–63* (London: BFI, 1986), chap. 7.

3 See John Hill, *British Cinema in the 1980s: Issues and Themes* (Oxford: Clarendon Press, 1999), chap. 8.

4 Some of the ensuing argument first appeared in John Hill, '"Every fuckin' choice stinks": Ken Loach', *Sight and Sound*, November 1998, pp. 18–21.

5 For a discussion of Loach's work in terms of 'naturalism', see Deborah Knight, 'Naturalism, Narration and Critical Perspective: Ken Loach and the Experimental Method' in George McKnight (ed.), *Agent of Challenge and Defiance: The Films of Ken Loach* (Trowbridge: Flicks Books, 1997).

6 Richard Dyer, 'Introduction', in Richard Dyer et al., *Coronation Street* (London: BFI, 1981), p. 5.

7 Geoff Eley, '*Distant Voices, Still Lives*. The Family is a Dangerous Place: Memory, Gender, and the Image of the Working Class' in Robert A. Rosenstone (ed.), *Revisioning History: Film and the Construction of a New Past* (Princeton, NJ: Princeton University Press, 1995), p. 17.

8 Richard Dyer, 'Don't look now – the male pin-up', *Screen*, vol. 23, nos 3–4, Sept.–Oct. 1982, p. 71.

9 Robert Colls and Philip Dodd, 'Representing the Nation – British Documentary Film, 1930–45', *Screen*, vol. 26, no. 1, Jan.–Feb. 1985, p. 24. The recovery of male self-respect through boxing in Shane Meadows' *TwentyFourSeven* (1998) provides a more sober variation on this theme.

10 Claire Monk, 'Underbelly UK: the underclass and the 1990s British cinema revival', Paper delivered to the *Cinema, Identity, History Conference on British Cinema*, University of East Anglia, 10–12 Jul. 1998. In describing these films, Monk employs the term 'underclass' which I have avoided. This is partly because of the way that the term became associated, during the 1980s and 1990s, with the neo-conservative positions of writers such as Charles Murray and partly because, as Stephen Edgell argues, it is more useful 'to regard the underclass as the underemployed and unemployed fraction of the working class' rather than as a separate social grouping. See Stephen Edgell, *Class* (London: Routledge, 1994), p. 80.

11 The fact that it is Guy who, the film implies, is the most well-endowed in terms of penis size also plays with the traditional association of physical prowess with conventionally 'masculine' (i.e. heterosexual) virility.

12 For a discussion of how Loach's stress on the primacy of class politics, as in *Riff-Raff*, has tended to be at the expense of women and blacks, see John Hill, *British Cinema in the 1980s*, chap. 9.

13 Nicholas Abercrombie and Alan Warde, *Contemporary British Society*, 2nd edn, (Cambridge: Polity Press, 1994), p. 172.

Select Bibliography

Abercrombie, Nicholas and Alan Warde, *Contemporary British Society*, 2nd edn, (Cambridge: Polity Press, 1994)

Allin, Paul, 'Statistics on film: what the official statistics show', *Cultural Trends 30* (London: Policy Studies Institute, 1998)

Arnold, Kevin and Onyekachi Wambu, *A Fuller Picture: The Commercial Impact of Six British Films With Black Themes in the 1990s* (London: BFI, 1999)

Berrington, Hugh, (ed.), *Britain in the Nineties: The Politics of Paradox* (London: Frank Cass, 1998)

Bhattacharya, Gargi, and John Gabriel, 'Gurinder Chadha and the *Apna* generation: Black British film in the 1990s', *Third Text*, 27, 1994

Blanchard, Simon, 'Cinema-going, going, gone?', *Screen*, vol. 24, nos 4–5, July–October 1983

British Film Institute, *BFI Television Industry Tracking Study. The First Year: An Interim Report* (London: BFI, 1995)

British Film Institute, *BFI Television Industry Tracking Study. Second Interim Report* (London: BFI, 1997)

Brooks, Xan, *Choose Life: Ewan McGregor and the British Film Revival* (London: Chameleon Books, 1998)

Chandler, Chris, 'Beyond a London thing', *Vertigo*, Autumn 1997, Issue 7

Chibnall, Steve and Robert Murphy (eds), *British Crime Cinema* (London and New York: Routledge, 1999)

Christie, Ian, 'Film for a Spanish republic', *Sight and Sound*, October 1995

Christie, Ian, 'Will Lottery money assure the British film industry? Or should Chris Smith be rediscovering the virtues of state intervention?', *New Statesman*, 20 June 1997

Cinema Advertisers' Association (CAA), *Cinema and Video Industry Audience Research (CAVIAR) Number 10* (London: CAA, 1993)

Cinema Advertisers' Association (CAA), *Cinema and Video Industry Audience Research (CAVIAR) Number 15* (London: CAA, 1998)

Claypole, Jonty, 'The underground', *Filmways*, issue 7, spring 1999

Dawtrey, Adam, 'Scripting a pic renaissance', *Variety*, 15 December 1997

Department of Culture, Media and Sport, *A Bigger Picture – The Report of the Film Policy Review Group* (London: DCMS, 1998)

Department of National Heritage, *The British Film Industry: a Policy Document, Incorporating the Government's Response to the House of Commons National Heritage Select Committee* (London: HMSO, 1995)

Dickinson, Margaret and Sarah Street, *Cinema and State: the Film Industry and the Government 1927–84* (London: BFI, 1985)

Dodona Research, 'Coming soon – a cinema near you?', presentation given at Jesus College, Cambridge, September 1997, www.dodona.co.uk/somethingtoread.html

Dyja, Eddie (ed.), *BFI Film and Television Handbook 1996* (London: BFI, 1995)

Dyja, Eddie (ed.), *BFI Film and Television Handbook 1997* (London: BFI, 1996)

Dyja, Eddie (ed.), *BFI Film and Television Handbook 1998* (London: BFI, 1997)

Dyja, Eddie (ed.), *BFI Film and Television Handbook 1999* (London: BFI, 1998)

Employment in the Film Industry in the UK – An Interim Report for the British Film Institute, (London: London Economics, 1993)

Eyles, Allen, *ABC The First Name in Entertainment* (London: Cinema Theatre Association/ BFI, 1993)

Eyles, Allen, *The Granada Theatres* (London: Cinema Theatre Association/ BFI, 1998)

Finney, Angus, *The Egos Have Landed* (London: Heinemann, 1996)

Finney, Angus, *The State of European Cinema: A New Dose of Reality* (London: Cassell, 1996)

Fonck, Vinciane, *Les Virtuoses/Brassed Off: Un Film de Mark Herman* (Liège, France: Le Centre Culturel les Grignoux, 1998)

Gilroy, Paul, 'Unwelcome', *Sight and Sound*, vol. 5.2, February 1995

Givanni, June (ed.), *Remote Control: Dilemmas of Black Intervention in British Film and TV* (London: BFI, 1995)

Glass, Honey, 'Queer', *Sight and Sound*, October 1997

Gray, Richard, *Cinemas in Britain: 100 Years of Cinema Architecture* (London: Cinema Theatre Association/ BFI, 1996)

Groves, Don, 'Cinema's multiplex fever cooling down', *Variety*, 21 January 1991

Hanson, Stuart, *The development and growth of the multiplex cinema: 1985–1992*, unpublished undergraduate dissertation, Department of Cultural Studies, University of Birmingham, July 1992

Hewison, Robert, *Culture and Consensus: England Art and Politics since 1940* (London: Methuen, 1995)

Higson, Andrew, *Waving the Flag: Constructing a National Cinema in Britain* (Oxford: Clarendon Press, 1995)

Higson, Andrew (ed.) *Dissolving Views: Key Writings on British Cinema* (London: Cassell, 1996)

Hill, John, Martin McLoone, and Paul Hainsworth (eds), *Border Crossing: Film in Ireland, Britain and Europe* (Belfast: Institute of Irish Studies/BFI, 1994)

Hill, John and Martin McLoone (eds), *Big Picture, Small Screen: The Relations Between Film and Television* (Luton: John Libbey Media, University of Luton Press, 1996)

Hill, John, 'Every fuckin' choice stinks: Ken Loach', *Sight and Sound*, November 1998

Hill, John, 'Filming in the north', *Cineaste*, vol. xxiv, nos 2/3, contemporary Irish cinema supplement, 1999

Hill, John, *British Cinema in the 1980s: Issues and Themes* (Oxford: Clarendon Press, 1999)

Ilott, Terry and David Leafe (eds), *BFI Film and Television Handbook 1994* (London: BFI, 1993)

James, Nick, 'Being there', *Sight and Sound*, October 1997

James, Nick, 'Farewell to Napoli', *Sight and Sound*, May 1999

Johnston, Sheila, 'British pic biz bounces back', *Variety*, 15 December 1997

Leafe, David (ed.), *BFI Film and Television Handbook 1991* (London: BFI, 1990)

Leafe, David (ed.), *BFI Film and Television Handbook 1992* (London: BFI, 1991)

Leafe, David (ed.), *BFI Film and Television Handbook 1993* (London: BFI, 1992)

McKnight, George (ed.), *Agent of Challenge and Defiance: the Films of Ken Loach* (Trowbridge: Flicks Books, 1997)

Medhurst, Andy, 'Mike Leigh: Beyond embarrassment', *Sight and Sound*, November 1993

Medhurst, Andy, 'Unhinged invention', *Sight and Sound*, October 1995

Medhurst, Andy, 'Licensed to check', *Sight and Sound*, October 1997

Medhurst, Andy, 'Spend a little time with me', *Sight and Sound*, January 1999

Monk, Claire, 'Heritage film and the British cinema audience in the 1990s', *Journal of Popular British Cinema*, no. 2, January 1999

Monopolies Commission, *A Report on the Supply of Films for Exhibition in Cinemas*, Cm. 2673 (London: HMSO, 1994)

Moran, Albert, (ed.), *Film Policy: International, National and Regional Perspectives* (London: Routledge, 1996)

Murphy, Robert (ed.), *The British Cinema Book* (London: BFI, 1997)

National Heritage Committee, *The British Film Industry, Vol. 1: Report and Minutes of Proceedings, Vol. II: Minutes of Evidence, Vol III: Appendices to the Minutes of Evidence* (London: HMSO, 1995)

Nowell Smith, Geoffrey and Stephen Ricci (eds), *Hollywood and Europe: Economics, Culture and National Identity 1945–95* (London: BFI, 1998)

Olins, Wally, 'The best place to see a film?', *Sight and Sound*, Autumn 1985

O'Pray, Michael, 'Cinephilia', *Art Monthly*, no. 224, March 1999

O'Pray, Michael (ed.), *The British Avant-Garde Film, 1926–1995: An Anthology of Writings* (Luton: University of Luton Press, 1997)

Petrie, Duncan (ed.), *New Questions of British Cinema* (London: BFI, 1992)

Pidduck, Julianne, 'Travels with Sally Potter's *Orlando*: gender, narrative, movement', *Screen*, vol. 38, no. 2, 1997

Pidduck, Julianne, 'Of women, windows and walks', *Screen*, vol. 39, no. 4, 1998

Puttnam, David with Neil Watson, *The Undeclared War: The Struggle for Control of the World's Film Industry* (London: HarperCollins, 1997)

Pym, John, *Film on Four, 1981–1992: A Survey* (London: BFI, 1992)

Pym, John, *Time Out Film Guide* (London: Penguin, 1999)

Rich, B. Ruby, 'New queer cinema', *Sight and Sound*, September 1992

Roddick, Nick 'Welcome to the multiplex', *Sight and Sound*, June 1994

Roddick, Nick, 'Show me the culture!', *Sight and Sound*, December 1998

Roddick, Nick, 'Shotguns and weddings', *Mediawatch 99*, with *Sight and Sound*, March 1999

Smith, Chris, *Creative Britain* (London: Faber and Faber, 1998)

Street, Sarah, *British National Cinema* (London and New York: Routledge, 1997)

Thomas, Nick (ed.), *BFI Film and Television Handbook 1995* (London: BFI, 1994)

Turner, Janice, 'Exposed: The great British film industry rip-off', *Stage, Screen & Radio*, Jul/Aug 1994

Willemen, Paul, *Looks and Frictions: Essays in Cultural Studies and Film Theory*, (London: BFI, 1994)

Wood, Robin, *The Wings of the Dove* (London: BFI, 1999)

Websites

AC Nielsen EDI – www.entdata.com

British Film Institute – www.bfi.org.uk

Department for Culture, Media and Sport – www.culture.gov.uk

Dodona – www.dodona.co.uk

Europa Cinemas – www.europa-cinemas.org

European Audiovisual Observatory – www.obs.coe.int

Eurostat – europa.eu.int/eurostat.html

Media Salles – www.mediasalles.it

Office of National Statistics – www.ons.gov.uk

Variety – www.variety.com

List of Illustrations

Whilst considerable effort had been made to identify correct copyright holders this has not been possible in all cases. We apologise for any apparent negligence and any omissions or corrections brought to our attention will be remedied in any future editions.

1 – *Shallow Grave* Figment Films/Channel Four; 2 – *Sliding Doors* © Mirage Enterprises and Intermedia Film Equities, Ltd; 3 – *Hideous Kinky* © The Film Consortium/L Films; 4 – *The Scar* Amber Productions; 5 – *Elizabeth* © Polygram Filmed Entertainment Inc. (Working Title); 6 – *Shakespeare in Love* © Miramax Films/Universal Pictures; 7 – *Lock Stock and Two Smoking Barrels* © Ska Films; 8 – *Shooting Fish* © The Gruber Brothers (Entrepreneurs) Ltd; 9 – *Orlando* Adventure Pictures; 10 – *Bean* © PolyGram Film Productions BV and NV Polygram SA; 11 – *Il Postino* Penta Film; 13 – *I Know What You Did Last Summer* © Mandalay Entertainment; 14 – *Festen* © Nimbus Films ApS 1998; 15 – *Land and Freedom* Parallax Pictures/Messidor Films/Road Movies Filmproduktion GmbH; 16 – *Prospero's Books* Allarts Enterprises (Amsterdam)/Cinea/Camera One(Paris)/Penta Pictures/Elsevier Vendex Film/Film Four International/VPRO Television/Canal Plus; 17 – *Little Voice* © 1998 Scala (Little Voice) Limited © 1998 Miramax Film Corporation; 18 – *Four Weddings and a Funeral* Polygram Filmed Entertainment (Universal)/ Channel Four/ Working Title Films; 19 – *Quadrophenia* Who Films/Polytel Films; 20 – *Twin Town* PolyGram Films (UK) Limited; 21 – *The Full Monty* © 1997 Twentieth Century Fox Film Corporation /Redwave Films; 22 – *Trainspotting* Channel Four/ Figment Films/ Universal/ Noel Gay Motion Picture Company Ltd; 23 – *Shopping* Impact Pictures; 24 – *Secrets and Lies* Film Four/CiBY 2000/Thin Man; 25 – *Bhaji on the Beach* Umbi Films; 26 – *Jude* © PolyGram Filmed Entertainment; 27 – *Wings of a Dove* © Miramax Films and Renaissance Dove Ltd; 28 – *Priest* © 1994 BBC; 29 – *Sister My Sister* NFH Productions/Film Four International/British Screen; 30 – *This Year's Love* © Entertainment Film Distributor's Limited; 31 – *Up 'n' Under* © Touchdown Film; 32 – *Victory* © The Recorded Picture Company Limited/UGC Images S.A./Studio Babelsberg GmbH; 33 – *Gallivant* Tall Stories/Channel Four/British Film Institute/Arts Council of England; 34 – *Robinson in Space* BBC Films; 35 – *Love is the Devil* © BBC Films and British Film Institute; 36 – *Brassed Off* © Channel Four Television Corporation/Miramax Film Corporation; 37 – *Nil by Mouth* © Twentieth Century Fox/ SE8 Group Limited; 38 – *Stella Does Tricks* © British Film Institute/Channel Four; 39 – *Under the Skin* © British Film Institute/Channel Four; 40 – *The Girl With Brains in Her Feet* © 1997 Lexington Films Ltd; 41 – *My Name is Joe* © Parallax (Joe) Ltd/Road Movies Vierte/Produktionen GmbH.

Cover Images:

Trainspotting Channel Four/ Figment Films/Noel Gay Motion Picture Company Ltd/Universal; *The Long Day Closes* British Film Institute/Film Four International; *Nil by Mouth* © Twentieth Century Fox/ SE8 Group Limited; *My Name is Joe* © Parallax (Joe) Ltd/Road Movies Vierte/Produktionen GmbH; *Elizabeth* © Polygram Filmed Entertainment Inc. (Working Title); *Sense and Sensibility* © Mirage/Columbia Pictures; *Shooting Fish* © The Gruber Brothers (Entrepreneurs) Ltd

Index